PUBLISHER'S NOTE

Wall Street and the Bolshevik Revolution was first published in 1974. Sadly, the author was not able to update it in his lifetime. It is reproduced here in its original form, as a classic study of the subject.

Wall Street
and the
Bolshevik Revolution

"DEE-LIGHTED!"

Cartoon by Robert Minor in St. Louis Post-Dispatch (1911). Karl Marx surrounded by an appreciative audience of Wall Street financiers: John D. Rockefeller, J. P. Morgan, John D. Ryan of National City Bank, and Morgan partner George W. Perkins. Immediately behind Karl Marx is Teddy Roosevelt, leader of the Progressive Party.

WALL STREET
AND THE
BOLSHEVIK REVOLUTION

ANTONY C. SUTTON

CLAIRVIEW

Clairview Books
Hillside House, The Square
Forest Row, RH18 5ES

www.clairviewbooks.com

Published by Clairview 2011
Reprinted 2013

First published in 1974 by Arlington House, New York

A catalogue record for this book is available from the British Library

ISBN 978 1 905570 35 5

Cover by Andrew Morgan Design
Printed and bound by Gutenberg Press Ltd., Malta

TO

those unknown Russian libertarians, also known as Greens, who in 1919 fought both the Reds and the Whites in their attempt to gain a free and voluntary Russia.

CONTENTS

PREFACE

Since the early 1920s, numerous pamphlets and articles, even a few books, have sought to forge a link between "international bankers" and "Bolshevik revolutionaries." Rarely have these attempts been supported by hard evidence, and never have such attempts been argued within the framework of a scientific methodology. Indeed, some of the "evidence" used in these efforts has been fraudulent, some has been irrelevant, much cannot be checked. Examination of the topic by academic writers has been studiously avoided; probably because the hypothesis offends the neat dichotomy of capitalists versus Communists (and everyone knows, of course, that these are bitter enemies). Moreover, because a great deal that has been written borders on the absurd, a sound academic reputation could easily be wrecked on the shoals of ridicule. Reason enough to avoid the topic.

Fortunately, the State Department Decimal File, particularly the 861.00 section, contains extensive documentation on the hypothesized link. When the evidence in these official papers is merged with nonofficial evidence from biographies, personal papers, and conventional histories, a truly fascinating story emerges.

We find there was a link between *some* New York international bankers and *many* revolutionaries, including Bolsheviks. These banking gentlemen—who are here identified—had a financial stake in, and were rooting for, the success of the Bolshevik Revolution.

Who, why—and for how much—is the story in this book.

ANTONY C. SUTTON

March 1974

Wall Street
and the
Bolshevik Revolution

.

Chapter 1

THE ACTORS ON THE REVOLUTIONARY STAGE

Dear Mr. President:
I am in sympathy with the Soviet form of government as that best suited for the Russian people . . .

Letter to President Woodrow Wilson (October 17, 1918) from William Lawrence Saunders, chairman, Ingersoll-Rand Corp.; director, American International Corp.; and deputy chairman, Federal Reserve Bank of New York

The frontispiece in this book was drawn by cartoonist Robert Minor in 1911 for the *St. Louis Post-Dispatch*. Minor was a talented artist and writer who doubled as a Bolshevik revolutionary, got himself arrested in Russia in 1915 for alleged subversion, and was later bankrolled by prominent Wall Street financiers. Minor's cartoon portrays a bearded, beaming Karl Marx standing in Wall Street with *Socialism* tucked under his arm and accepting the congratulations of financial luminaries J. P. Morgan, Morgan partner George W. Perkins, a smug John D. Rockefeller, John D. Ryan of National City Bank, and Teddy Roosevelt—prominently identified by his famous teeth—in the background. Wall Street is decorated by Red flags. The cheering crowd and the airborne hats suggest that Karl Marx must have been a fairly popular sort of fellow in the New York financial district.

15

Was Robert Minor dreaming? On the contrary, we shall see that Minor was on firm ground in depicting an enthusiastic alliance of Wall Street and Marxist socialism. The characters in Minor's cartoon— Karl Marx (symbolizing the future revolutionaries Lenin and Trotsky), J. P. Morgan, John D. Rockefeller—and indeed Robert Minor himself, are also prominent characters in this book.

The contradictions suggested by Minor's cartoon have been brushed under the rug of history because they do not fit the accepted conceptual spectrum of political left and political right. Bolsheviks are at the left end of the political spectrum and Wall Street financiers are at the right end; *therefore,* we implicitly reason, the two groups have nothing in common and any alliance between the two is absurd. Factors contrary to this neat conceptual arrangement are usually rejected as bizarre observations or unfortunate errors. Modern history possesses such a built-in duality and certainly if too many uncomfortable facts have been rejected and brushed under the rug, it is an inaccurate history.

On the other hand, it may be observed that both the extreme right and the extreme left of the conventional political spectrum are absolutely collectivist. The national socialist (for example, the fascist) and the international socialist (for example, the Communist) both recommend totalitarian politico-economic systems based on naked, unfettered political power and individual coercion. Both systems require monopoly control of society. While monopoly control of industries was once the objective of J. P. Morgan and J. D. Rockefeller, by the late nineteenth century the inner sanctums of Wall Street understood that the most efficient way to gain an unchallenged monopoly was to "go political" and make society go to work for the monopolists— under the name of the public good and the public interest. This strategy was detailed in 1906 by Frederick C. Howe in his *Confessions of a Monopolist.*[1] Howe, by the way, is also a figure in the story of the Bolshevik Revolution.

Therefore, an alternative conceptual packaging of political ideas and politico-economic systems would be that of ranking the degree of individual freedom versus the degree of centralized political control.

1. "These are the rules of big business. They have superseded the teachings of our parents and are reducible to a simple maxim: Get a monopoly; let Society work for you: and remember that the best of all business is politics, for a legislative grant, franchise, subsidy or tax exemption is worth more than a Kimberly or Comstock lode, since it does not require any labor, either mental or physical, for its exploitation" (Chicago: Public Publishing, 1906), p. 157.

Under such an ordering the corporate welfare state and socialism are at the same end of the spectrum. Hence we see that attempts at monopoly control of society can have different labels while owning common features.

Consequently, one barrier to mature understanding of recent history is the notion that all capitalists are the bitter and unswerving enemies of all Marxists and socialists. This erroneous idea originated with Karl Marx and was undoubtedly useful to his purposes. In fact, the idea is nonsense. There has been a continuing, albeit concealed, alliance between international political capitalists and international revolutionary socialists—to their mutual benefit. This alliance has gone unobserved largely because historians—with a few notable exceptions—have an unconscious Marxian bias and are thus locked into the impossibility of any such alliance existing. The open-minded reader should bear two clues in mind: monopoly capitalists are the bitter enemies of laissez-faire entrepreneurs; and, given the weaknesses of socialist central planning, the totalitarian socialist state is a perfect captive market for monopoly capitalists, if an alliance can be made with the socialist powerbrokers. Suppose—and it is only hypothesis at this point—that American monopoly capitalists were able to reduce a planned socialist Russia to the status of a captive technical colony? Would not this be the logical twentieth-century internationalist extension of the Morgan railroad monopolies and the Rockefeller petroleum trust of the late nineteenth century?

Apart from Gabriel Kolko, Murray Rothbard, and the revisionists, historians have not been alert for such a combination of events. Historical reporting, with rare exceptions, has been forced into a dichotomy of capitalists versus socialists. George Kennan's monumental and readable study of the Russian Revolution consistently maintains this fiction of a Wall Street-Bolshevik dichotomy.[2] *Russia Leaves the War* has a single incidental reference to the J. P. Morgan firm and no reference at all to Guaranty Trust Company. Yet both organizations are prominently mentioned in the State Department files, to which frequent reference is made in this book, and both are part of the core of the evidence presented here. Neither self-admitted "Bolshevik banker" Olof Aschberg nor Nya Banken in Stockholm is mentioned in Kennan yet both were central to Bolshe-

2. George F. Kennan, *Russia Leaves the War* (New York: Atheneum, 1967); and *Decision to Intervene: Soviet-American Relations, 1917-1920* (Princeton, N.J.: Princeton University Press, 1958).

vik funding. Moreover, in minor yet crucial circumstances, at least crucial for *our* argument, Kennan is factually in error. For example, Kennan cites Federal Reserve Bank director William Boyce Thompson as leaving Russia on November 27, 1917. This departure date would make it physically impossible for Thompson to be in Petrograd on December 2, 1917, to transmit a cable request for $1 million to Morgan in New York. Thompson in fact left Petrograd on December 4, 1918, two days after sending the cable to New York. Then again, Kennan states that on November 30, 1917, Trotsky delivered a speech before the Petrograd Soviet in which he observed, "Today I had here in the Smolny Institute two Americans closely connected with American Capitalist elements. . . ." According to Kennan, it "is difficult to imagine" who these two Americans "could have been, if not Robins and Gumberg." But in fact Alexander Gumberg was Russian, not American. Further, as Thompson was still in Russia on November 30, 1917, then the two Americans who visited Trotsky were more than likely Raymond Robins, a mining promoter turned do-gooder, and Thompson, of the Federal Reserve Bank of New York.

The Bolshevization of Wall Street was known among well informed circles as early as 1919. The financial journalist Barron recorded a conversation with oil magnate E. H. Doheny in 1919 and specifically named three prominent financiers, William Boyce Thompson, Thomas Lamont and Charles R. Crane:

Aboard S. S. Aquitania, Friday Evening, February 1, 1919.
Spent the evening with the Dohenys in their suite. Mr. Doheny said:
If you believe in democracy you cannot believe in Socialism. Socialism is the poison that destroys democracy. Democracy means opportunity for all. Socialism holds out the hope that a man can quit work and be better off. Bolshevism is the true fruit of socialism and if you will read the interesting testimony before the Senate Committee about the middle of January that showed up all these pacifists and peace-makers as German sympathizers, Socialists, and Bolsheviks, you will see that a majority of the college professors in the United States are teaching socialism and Bolshevism and that fifty-two college professors were on so-called peace committees in 1914. President Eliot of Harvard is teaching Bolshevism. The worst Bolshevists in the United States are not only college professors, of whom President Wilson is one, but capitalists and the wives of capitalists and neither seem to know what they are talking about. William Boyce Thompson is teaching Bolshevism and he may yet convert Lamont of J. P. Morgan & Company. Vanderlip is a Bolshevist, so is Charles R. Crane. Many women are joining the movement and neither they, nor their husbands, know what it is, or what it leads to.

18

Henry Ford is another and so are most of those one hundred historians Wilson took abroad with him in the foolish idea that history can teach youth proper demarcations of races, peoples, and nations geographically.[3]

In brief, this is a story of the Bolshevik Revolution and its aftermath, but a story that departs from the usual conceptual straitjacket approach of capitalists versus Communists. Our story postulates a partnership between international monopoly capitalism and international revolutionary socialism for their mutual benefit. The final human cost of this alliance has fallen upon the shoulders of the individual Russian and the individual American. Entrepreneurship has been brought into disrepute and the world has been propelled toward inefficient socialist planning as a result of these monopoly maneuverings in the world of politics and revolution.

This is also a story reflecting the betrayal of the Russian Revolution. The tsars and their corrupt political system were ejected only to be replaced by the new powerbrokers of another corrupt political system. Where the United States could have exerted its dominant influence to bring about a free Russia it truckled to the ambitions of a few Wall Street financiers who, for their own purposes, could accept a centralized tsarist Russia or a centralized Marxist Russia but not a decentralized free Russia. And the reasons for these assertions will unfold as we develop the underlying and, so far, untold history of the Russian Revolution and its aftermath.[4]

3. Arthur Pound and Samuel Taylor Moore, *They Told Barron* (New York: Harper & Brothers, 1930), pp. 13-14.
4. There is a parallel, and also unknown, history with respect to the Makhanovite movement that fought both the "Whites" and the "Reds" in the Civil War of 1919-20 (see Voline, *The Unknown Revolution* [New York: Libertarian Book Club, 1953]). There was also the "Green" movement, which fought both Whites and Reds. The author has never seen even one isolated mention of the Greens in any history of the Bolshevik Revolution. Yet the Green Army was at least 700,000 strong!

Chapter 2

TROTSKY LEAVES NEW YORK TO COMPLETE THE REVOLUTION

You will have a revolution, a terrible revolution. What course it takes will depend much on what Mr. Rockefeller tells Mr. Hague to do. Mr. Rockefeller is a symbol of the American ruling class and Mr. Hague is a symbol of its political tools.

Leon Trotsky, in New York Times, *December 13, 1938. (Hague was a New Jersey politician)*

In 1916, the year preceding the Russian Revolution, internationalist Leon Trotsky was expelled from France, officially because of his participation in the Zimmerwald conference but also no doubt because of inflammatory articles written for *Nashe Slovo,* a Russian-language newspaper printed in Paris. In September 1916 Trotsky was politely escorted across the Spanish border by French police. A few days later Madrid police arrested the internationalist and lodged him in a "first-class cell" at a charge of one-and-one-half pesetas per day. Subsequently Trotsky was taken to Cadiz, then to Barcelona finally to be placed on board the Spanish Transatlantic Company steamer *Monserrat.* Trotsky and family crossed the Atlantic Ocean and landed in New York on January 13, 1917.

Other Trotskyites also made their way westward across the Atlantic. Indeed, one Trotskyite group acquired sufficient immediate influence in Mexico to write the Constitution of Querétaro for the revolutionary 1917 Carranza government, giving Mexico the dubious distinction of being the first government in the world to adopt a Soviet-type constitution.

How did Trotsky, who knew only German and Russian, survive in capitalist America? According to his autobiography, *My Life,* "My only profession in New York was that of a revolutionary socialist." In other words, Trotsky wrote occasional articles for *Novy Mir,* the New York Russian socialist journal. Yet we know that the Trotsky family apartment in New York had a refrigerator and a telephone, and, according to Trotsky, that the family occasionally traveled in a chauffered limousine. This mode of living puzzled the two young Trotsky boys. When they went into a tearoom, the boys would anxiously demand of their mother, "Why doesn't the chauffeur come in?"[1] The stylish living standard is also at odds with Trotsky's reported income. The only funds that Trotsky admits receiving in 1916 and 1917 are $310, and, said Trotsky, "I distributed the $310 among five emigrants who were returning to Russia." Yet Trotsky had paid for a first-class cell in Spain, the Trotsky family had traveled across Europe to the United States, they had acquired an excellent apartment in New York—paying rent three months in advance—and they had use of a chauffered limousine. All this on the earnings of an impoverished revolutionary for a few articles for the low-circulation Russian-language newspaper *Nashe Slovo* in Paris and *Novy Mir* in New York!

Joseph Nedava estimates Trotsky's 1917 income at $12.00 per week, "supplemented by some lecture fees."[2] Trotsky was in New York in 1917 for three months, from January to March, so that makes $144.00 in income from *Novy Mir* and, say, another $100.00 in lecture fees, for a total of $244.00. Of this $244.00 Trotsky was able to give away $310.00 to his friends, pay for the New York apartment, provide for his family—and find the $10,000 that was taken from him in April 1917 by Canadian authorities in Halifax. Trotsky claims that those who said he had other sources of income are "slanderers" spreading "stupid calumnies" and "lies," but unless Trotsky was playing the horses at the Jamaica racetrack, it can't be done. Obviously Trotsky had an unreported source of income.

What was that source? In *The Road to Safety,* author Arthur

1. Leon Trotsky, *My Life* (New York: Scribner's, 1930), chap. 22.
2. Joseph Nedava, *Trotsky and the Jews* (Philadelphia: Jewish Publication Society of America, 1972), p. 163.

Willert says Trotsky earned a living by working as an electrician for Fox Film Studios. Other writers have cited other occupations, but there is no evidence that Trotsky occupied himself for remuneration otherwise than by writing and speaking.

Most investigation has centered on the verifiable fact that when Trotsky left New York in 1917 for Petrograd, to organize the Bolshevik phase of the revolution, he left with $10,000. In 1919 the U.S. Senate Overman Committee investigated Bolshevik propaganda and German money in the United States and incidentally touched on the source of Trotsky's $10,000. Examination of Colonel Hurban, Washington attaché to the Czech legation, by the Overman Committee yielded the following:

> COL. HURBAN: Trotsky, perhaps, took money from Germany, but Trotsky will deny it. Lenin would not deny it. Miliukov proved that he got $10,000 from some Germans while he was in America. Miliukov had the proof, but he denied it. Trotsky did, although Miliukov had the proof.
>
> SENATOR OVERMAN: It was charged that Trotsky got $10,000 here.
>
> COL.HURBAN: I do not remember how much it was, but I know it was a question between him and Miliukov.
>
> SENATOR OVERMAN: Miliukov proved it, did he?
>
> COL. HURBAN: Yes, sir.
>
> SENATOR OVERMAN: Do you know where he got it from?
>
> COL. HURBAN: I remember it was $10,000; but it is no matter. I will speak about their propaganda. The German Government knew Russia better than anybody, and they knew that with the help of those people they could destroy the Russian army.
>
> (At 5:45 o'clock p.m. the subcommittee adjourned until tomorrow, Wednesday, February 19, at 10:30 o'clock a.m.)[3]

It is quite remarkable that the committee adjourned abruptly before the *source* of Trotsky's funds could be placed into the Senate record. When questioning resumed the next day, Trotsky and his $10,000 were no longer of interest to the Overman Committee. We shall later develop evidence concerning the financing of German and revolutionary activities in the United States by New York financial houses; the origins of Trotsky's $10,000 will then come into focus.

An amount of $10,000 of German origin is also mentioned in the official British telegram to Canadian naval authorities in Halifax, who requested that Trotsky and party en route to the revolution be

---

3. United States, Senate, *Brewing and Liquor Interests and German and Bolshevik Propaganda* (Subcommittee on the Judiciary), 65th Cong., 1919.

taken off the S.S. *Kristianiafjord* (see page 28). We also learn from a British Directorate of Intelligence report[4] that Gregory Weinstein, who in 1919 was to become a prominent member of the Soviet Bureau in New York, collected funds for Trotsky in New York. These funds originated in Germany and were channeled through the *Volkszeitung*, a German daily newspaper in New York and subsidized by the German government.

While Trotsky's funds are officially reported as German, Trotsky was actively engaged in American politics immediately prior to leaving New York for Russia and the revolution. On March 5, 1917, American newspapers headlined the increasing possibility of war with Germany; the same evening Trotsky proposed a resolution at the meeting of the New York County Socialist Party "pledging Socialists to encourage strikes and resist recruiting in the event of war with Germany."[5] Leon Trotsky was called by the *New York Times* "an exiled Russian revolutionist." Louis C. Fraina, who cosponsored the Trotsky resolution, later—under an alias—wrote an uncritical book on the Morgan financial empire entitled *House of Morgan*.[6] The Trotsky-Fraina proposal was opposed by the Morris Hillquit faction, and the Socialist Party subsequently voted opposition to the resolution.[7]

More than a week later, on March 16, at the time of the deposition of the tsar, Leon Trotsky was interviewed in the offices of *Novy Mir*. The interview contained a prophetic statement on the Russian revolution:

". . . the committee which has taken the place of the deposed Ministry in Russia did not represent the interests or the aims of the revolutionists, that it would probably be shortlived and step down in favor of men who would be more sure to carry forward the democratization of Russia."[8]

---

4. Special Report No. 5, *The Russian Soviet Bureau in the United States*, July 14, 1919, Scotland House, London S.W.I. Copy in U.S. State Dept. Decimal File, 316-23-1145.
5. *New York Times*, March 5, 1917.
6. Lewis Corey, *House of Morgan: A Social Biography of the Masters of Money* (New York: G. W. Watt, 1930).
7. Morris Hillquit (formerly Hillkowitz) had been defense attorney for Johann Most, after the assassination of President McKinley, and in 1917 was a leader of the New York Socialist Party. In the 1920s Hillquit established himself in the New York banking world by becoming a director of, and attorney for, the International Union Bank. Under President Franklin D. Roosevelt, Hillquit helped draw up the NRA codes for the garment industry.
8. *New York Times*, March 16, 1917.

The "men who would be more sure to carry forward the democratization of Russia," that is, the Mensheviks and the Bolsheviks, were then in exile abroad and needed first to return to Russia. The temporary "committee" was therefore dubbed the Provisional Government, a title, it should be noted, that was used from the start of the revolution in March and not applied ex post facto by historians.

WOODROW WILSON AND A PASSPORT FOR TROTSKY

President Woodrow Wilson was the fairy godmother who provided Trotsky with a passport to return to Russia to "carry forward" the revolution. This American passport was accompanied by a Russian entry permit and a British transit visa. Jennings C. Wise, in *Woodrow Wilson: Disciple of Revolution,* makes the pertinent comment, "Historians must never forget that Woodrow Wilson, despite the efforts of the British police, made it possible for Leon Trotsky to enter Russia with an American passport."

President Wilson facilitated Trotsky's passage to Russia at the same time careful State Department bureaucrats, concerned about such revolutionaries entering Russia, were unilaterally attempting to tighten up passport procedures. The Stockholm legation cabled the State Department on June 13, 1917, just *after* Trotsky crossed the Finnish-Russian border, "Legation confidentially informed Russian, English and French passport offices at Russian frontier, Tornea, considerably worried by passage of suspicious persons bearing American passports."[9]

To this cable the State Department replied, on the same day, "Department is exercising special care in issuance of passports for Russia"; the department also authorized expenditures by the legation to establish a passport-control office in Stockholm and to hire an "absolutely dependable American citizen" for employment on control work.[10] But the bird had flown the coop. Menshevik Trotsky with Lenin's Bolsheviks were already in Russia preparing to "carry forward" the revolution. The passport net erected caught only more legitimate birds. For example, on June 26, 1917, Herman Bernstein, a reputable New York newspaperman on his way to Petrograd to represent the *New York Herald,* was held at the border and refused entry to Russia. Somewhat tardily, in mid-August 1917 the Russian embassy in Washington requested the State Department (and State agreed) to "prevent the entry into Russia of criminals and anarchists . . . numbers of whom have already gone to Russia."[11]

9. U. S. State Dept. Decimal File, 316-85-1002.
10. Ibid.
11. Ibid., 861.111/315.

Consequently, by virtue of preferential treatment for Trotsky, when the S.S. *Kristianiafjord* left New York on March 26, 1917, Trotsky was aboard and holding a U.S. passport—and in company with other Trotskyite revolutionaries, Wall Street financiers, American Communists, and other interesting persons, few of whom had embarked for legitimate business. This mixed bag of passengers has been described by Lincoln Steffens, the American Communist:

> The passenger list was long and mysterious. Trotsky was in the steerage with a group of revolutionaries; there was a Japanese revolutionist in my cabin. There were a lot of Dutch hurrying home from Java, the only innocent people aboard. The rest were war messengers, two from Wall Street to Germany . . . .[12]

Notably, Lincoln Steffens was on board en route to Russia at the specific invitation of Charles Richard Crane, a backer and a former chairman of the Democratic Party's finance committee. Charles Crane, vice president of the Crane Company, had organized the Westinghouse Company in Russia, was a member of the Root mission to Russia, and had made no fewer than twenty-three visits to Russia between 1890 and 1930. Richard Crane, his son, was confidential assistant to then Secretary of State Robert Lansing. According to the former ambassador to Germany William Dodd, Crane "did much to bring on the Kerensky revolution which gave way to Communism."[13] And so Steffens' comments in his diary about conversations aboard the S.S. *Kristianiafjord* are highly pertinent: " . . . all agree that the revolution is in its first phase only, that it must grow. Crane and Russian radicals on the ship think we shall be in Petrograd for the re-revolution."[14]

Crane returned to the United States when the Bolshevik Revolution (that is, "the re-revolution") had been completed and, although a private citizen, was given firsthand reports of the progress of the Bolshevik Revolution as cables were received at the State Department. For example, one memorandum, dated December 11, 1917, is entitled "Copy of report on Maximalist uprising for Mr Crane." It originated with Maddin Summers, U.S. consul general in Moscow, and the covering letter from Summers reads in part:

12. Lincoln Steffens, *Autobiography* (New York: Harcourt, Brace, 1931), p. 764. Steffens was the "go-between" for Crane and Woodrow Wilson.
13. William Edward Dodd, *Ambassador Dodd's Diary, 1933-1938* (New York: Harcourt, Brace, 1941), pp. 42-43.
14. Lincoln Steffens, *The Letters of Lincoln Steffens* (New York: Harcourt, Brace, 1941), p. 396.

I have the honor to enclose herewith a copy of same [above report] with the request that it be sent for the confidential information of Mr. Charles R. Crane. It is assumed that the Department will have no objection to Mr. Crane seeing the report. . . . [15]

In brief, the unlikely and puzzling picture that emerges is that Charles Crane, a friend and backer of Woodrow Wilson and a prominent financier and politician, had a known role in the "first" revolution and traveled to Russia in mid-1917 in company with the American Communist Lincoln Steffens, who was in touch with both Woodrow Wilson and Trotsky. The latter in turn was carrying a passport issued at the orders of Wilson and $10,000 from supposed German sources. On his return to the U.S. after the "re-revolution," Crane was granted access to official documents concerning consolidation of the Bolshevik regime. This is a pattern of interlocking—if puzzling—events that warrants further investigation and suggests, though without at this point providing evidence, some link between the financier Crane and the revolutionary Trotsky.

CANADIAN GOVERNMENT DOCUMENTS ON TROTSKY'S RELEASE[16]

Documents on Trotsky's brief stay in Canadian custody are now declassified and available from the Canadian government archives. According to these archives, Trotsky was removed by Canadian and British naval personnel from the S.S. *Kristianiafjord* at Halifax, Nova Scotia, on April 3, 1917, listed as a German prisoner of war, and interned at the Amherst, Nova Scotia, internment station for German prisoners. Mrs. Trotsky, the two Trotsky boys, and five other men described as "Russian Socialists" were also taken off and interned. Their names are recorded by the Canadian files as: Nickita Muchin, Leiba Fisheleff, Konstantin Romanchanco, Gregor Teheodnovski, Gerchon Melintchansky and Leon Bronstein Trotsky (all spellings from original Canadian documents).

Canadian Army form LB-1, under serial number 1098 (including thumb prints), was completed for Trotsky, with a description as follows: "37 years old, a political exile, occupation journalist, born in Gromskty, Chuson, Russia, Russian citizen." The form was signed by Leon Trotsky and his full name given as Leon Bromstein (*sic*) Trotsky.

The Trotsky party was removed from the S.S. *Kristianiafjord* under

15. U.S. State Dept. Decimal File, 861.00/1026.
16. This section is based on Canadian government records.

official instructions received by cablegram of March 29, 1917, London, presumably originating in the Admiralty with the naval control officer, Halifax. The cablegram reported that the Trotsky party was on the *"Christianiafjord"* (*sic*) and should be "taken off and retained pending instructions." The reason given to the naval control officer at Halifax was that "these are Russian Socialists leaving for purposes of starting revolution against present Russian government for which Trotsky is reported to have 10,000 dollars subscribed by Socialists and Germans."

On April 1, 1917, the naval control officer, Captain O. M. Makins, sent a confidential memorandum to the general officer commanding at Halifax, to the effect that he had "examined all Russian passengers" aboard the S.S. *Kristianiafjord* and found six men in the second-class section: "They are all avowed Socialists, and though professing a desire to help the new Russian Govt., might well be in league with German Socialists in America, and quite likely to be a great hindrance to the Govt. in Russia just at present." Captain Makins added that he was going to remove the group, as well as Trotsky's wife and two sons, in order to intern them at Halifax. A copy of this report was forwarded from Halifax to the chief of the General Staff in Ottawa on April 2, 1917.

The next document in the Canadian files is dated April 7, from the chief of the General Staff, Ottawa, to the director of internment operations, and acknowledges a previous letter (not in the files) about the internment of Russian socialists at Amherst, Nova Scotia: " . . . in this connection, have to inform you of the receipt of a long telegram yesterday from the Russian Consul General, MONTREAL, protesting against the arrest of these men as they were in possession of passports issued by the Russian Consul General, NEW YORK, U.S.A."

The reply to this Montreal telegram was to the effect that the men were interned "on suspicion of being German," and would be released only upon definite proof of their nationality and loyalty to the Allies. No telegrams from the Russian consul general in New York are in the Canadian files, and it is known that this office was reluctant to issue Russian passports to Russian political exiles. However, there *is* a telegram in the files from a New York attorney, N. Aleinikoff, to R. M. Coulter, then deputy postmaster general of Canada. The postmaster general's office in Canada had no connection with either internment of prisoners of war or military activities. Accordingly, this telegram was in the nature of a personal, nonofficial intervention. It reads:

DR. R. M. COULTER, Postmaster Genl. OTTAWA Russian political exiles returning to Russia detained Halifax interned Amherst camp. Kindly investigate and advise cause of the detention and names of all detained. Trust as champion of freedom you will intercede on their behalf. Please wire collect. NICHOLAS ALEINIKOFF

On April 11, Coulter wired Aleinikoff, "Telegram received. Writing you this afternoon. You should receive it to-morrow evening. R. M. Coulter." This telegram was sent by the Canadian Pacific Railway Telegraph but charged to the Canadian Post Office Department. Normally a private business telegram would be charged to the recipient and this was not official business. The follow-up Coulter letter to Aleinikoff is interesting because, after confirming that the Trotsky party was held at Amherst, it states that they were suspected of propaganda against the present Russian government and "are supposed to be agents of Germany." Coulter then adds, " . . . they are not what they represent themselves to be"; the Trotsky group is " . . . not detained by Canada, but by the Imperial authorities." After assuring Aleinikoff that the detainees would be made comfortable, Coulter adds that any information "in their favour" would be transmitted to the military authorities. The general impression of the letter is that while Coulter is sympathetic and fully aware of Trotsky's pro-German links, he is unwilling to get involved. On April 11 Arthur Wolf of 134 East Broadway, New York, sent a telegram to Coulter. Though sent from New York, this telegram, after being acknowledged, was also charged to the Canadian Post Office Department.

Coulter's reactions, however, reflect more than the detached sympathy evident in his letter to Aleinikoff. They must be considered in the light of the fact that these letters in behalf of Trotsky came from two American residents of New York City and involved a Canadian or Imperial military matter of international importance. Further, Coulter, as deputy postmaster general, was a Canadian government official of some standing. Ponder, for a moment, what would happen to someone who similarly intervened in United States affairs! In the Trotsky affair we have two American residents corresponding with a Canadian deputy postmaster general in order to intervene in behalf of an interned Russian revolutionary.

Coulter's subsequent action also suggests something more than casual intervention. After Coulter acknowledged the Aleinikoff and Wolf telegrams, he wrote to Major General Willoughby Gwatkin of the Department of Militia and Defense in Ottawa—a man of significant influence in the Canadian military—and attached copies of the Aleinikoff and Wolf telegrams:

These men have been hostile to Russia because of the way the Jews have been treated, and are now strongly in favor of the present Administration, so far as I know. Both are responsible men. Both are reputable men, and I am sending their telegrams to you for what they may be worth, and so that you may represent them to the English authorities if you deem it wise.

Obviously Coulter knows—or intimates that he knows—a great deal about Aleinikoff and Wolf. His letter was in effect a character reference, and aimed at the root of the internment problem—London. Gwatkin was well known in London, and in fact was on loan to Canada from the War Office in London.[17]

Aleinikoff then sent a letter to Coulter to thank him

most heartily for the interest you have taken in the fate of the Russian Political Exiles. . . . You know me, esteemed Dr. Coulter, and you also know my devotion to the cause of Russian freedom. . . . Happily I know Mr. Trotsky, Mr. Melnichahnsky, and Mr. Chudnowsky . . . intimately.

It might be noted as an aside that if Aleinikoff knew Trotsky "intimately," then he would also probably be aware that Trotsky had declared his intention to return to Russia to overthrow the Provisional Government and institute the "re-revolution." On receipt of Aleinikoff's letter, Coulter immediately (April 16) forwarded it to Major General Gwatkin, adding that he became acquainted with Aleinikoff "in connection with Departmental action on United States papers in the Russian language" and that Aleinikoff was working "on the same lines as Mr. Wolf . . . who was an escaped prisoner from Siberia."

Previously, on April 14, Gwatkin sent a memorandum to his naval counterpart on the Canadian Military Interdepartmental Committee repeating that the internees were Russian socialists with "10,000 dollars subscribed by socialists and Germans." The concluding paragraph stated: "On the other hand there are those who declare that an act of high-handed injustice has been done." Then on April 16, Vice Admiral C. E. Kingsmill, director of the Naval Service, took Gwatkin's intervention at face value. In a letter to Captain Makins, the naval control officer at Halifax, he stated, "The Militia authori-

17. Gwatkin's memoranda in the Canadian government files are not signed, but initialed with a cryptic mark or symbol. The mark has been identified as Gwatkin's because one Gwatkin letter (that of April 21) with that cryptic mark was acknowledged.

ties request that a decision as to their (that is, the six Russians) disposal may be hastened." A copy of this instruction was relayed to Gwatkin who in turn informed Deputy Postmaster General Coulter. Three days later Gwatkin applied pressure. In a memorandum of April 20 to the naval secretary, he wrote, "Can you say, please, whether or not the Naval Control Office has given a decision?"

On the same day (April 20) Captain Makins wrote Admiral Kingsmill explaining his reasons for removing Trotsky; he refused to be pressured into making a decision, stating, "I will cable to the Admiralty informing them that the Militia authorities are requesting an early decision as to their disposal." However, the next day, April 21, Gwatkin wrote Coulter: "Our friends the Russian socialists are to be released; and arrangements are being made for their passage to Europe." The order to Makins for Trotsky's release originated in the Admiralty, London. Coulter acknowledged the information, "which will please our New York correspondents immensely."

While we can, on the one hand, conclude that Coulter and Gwatkin were intensely interested in the release of Trotsky, we do not, on the other hand, know why. There was little in the career of either Deputy Postmaster General Coulter or Major General Gwatkin that would explain an urge to release the Menshevik Leon Trotsky.

Dr. Robert Miller Coulter was a medical doctor of Scottish and Irish parents, a liberal, a Freemason, and an Odd Fellow. He was appointed deputy postmaster general of Canada in 1897. His sole claim to fame derived from being a delegate to the Universal Postal Union Convention in 1906 and a delegate to New Zealand and Australia in 1908 for the "All Red" project. All Red had nothing to do with Red revolutionaries; it was only a plan for all-red or all-British fast steamships between Great Britain, Canada, and Australia.

Major General Willoughby Gwatkin stemmed from a long British military tradition (Cambridge and then Staff College). A specialist in mobilization, he served in Canada from 1905 to 1918. Given only the documents in the Canadian files, we can but conclude that their intervention in behalf of Trotsky is a mystery.

CANADIAN MILITARY INTELLIGENCE VIEWS TROTSKY

We can approach the Trotsky release case from another angle: Canadian intelligence. Lieutenant Colonel John Bayne MacLean, a prominent Canadian publisher and businessman, founder and president of MacLean Publishing Company, Toronto, operated numerous

Canadian trade journals, including the *Financial Post*. MacLean also had a long-time association with Canadian Army Intelligence.[18]

In 1918 Colonel MacLean wrote for his own *MacLean's* magazine an article entitled "Why Did We Let Trotsky Go? How Canada Lost an Opportunity to Shorten the War."[19] The article contained detailed and unusual information about Leon Trotsky, although the last half of the piece wanders off into space remarking about barely related matters. We have two clues to the authenticity of the information. First, Colonel MacLean was a man of integrity with excellent connections in Canadian government intelligence. Second, government records since released by Canada, Great Britain, and the United States confirm MacLean's statement to a significant degree. Some MacLean statements remain to be confirmed, but information available in the early 1970s is not necessarily inconsistent with Colonel MacLean's article.

MacLean's opening argument is that "some Canadian politicians or officials were chiefly responsible for the prolongation of the war [World War I], for the great loss of life, the wounds and sufferings of the winter of 1917 and the great drives of 1918."

Further, states MacLean, these persons were (in 1919) doing everything possible to prevent Parliament and the Canadian people from getting the related facts. Official reports, including those of Sir Douglas Haig, demonstrate that but for the Russian break in 1917 the war would have been over a year earlier, and that "the man chiefly responsible for the defection of Russia was Trotsky . . . acting under German instructions."

Who was Trotsky? According to MacLean, Trotsky was not Russian, but German. Odd as this assertion may appear it does coincide with other scraps of intelligence information: to wit, that Trotsky spoke better German than Russian, and that he was the Russian executive of the German "Black Bond." According to MacLean, Trotsky in August 1914 had been "ostentatiously" expelled from Berlin;[20] he finally arrived in the United States where he organized Russian revolutionaries, as well as revolutionaries in Western Canada, who "were largely Germans and Austrians traveling as Russians." MacLean continues:

18. H.J. Morgan, *Canadian Men and Women of the Times, 1912,* 2 vols. (Toronto: W. Briggs, 1898-1912).
19. June 1919, pp. 66a-666. Toronto Public Library has a copy; the issue of *MacLean's* in which Colonel MacLean's article appeared is not easy to find and a full summary is provided below.
20. See also Trotsky, *My Life,* p. 236.

Originally the British found through Russian associates that Kerensky,[21] Lenin and some lesser leaders were practically in German pay as early as 1915 and they uncovered in 1916 the connections with Trotsky then living in New York. From that time he was closely watched by . . . the Bomb Squad. In the early part of 1916 a German official sailed for New York. British Intelligence officials accompanied him. He was held up at Halifax; but on their instruction he was passed on with profuse apologies for the necessary delay. After much manoeuvering he arrived in a dirty little newspaper office in the slums and there found Trotsky, to whom he bore important instructions. From June 1916, until they passed him on [to] the British, the N.Y. Bomb Squad never lost touch with Trotsky. They discovered that his real name was Braunstein and that he was a German, not a Russian.[22]

Such German activity in neutral countries is confirmed in a State Department report (316-9-764-9) describing organization of Russian refugees for revolutionary purposes.

Continuing, MacLean states that Trotsky and four associates sailed on the "S.S. *Christiania*" (*sic*), and on April 3 reported to "Captain Making" (*sic*) and were taken off the ship at Halifax under the direction of Lieutenant Jones. (Actually a party of nine, including six men, were taken off the S.S. *Kristianiafjord.* The name of the naval control officer at Halifax was Captain O. M. Makins, R.N. The name of the officer who removed the Trotsky party from the ship is not in the Canadian government documents; Trotsky said it was "Machen.") Again, according to MacLean, Trotsky's money came "from German sources in New York." Also:

> generally the explanation given is that the release was done at the reque t of Kerensky but months before this British officers and one Canadian serving in Russia, who could speak the Russian language, reported to London and Washington that Kerensky was in German service.[23]

Trotsky was released "at the request of the British Embassy at Washington . . . [which] acted on the request of the U.S. State Department, who were acting for someone else." Canadian officials "were

21. See Appendix 3.
22. According to his own account, Trotsky did not arrive in the U.S. until January 1917. Trotsky's real name was Bronstein; he invented the name "Trotsky." "Bronstein" is German and "Trotsky" is Polish rather than Russian. His first name is usually given as "Leon"; however, Trotsky's first book, which was published in Geneva, has the initial "N," not "L."
23. See Appendix 3; this document was obtained in 1971 from the British Foreign Office but apparently was known to MacLean.

instructed to inform the press that Trotsky was an American citizen travelling on an American passport; that his release was specially demanded by the Washington State Department." Moreover, writes MacLean, in Ottawa "Trotsky had, and continues to have, strong underground influence. There his power was so great that orders were issued that he must be given every consideration."

The theme of MacLean's reporting is, quite evidently, that Trotsky had intimate relations with, and probably worked for, the German General Staff. While such relations have been established regarding Lenin—to the extent that Lenin was subsidized and his return to Russia facilitated by the Germans—it appears certain that Trotsky was similarly aided. The $10,000 Trotsky fund in New York was from German sources, and a recently declassified document in the U.S. State Department files reads as follows:

> March 9, 1918 to: American Consul, Vladivostok from Polk, Acting Secretary of State, Washington D.C.
> For your confidential information and prompt attention: Following is substance of message of January twelfth from Von Schanz of German Imperial Bank to Trotsky, quote Consent imperial bank to appropriation from credit general staff of five million roubles for sending assistant chief naval commissioner Kudrisheff to Far East.

This message suggests some liaison between Trotsky and the Germans in January 1918, a time when Trotsky was proposing an alliance with the West. The State Department does not give the provenance of the telegram, only that it originated with the War College Staff. The State Department did treat the message as authentic and acted on the basis of assumed authenticity. It is consistent with the general theme of Colonel MacLean's article.

TROTSKY'S INTENTIONS AND OBJECTIVES

Consequently, we can derive the following sequence of events: Trotsky traveled from New York to Petrograd on a passport supplied by the intervention of Woodrow Wilson, and with the declared intention to "carry forward" the revolution. The British government was the immediate source of Trotsky's release from Canadian custody in April 1917, but there may well have been "pressures." Lincoln Steffens, an American Communist, acted as a link between Wilson and Charles R. Crane and between Crane and Trotsky. Further, while Crane had no official position, his son Richard was confidential assistant to Secretary of State Robert Lansing, and Crane senior was provided with prompt and detailed reports on the progress of the

Bolshevik Revolution. Moreover, Ambassador William Dodd (U.S. ambassador to Germany in the Hitler era) said that Crane had an active role in the Kerensky phase of the revolution; the Steffens letters confirm that Crane saw the Kerensky phase as only one step in a continuing revolution.

The interesting point, however, is not so much the communication among dissimilar persons like Crane, Steffens, Trotsky, and Woodrow Wilson as the existence of at least a measure of agreement on the procedure to be followed—that is, the Provisional Government was seen as "provisional," and the "re-revolution" was to follow.

On the other side of the coin, interpretation of Trotsky's intentions should be cautious: he was adept at double games. Official documentation clearly demonstrates contradictory actions. For example, the Division of Far Eastern Affairs in the U.S. State Department received on March 23, 1918, two reports stemming from Trotsky; one is inconsistent with the other. One report, dated March 20 and from Moscow, originated in the Russian newspaper *Russkoe Slovo*. The report cited an interview with Trotsky in which he stated that any alliance with the United States was impossible:

> The Russia of the Soviet cannot align itself . . . with capitalistic America for this would be a betrayal. . . . It is possible that Americans seek such an rapproachment with us, driven by its antagonism towards Japan, but in any case there can be no question of an alliance by us of any nature with a bourgeoisie nation.[24]

The other report, also originating in Moscow, is a message dated March 17, 1918, three days earlier, and from Ambassador Francis: "Trotsky requests five American officers as inspectors of army being organized for defense also requests railroad operating men and equipment."[25]

This request to the U.S. is of course inconsistent with rejection of an "alliance."

Before we leave Trotsky some mention should be made of the Stalinist show trials of the 1930s and, in particular, the 1938 accusations and trial of the "Anti-Soviet bloc of rightists and Trotskyites." These forced parodies of the judicial process, almost unanimously rejected in the West, may throw light on Trotsky's intentions.

The crux of the Stalinist accusation was that Trotskyites were

24. U.S. State Dept. Decimal File, 861.00/1351.
25. U.S. State Dept. Decimal File, 861.00/1341.

paid agents of international capitalism. K. G. Rakovsky, one of the 1938 defendants, said, or was induced to say, "We were the vanguard of foreign aggression, of international fascism, and not only in the USSR but also in Spain, China, throughout the world." The summation of the "court" contains the statement, "There is not a single man in the world who brought so much sorrow and misfortune to people as Trotsky. He is the vilest agent of fascism. . . . "[26]

Now while this may be no more than verbal insults routinely traded among the international Communists of the 1930s and 40s, it is also notable that the threads behind the self-accusation are consistent with the evidence in this chapter. And further, as we shall see later, Trotsky was able to generate support among international capitalists, who, incidentally, were also supporters of Mussolini and Hitler.[27]

So long as we see all international revolutionaries and all international capitalists as implacable enemies of one another, then we miss a crucial point—that there has indeed been some operational cooperation between international capitalists, including fascists. And there is no a priori reason why we should reject Trotsky as a part of this alliance.

This tentative, limited reassessment will be brought into sharp focus when we review the story of Michael Gruzenberg, the chief Bolshevik agent in Scandinavia who under the alias of Alexander Gumberg was also a confidential adviser to the Chase National Bank in New York and later to Floyd Odlum of Atlas Corporation. This dual role was known to and accepted by both the Soviets and his American employers. The Gruzenberg story is a case history of international revolution allied with international capitalism.

Colonel MacLean's observations that Trotsky had "strong underground influence" and that his "power was so great that orders were issued that he must be given every consideration" are not at all inconsistent with the Coulter-Gwatkin intervention in Trotsky's behalf; or, for that matter, with those later occurrences, the Stalinist accusations in the Trotskyite show trials of the 1930s. Nor are they inconsistent with the Gruzenberg case. On the other hand, the only

26. *Report of Court Proceedings in the Case of the Anti-Soviet "Bloc of Rightists and Trotskyites" Heard Before the Military Collegium of the Supreme Court of the USSR* (Moscow: People's Commissariat of Justice of the USSR, 1938), p. 293.
27. See p. 174. Thomas Lamont of the Morgans was an early supporter of Mussolini.

known direct link between Trotsky and international banking is through his cousin Abram Givatovzo, who was a private banker in Kiev before the Russian Revolution and in Stockholm after the revolution. While Givatovzo professed antibolshevism, he was in fact acting in behalf of the Soviets in 1918 in currency transactions.[28]

Is it possible an international web can be spun from these events? First there's Trotsky, a Russian internationalist revolutionary with German connections who sparks assistance from two supposed supporters of Prince Lvov's government in Russia (Aleinikoff and Wolf, Russians resident in New York). These two ignite the action of a liberal Canadian deputy postmaster general, who in turn intercedes with a prominent British Army major general on the Canadian military staff. These are all verifiable links.

In brief, allegiances may not always be what they are called, or appear. We can, however, *surmise* that Trotsky, Aleinikoff, Wolf, Coulter, and Gwatkin in acting for a common limited objective also had some common higher goal than national allegiance or political label. To emphasize, there is no absolute proof that this is so. It is, at the moment, only a logical supposition from the facts. A loyalty higher than that forged by a common immediate goal need have been no more than that of friendship, although that strains the imagination when we ponder such a polyglot combination. It may also have been promoted by other motives. The picture is yet incomplete.

28. See p. 122.

Chapter 3

LENIN AND GERMAN ASSISTANCE FOR THE BOLSHEVIK REVOLUTION

It was not until the Bolsheviks had received from us a steady flow of funds through various channels and under varying labels that they were in a position to be able to build up their main organ *Pravda,* **to conduct energetic propaganda and appreciably to extend the originally narrow base of their party.**

Von Kühlmann, minister of foreign affairs, to the kaiser, December 3, 1917

In April 1917 Lenin and a party of 32 Russian revolutionaries, mostly Bolsheviks, journeyed by train from Switzerland across Germany through Sweden to Petrograd, Russia. They were on their way to join Leon Trotsky to "complete the revolution." Their trans-Germany transit was approved, facilitated, and financed by the German General Staff. Lenin's transit to Russia was part of a plan approved by the German Supreme Command, apparently not immediately known to the kaiser, to aid in the disintegration of the Russian army and so eliminate Russia from World War I. The possibility that the Bolsheviks might be turned against Germany and Europe did not occur to the German General Staff. Major General Hoffman has written, "We neither knew nor foresaw the danger to humanity from the consequences of this journey of the Bolsheviks to Russia."[1]

At the highest level the German political officer who approved Lenin's journey to Russia was Chancellor Theobald von Bethmann-Hollweg, a descendant of the Frankfurt banking family Bethmann, which achieved great prosperity in the nineteenth century. Bethmann-Hollweg was appointed chancellor in 1909 and in November 1913 became the subject of the first vote of censure ever passed by the German Reichstag on a chancellor. It was Bethmann-Hollweg who in 1914 told the world that the German guarantee to Belgium was a mere "scrap of paper." Yet on other war matters—such as the use of unrestricted submarine warfare—Bethmann-Hollweg was ambivalent; in January 1917 he told the kaiser, "I can give Your Majesty neither my assent to the unrestricted submarine warfare nor my refusal." By 1917 Bethmann-Hollweg had lost the Reichstag's support and resigned—but not before approving transit of Bolshevik revolutionaries to Russia. The transit instructions from Bethmann-Hollweg went through the state secretary Arthur Zimmermann—who was immediately under Bethmann-Hollweg and who handled day-to-day operational details with the German ministers in both Bern and Copenhagen—to the German minister to Bern in early April 1917. The kaiser himself was not aware of the revolutionary movement until after Lenin had passed into Russia.

While Lenin himself did not know the precise source of the assistance, he certainly knew that the German government was providing some funding. There were, however, intermediate links between the German foreign ministry and Lenin, as the following shows:

LENIN'S TRANSFER TO RUSSIA IN APRIL 1917

Final decision	BETHMANN-HOLLWEG (Chancellor)
Intermediary I	ARTHUR ZIMMERMANN (State Secretary)
Intermediary II	BROCKDORFF-RANTZAU (German Minister in Copenhagen)
Intermediary III	ALEXANDER ISRAEL HELPHAND (alias PARVUS)
Intermediary IV	JACOB FÜRSTENBERG (alias GANETSKY)
	LENIN, in Switzerland

1. Max Hoffman, *War Diaries and Other Papers* (London: M. Secker, 1929), 2:177.

From Berlin Zimmermann and Bethmann-Hollweg communicated with the German minister in Copenhagen, Brockdorff-Rantzau. In turn, Brockdorff-Rantzau was in touch with Alexander Israel Helphand (more commonly known by his alias, Parvus), who was located in Copenhagen.[2] Parvus was the connection to Jacob Fürstenberg, a Pole descended from a wealthy family but better known by his alias, Ganetsky. And Jacob Fürstenberg was the immediate link to Lenin.

Although Chancellor Bethmann-Hollweg was the final authority for Lenin's transfer, and although Lenin was probably aware of the German origins of the assistance, Lenin cannot be termed a German agent. The German Foreign Ministry assessed Lenin's probable actions in Russia as being consistent with their own objectives in the dissolution of the existing power structure in Russia. Yet both parties also had hidden objectives: Germany wanted priority access to the postwar markets in Russia, and Lenin intended to establish a Marxist dictatorship.

The idea of using Russian revolutionaries in this way can be traced back to 1915. On August 14 of that year, Brockdorff-Rantzau wrote the German state undersecretary about a conversation with Helphand (Parvus), and made a strong recommendation to employ Helphand, "an extraordinarily important man whose unusual powers I feel we *must* employ for duration of the war. . . . "[3] Included in the report was a warning: "It *might perhaps* be risky to want to use the powers ranged behind Helphand, but it would certainly be an admission of our own weakness if we were to refuse their services out of fear of not being able to *direct* them."[4]

Brockdorff-Rantzau's ideas of directing or controlling the revolutionaries parallel, as we shall see, those of the Wall Street financiers. It was J. P. Morgan and the American International Corporation that attempted to control both domestic and foreign revolutionaries in the United States for their own purposes.

A subsequent document[5] outlined the terms demanded by Lenin,

2. Z. A. B. Zeman and W. B. Scharlau, *The Merchant of Revolution: The Life of Alexander Israel Helphand (Parvus), 1867-1924* (New York: Oxford University Press, 1965).

3. Z. A. B. Zeman, *Germany and the Revolution in Russia, 1915-1918: Documents from the Archives of the German Foreign Ministry* (London: Oxford University Press, 1958), p. 4, doc. 5.

4. Ibid.

5. Ibid., p. 6, doc. 6, reporting a conversation with the Estonian intermediary Kesküla.

of which the most interesting was point number seven, which allowed "Russian troops to move into India"; this suggested that Lenin intended to continue the tsarist expansionist program. Zeman also records the role of Max Warburg in establishing a Russian publishing house and adverts to an agreement dated August 12, 1916, in which the German industrialist Stinnes agreed to contribute two million rubles for financing a publishing house in Russia.[6]

Consequently, on April 16, 1917, a trainload of thirty-two, including Lenin, his wife Nadezhda Krupskaya, Grigori Zinoviev, Sokolnikov, and Karl Radek, left the Central Station in Bern en route to Stockholm. When the party reached the Russian frontier only Fritz Plattan and Radek were denied entrance into Russia. The remainder of the party was allowed to enter. Several months later they were followed by almost 200 Mensheviks, including Martov and Axelrod.

It is worth noting that Trotsky, at that time in New York, also had funds traceable to German sources. Further, Von Kühlmann alludes to Lenin's inability to broaden the base of his Bolshevik party until the Germans supplied funds. Trotsky was a Menshevik who turned Bolshevik only in 1917. This suggests that German funds were perhaps related to Trotsky's change of party label.

THE SISSON DOCUMENTS

In early 1918 Edgar Sisson, the Petrograd representative of the U.S. Committee on Public Information, bought a batch of Russian documents purporting to prove that Trotsky, Lenin, and the other Bolshevik revolutionaries were not only in the pay of, but also agents of, the German government.

These documents, later dubbed the "Sisson Documents," were shipped to the United States in great haste and secrecy. In Washington, D.C. they were submitted to the National Board for Historical Service for authentication. Two prominent historians, J. Franklin Jameson and Samuel N. Harper, testified to their genuineness. These historians divided the Sisson papers into three groups. Regarding Group I, they concluded:

> We have subjected them with great care to all the applicable tests to which historical students are accustomed and . . . upon the basis of these investigations, we have no hesitation in declaring that

6. Ibid., p. 92, n. 3.

we see no reason to doubt the genuineness or authenticity of these fifty-three documents.[7]

The historians were less confident about material in Group II. This group was not rejected as outright forgeries, but it was suggested that they were copies of original documents. Although the historians made "no confident declaration" on Group III, they were not prepared to reject the documents as outright forgeries.

The Sisson Documents were published by the Committee on Public Information, whose chairman was George Creel, a former contributor to the pro-Bolshevik *Masses*. The American press in general accepted the documents as authentic. The notable exception was the *New York Evening Post*, at that time owned by Thomas W. Lamont, a partner in the Morgan firm. When only a few installments had been published, the *Post* challenged the authenticity of all the documents.[8]

We now know that the Sisson Documents were almost all forgeries: only one or two of the minor German circulars were genuine. Even casual examination of the German letterhead suggests that the forgers were unusually careless forgers perhaps working for the gullible American market. The German text was strewn with terms verging on the ridiculous: for example, *Bureau* instead of the German word *Büro*; *Central* for the German *Zentral*; etc.

That the documents are forgeries is the conclusion of an exhaustive study by George Kennan[9] and of studies made in the 1920s by the British government. Some documents were based on authentic information and, as Kennan observes, those who forged them certainly had access to some unusually good information. For example, Documents 1, 54, 61, and 67 mention that the Nya Banken in Stockholm served as the conduit for Bolshevik funds from Germany. This conduit has been confirmed in more reliable sources. Documents 54, 63, and 64 mention Fürstenberg as the banker-intermediary between the Germans and the Bolshevists; Fürstenberg's name appears elsewhere in authentic documents. Sisson's Document

---

7. U.S., Committee on Public Information, *The German-Bolshevik Conspiracy*, War Information Series, no. 20, October 1918.
8. *New York Evening Post*, September 16-18, 21; October 4, 1918. It is also interesting, but not conclusive of anything, that the Bolsheviks also stoutly questioned the authenticity of the documents.
9. George F. Kennan, "The Sisson Documents," *Journal of Modern History* 27-28 (1955-56): 130-154.

54 mentions Olof Aschberg, and Olof Aschberg by his own statements was the "Bolshevik Banker." Aschberg in 1917 was the director of Nya Banken. Other documents in the Sisson series list names and institutions, such as the German Naptha-Industrial Bank, the Disconto Gesellschaft, and Max Warburg, the Hamburg banker, but hard supportive evidence is more elusive. In general, the Sisson Documents, while themselves outright forgeries, are nonetheless based partly on generally authentic information.

One puzzling aspect in the light of the story in this book is that the documents came to Edgar Sisson from Alexander Gumberg (alias Berg, real name Michael Gruzenberg), the Bolshevik agent in Scandinavia and later a confidential assistant to Chase National Bank and Floyd Odlum of Atlas Corporation. The Bolshevists, on the other hand, stridently repudiated the Sisson material. So did John Reed, the American representative on the executive of the Third International and whose paycheck came from *Metropolitan* magazine, which was owned by J. P. Morgan interests.[10] So did Thomas Lamont, the Morgan partner who owned the *New York Evening Post*. There are several possible explanations. Probably the connections between the Morgan interests in New York and such agents as John Reed and Alexander Gumberg were highly flexible. This *could* have been a Gumberg maneuver to discredit Sisson and Creel by planting forged documents; or perhaps Gumberg was working in his own interest.

The Sisson Documents "prove" exclusive German involvement with the Bolsheviks. They also have been used to "prove" a Jewish-Bolshevik conspiracy theory along the lines of that of the Protocols of Zion. In 1918 the U.S. government wanted to unite American opinion behind an unpopular war with Germany, and the Sisson Documents dramatically "proved" the exclusive complicity of Germany with the Bolshevists. The documents also provided a smoke screen against public knowledge of the events to be described in this book.

THE TUG-OF-WAR IN WASHINGTON[11]
A review of documents in the State Department Decimal File suggests that the State Department and Ambassador Francis in Petrograd were quite well informed about the intentions and progress of

10. John Reed, *The Sisson Documents* (New York: Liberator Publishing, n.d.).
11. This part is based on section 861.00 of the U.S. State Dept. Decimal File, also available as National Archives rolls 10 and 11 of microcopy 316.

the Bolshevik movement. In the summer of 1917, for example, the State Department wanted to stop the departure from the U.S. of "injurious persons" (that is, returning Russian revolutionaries) but was unable to do so because they were using new Russian and American passports. The preparations for the Bolshevik Revolution itself were well known at least six weeks before it came about. One report in the State Department files states, in regard to the Kerensky forces, that it was "doubtful whether government . . . [can] suppress outbreak." Disintegration of the Kerensky government was reported throughout September and October as were Bolshevik preparations for a coup. The British government warned British residents in Russia to leave at least six weeks before the Bolshevik phase of the revolution.

The first full report of the events of early November reached Washington on December 9, 1917. This report described the low-key nature of the revolution itself, mentioned that General William V. Judson had made an unauthorized visit to Trotsky, and pointed out the presence of Germans in Smolny—the Soviet headquarters.

On November 28, 1917, President Woodrow Wilson ordered no interference with the Bolshevik Revolution. This instruction was apparently in response to a request by Ambassador Francis for an Allied conference, to which Britain had already agreed. The State Department argued that such a conference was impractical. There were discussions in Paris between the Allies and Colonel Edward M. House, who reported these to Woodrow Wilson as "long and frequent discussions on Russia." Regarding such a conference, House stated that England was "passively willing," France "indifferently against," and Italy "actively so." Woodrow Wilson, shortly thereafter, approved a cable authored by Secretary of State Robert Lansing, which provided financial assistance for the Kaledin movement (December 12, 1917). There were also rumors filtering into Washington that "monarchists working with the Bolsheviks and same supported by various occurrences and circumstances"; that the Smolny government was absolutely under control of the German General Staff; and rumors elsewhere that "many or most of them [that is, Bolshevists] are from America."

In December, General Judson again visited Trotsky; this was looked upon as a step towards recognition by the U.S., although a report dated February 5, 1918, from Ambassador Francis to Washington, recommended against recognition. A memorandum originating with Basil Miles in Washington argued that "we should deal with all authorities in Russia including Bolsheviks." And on February 15, 1918, the State Department cabled Ambassador Francis in Petrograd, stating that the "department desires you gradually to keep in somewhat closer and informal touch with the Bolshevik authorities using such channels as will avoid any official recognition."

The next day Secretary of State Lansing conveyed the following to the French ambassador J. J. Jusserand in Washington: "It is considered inadvisable to take any action which will antagonize at this time any of the various elements of the people which now control the power in Russia. . . . "[12]

On February 20, Ambassador Francis cabled Washington to report the approaching end of the Bolshevik government. Two weeks later, on March 7, 1918, Arthur Bullard reported to Colonel House that German money was subsidizing the Bolsheviks and that this subsidy was more substantial than previously thought. Arthur Bullard (of the U.S. Committee on Public Information) argued: "we ought to be ready to help any honest national government. But men or money or equipment sent to the present rulers of Russia will be used against Russians at least as much as against Germans."[13]

This was followed by another message from Bullard to Colonel House: "I strongly advise against giving material help to the present Russian government. Sinister elements in Soviets seem to be gaining control."

But there were influential counterforces at work. As early as November 28, 1917, Colonel House cabled President Woodrow Wilson from Paris that it was "exceedingly important" that U.S. newspaper comments advocating that "Russia should be treated as an enemy" be "suppressed." Then next month William Franklin Sands, executive secretary of the Morgan-controlled American International Corporation and a friend of the previously mentioned Basil Miles, submitted a memorandum that described Lenin and Trotsky as appealing to the masses and that urged the U.S. to recognize Russia. Even American socialist Walling complained to the Department of State about the pro-Soviet attitude of George Creel (of the U.S. Committee on Public Information), Herbert Swope, and William Boyce Thompson (of the Federal Reserve Bank of New York).

On December 17, 1917, there appeared in a Moscow newspaper

12. U.S. State Dept. Decimal File, 861.00/1117a. The same message was conveyed to the Italian ambassador.
13. See Arthur Bullard papers at Princeton University.

an attack on Red Cross colonel Raymond Robins and Thompson, alleging a link between the Russian Revolution and American bankers:

Why are they so interested in enlightenment? Why was the money given the socialist revolutionaries and not to the constitutional democrats? One would suppose the latter nearer and dearer to hearts of bankers.

The article goes on to argue that this was because American capital viewed Russia as a future market and thus wanted to get a firm foothold. The money was given to the revolutionaries because

the backward working men and peasants trust the social revolutionaries. At the time when the money was passed the social revolutionaries were in power and it was supposed they would remain in control in Russia for some time.

Another report, dated December 12, 1917, and relating to Raymond Robins, details "negotiation with a group of American bankers of the American Red Cross Mission"; the "negotiation" related to a payment of two million dollars. On January 22, 1918, Robert L. Owen, chairman of the U.S. Senate Committee on Banking and Currency and linked to Wall Street interests, sent a letter to Woodrow Wilson recommending de facto recognition of Russia, permission for a shipload of goods urgently needed in Russia, the appointment of representatives to Russia to offset German influence, and the establishment of a career-service group in Russia.

This approach was consistently aided by Raymond Robins in Russia. For example, on February 15, 1918, a cable from Robins in Petrograd to Davison in the Red Cross in Washington (and to be forwarded to William Boyce Thompson) argued that support be given to the Bolshevik authority for as long as possible, and that the new revolutionary Russia will turn to the United States as it has "broken with the German imperialism." According to Robins, the Bolsheviks wanted United States assistance and cooperation together with railroad reorganization, because "by generous assistance and technical advice in reorganizing commerce and industry America may entirely exclude German commerce during balance of war."

In brief, the tug-of-war in Washington reflected a struggle between, on one side, old-line diplomats (such as Ambassador Francis) and lower-level departmental officials, and, on the other, financiers like Robins, Thompson, and Sands with allies such as Lansing and Miles in the State Department and Senator Owen in the Congress.

Chapter 4

WALL STREET AND WORLD REVOLUTION

What you Radicals and we who hold opposing views differ about, is not so much the end as the means, not so much what should be brought about as how it should, and can, be brought about. . . .

*Otto H. Kahn, director, American International Corp., and part-
ner, Kuhn, Loeb & Co., speaking to the League for Industrial
Democracy, New York, December 30, 1924*

Before World War I, the financial and business structure of the
United States was dominated by two conglomerates: Standard Oil,
or the Rockefeller enterprise, and the Morgan complex of industries—finance and transportation companies. Rockefeller and Morgan
trust alliances dominated not only Wall Street but, through interlocking directorships, almost the entire economic fabric of the
United States.[1] Rockefeller interests monopolized the petroleum and
allied industries, and controlled the copper trust, the smelters trust,
and the gigantic tobacco trust, in addition to having influence in
some Morgan properties such as the U.S. Steel Corporation as well
as in hundreds of smaller industrial trusts, public service operations,
railroads, and banking institutions. National City Bank was the

1. John Moody, *The Truth about the Trusts* (New York: Moody Publishing, 1904).

largest of the banks influenced by Standard Oil-Rockefeller, but financial control extended to the United States Trust Company and Hanover National Bank as well as to major life insurance companies—Equitable Life and Mutual of New York.

The great Morgan enterprises were in steel, shipping, and the electrical industry; they included General Electric, the rubber trust, and railroads. Like Rockefeller, Morgan controlled financial corporations—the National Bank of Commerce and the Chase National Bank, New York Life Insurance, and the Guaranty Trust Company. The names J. P. Morgan and Guaranty Trust Company occur repeatedly throughout this book. In the early part of the twentieth century the Guaranty Trust Company was dominated by the Harriman interests. When the elder Harriman (Edward Henry) died in 1909, Morgan and associates bought into Guaranty Trust as well as into Mutual Life and New York Life. In 1919 Morgan also bought control of Equitable Life, and the Guaranty Trust Company absorbed an additional six lesser trust companies. Therefore, at the end of World War I the Guaranty Trust and Bankers Trust were, respectively, the first and second largest trust companies in the United States, both dominated by Morgan interests.[2]

American financiers associated with these groups were involved in financing revolution even before 1917. Intervention by the Wall Street law firm of Sullivan & Cromwell into the Panama Canal controversy is recorded in 1913 congressional hearings. The episode is summarized by Congressman Rainey:

> It is my contention that the representatives of this Government [United States] made possible the revolution on the isthmus of Panama. That had it not been for the interference of this Government a successful revolution could not possibly have occurred, and I contend that this Government violated the treaty of 1846. I will be able to produce evidence to show that the declaration of independence which was promulgated in Panama on the 3rd day of November, 1903, was prepared right here in New York City and carried down there—prepared in the office of Wilson (sic) Nelson Cromwell. . . .[3]

2. The J. P. Morgan Company was originally founded in London as George Peabody and Co. in 1838. It was not incorporated until March 21, 1940. The company ceased to exist in April 1954 when it merged with the Guaranty Trust Company, then its most important commercial bank subsidiary, and is today known as the Morgan Guaranty Trust Company of New York.
3. United States, House, Committee on Foreign Affairs, *The Story of Panama,* Hearings on the Rainey Resolution, 1913, p. 53.

Congressman Rainey went on to state that only ten or twelve of the top Panamanian revolutionists plus "the officers of the Panama Railroad & Steamship Co., who were under the control of William Nelson Cromwell, of New York and the State Department officials in Washington," knew about the impending revolution.[4] The purpose of the revolution was to deprive Colombia, of which Panama was then a part, of $40 million and to acquire control of the Panama Canal.

The best-documented example of Wall Street intervention in revolution is the operation of a New York syndicate in the Chinese revolution of 1912, which was led by Sun Yat-sen. Although the final gains of the syndicate remain unclear, the intention and role of the New York financing group are fully documented down to amounts of money, information on affiliated Chinese secret societies, and shipping lists of armaments to be purchased. The New York bankers syndicate for the Sun Yat-sen revolution included Charles B. Hill, an attorney with the law firm of Hunt, Hill & Betts. In 1912 the firm was located at 165 Broadway, New York, but in 1917 it moved to 120 Broadway (see chapter eight for the significance of this address). Charles B. Hill was director of several Westinghouse subsidiaries, including Bryant Electric, Perkins Electric Switch, and Westinghouse Lamp—all affiliated with Westinghouse Electric whose New York office was also located at 120 Broadway. Charles R. Crane, organizer of Westinghouse subsidiaries in Russia, had a known role in the first and second phases of the Bolshevik Revolution (see page 26).

The work of the 1910 Hill syndicate in China is recorded in the Laurence Boothe Papers at the Hoover Institution.[5] These papers contain over 110 related items, including letters of Sun Yat-sen to and from his American backers. In return for financial support, Sun Yat-sen promised the Hill syndicate railroad, banking, and commercial concessions in the new revolutionary China.

Another case of revolution supported by New York financial institutions concerned that of Mexico in 1915-16. Von Rintelen, a German espionage agent in the United States,[6] was accused during his May 1917 trial in New York City of attempting to "embroil" the

4. Ibid., p. 60.
5. Stanford, Calif. See also the *Los Angeles Times,* October 13, 1966.
6. Later codirector with Hjalmar Schacht (Hitler's banker) and Emil Wittenberg of the Nationalbank für Deutschland.

U.S. with Mexico and Japan in order to divert ammunition then flowing to the Allies in Europe.[7] Payment for the ammunition that was shipped from the United States to the Mexican revolutionary Pancho Villa, was made through Guaranty Trust Company. Von Rintelen's adviser, Sommerfeld, paid $380,000 via Guaranty Trust and Mississippi Valley Trust Company to the Western Cartridge Company of Alton, Illinois, for ammunition shipped to El Paso, for forwarding to Villa. This was in mid-1915. On January 10, 1916, Villa murdered seventeen American miners at Santa Isabel and on March 9, 1916, Villa raided Columbus, New Mexico, and killed eighteen more Americans.

Wall Street involvement in these Mexican border raids was the subject of a letter (October 6, 1916) from Lincoln Steffens, an American Communist, to Colonel House, an aide to Woodrow Wilson:

> My dear Colonel House:
> Just before I left New York last Monday, I was told convincingly that "Wall Street" had completed arrangements for one more raid of Mexican bandits into the United States: to be so timed and so atrocious that it would settle the election. . . . [8]

Once in power in Mexico, the Carranza government purchased additional arms in the United States. The American Gun Company contracted to ship 5,000 Mausers and a shipment license was issued by the War Trade Board for 15,000 guns and 15,000,000 rounds of ammunition. The American ambassador to Mexico, Fletcher, "flatly refused to recommend or sanction the shipment of any munitions, rifles, etc., to Carranza."[9] However, intervention by Secretary of State Robert Lansing reduced the barrier to one of a temporary delay, and "in a short while . . . [the American Gun Company] would be permitted to make the shipment and deliver."[10]

The raids upon the U.S. by the Villa and the Carranza forces were reported in the *New York Times* as the "Texas Revolution" (a kind of dry run for the Bolshevik Revolution) and were undertaken jointly by Germans and Bolsheviks. The testimony of John A. Walls, district attorney of Brownsville, Texas, before the 1919 Fall

7. United States, Senate, Committee on Foreign Relations, *Investigation of Mexican Affairs*, 1920.
8. Lincoln Steffens, *The Letters of Lincoln Steffens* (New York: Harcourt, Brace, (1941), 1:386.
9. U.S., Senate, Committee on Foreign Relations, *Investigation of Mexican Affairs*, 1920, pts. 2, 18, p. 681.
10. Ibid.

Committee yielded documentary evidence of the link between Bolshevik interests in the United States, German activity, and the Carranza forces in Mexico.[11] Consequently, the Carranza government, the first in the world with a Soviet-type constitution (which was written by Trotskyites), was a government with support on Wall Street. The Carranza revolution probably could not have succeeded without American munitions and Carranza would not have remained in power as long as he did without American help.[12]

Similar intervention in the 1917 Bolshevik Revolution in Russia revolves around Swedish banker and intermediary Olof Aschberg. Logically the story begins with prerevolutionary tsarist loans by Wall Street bank syndicates.

AMERICAN BANKERS AND TSARIST LOANS

In August 1914 Europe went to war. Under international law neutral countries (and the United States was neutral until April 1917) could not raise loans for belligerent countries. This was a question of law as well as morality.

When the Morgan house floated war loans for Britain and France in 1915, J. P. Morgan argued that these were not war loans at all but merely a means of facilitating international trade. Such a distinction had indeed been elaborately made by President Wilson in October 1914; he explained that the sale of bonds in the U.S. for foreign governments was in effect a loan of savings to belligerent governments and did not finance a war. On the other hand, acceptance of Treasury notes or other evidence of debt in payment for articles was only a means of facilitating trade and not of financing a war effort.[13]

Documents in the State Department files demonstrate that the National City Bank, controlled by Stillman and Rockfeller interests, and the Guaranty Trust, controlled by Morgan interests, jointly raised substantial loans for the belligerent Russia before U.S. entry into the war, and that these loans were raised *after* the State Department pointed out to these firms that they were contrary to international law. Further, negotiations for the loans were undertaken through official U.S. government communications facilities under cover of the top-level "Green Cipher" of the State Department. Be-

11. *New York Times,* January 23, 1919.
12. U.S., Senate, Committee on Foreign Relations, op. cit., pp. 795-96.
13. U.S., Senate, *Hearings Before the Special Committee Investigating the Munitions Industry,* 73-74th Cong., 1934-37, pt. 25, p. 7666.

53

low are extracts from State Department cables that will make the case.

On May 24, 1916, Ambassador Francis in Petrograd sent the following cable to the State Department in Washington for forwarding to Frank Arthur Vanderlip, then chairman of the National City Bank in New York. The cable was sent in Green Cipher and was enciphered and deciphered by U.S. State Department officers in Petrograd and Washington at the taxpayers' expense (file 861.51/110).

563, May 24, 1 p.m.
For Vanderlip National City Bank New York. Five. Our previous opinions credit strengthened. We endorse plan cabled as safe investment plus very attractive speculation in roubles. In view of guarantee of exchange rate have placed rate somewhat above present market. Owing unfavorable opinion created by long delay have on own responsibility offered take twenty-five million dollars. We think large portion of all should be retained by bank and allied institutions. With clause respect customs bonds become practical lien on more than one hundred and fifty million dollars per annum customs making absolute security and secures market even if *defect*. We consider three [years?] option on bonds very valuable and for that reason amount of rouble credit should be enlarged by group or by distribution to close friends. American International should take block and we would inform Government. Think group should be formed at once to take and issue of bonds . . . should secure full cooperation guaranty. Suggest you see Jack personally, use every endeavor to get them really work otherwise cooperate guarantee form new group. Opportunities here during the next ten years very great along state and industrial financiering and if this transaction consummated doubtless should be established. In answering bear in mind situation regarding cable. MacRoberts Rich.

FRANCIS, AMERICAN AMBASSADOR[14]

There are several points to note about the above cable to understand the story that follows. First, note the reference to American International Corporation, a Morgan firm, and a name that turns up again and again in this story. Second, "guarantee" refers to Guaranty Trust Company. Third, "MacRoberts" was Samuel MacRoberts, a vice president and the executive manager of National City Bank.

On May 24, 1916, Ambassador Francis cabled a message from Rolph Marsh of Guaranty Trust in Petrograd to Guaranty Trust in

14. U.S. State Dept. Decimal File, 861.51/110 (316-116-682).

New York, again in the special Green Cipher and again using the facilities of the State Department. This cable reads as follows:

565, May 24, 6 p.m.
for Guaranty Trust Company New York:
Three.
Olof and self consider the new proposition takes care Olof and will help rather than harm your prestige. Situation such co-operation necessary if big things are to be accomplished here. Strongly urge your arranging with City to consider and act jointly in all big propositions here. Decided advantages for both and prevents playing one against other. City representatives here desire (hand written) such co-operation. Proposition being considered eliminates our credit in name also option but we both consider the rouble credit with the bond option in propositions. Second paragraph offers wonderful profitable opportunity, strongly urge your acceptance. Please cable me full authority to act in connection with City. Consider our entertaining proposition satisfactory situation for us and permits doing big things. Again strongly urge your taking twenty-five million of rouble credit. No possibility loss and decided speculative advantages. Again urge having Vice President upon the ground. Effect here will be decidedly good. Resident Attorney does not carry same prestige and weight. This goes through Embassy by code answer same way. See cable on possibilities.

ROLPH MARSH.
FRANCIS,
AMERICAN AMBASSADOR
Note:—
Entire Message in Green Cipher.
TELEGRAPH ROOM[15]

"Olof" in the cable was Olof Aschberg, Swedish banker and head of the Nya Banken in Stockholm. Aschberg had been in New York in 1915 conferring with the Morgan firm on these Russian loans. Now, in 1916, he was in Petrograd with Rolph Marsh of Guaranty Trust and Samuel MacRoberts and Rich of National City Bank ("City" in cable) arranging loans for a Morgan-Rockefeller consortium. The following year, Aschberg, as we shall see later, would be known as the "Bolshevik Banker," and his own memoirs reproduce evidence of his right to the title.

The State Department files also contain a series of cables between Ambassador Francis, Acting Secretary Frank Polk, and Secretary of State Robert Lansing concerning the legality and propriety of transmitting National City Bank and Guaranty Trust cables at pub-

15. U.S. State Dept. Decimal File, 861.51/112.

lic expense. On May 25, 1916, Ambassador Francis cabled Washington as follows and referred to the two previous cables:

569, May 25, one p.m.

My telegram 563 and 565 May twenty-fourth are sent for local representatives of institutions addressed in the hope of consummating loan which would largely increase international trade and greatly benefit [diplomatic relations?]. Prospect for success promising. Petrograd representatives consider terms submitted very satisfactory but fear such representations to their institutions would prevent consummation loan if Government here acquainted these proposals.

FRANCIS, AMERICAN AMBASSADOR.[16]

The basic reason cited by Francis for facilitating the cables is "the hope of consummating loan which would largely increase international trade." Transmission of commercial messages using State Department facilities had been prohibited, and on June 1, 1916, Polk cabled Francis:

842

In view of Department's regulation contained in its circular telegraphic instruction of March fifteenth, (discontinuance of forwarding Commercial messages)[17] 1915, please explain why messages in your 563, 565 and 575, should be communicated.

Hereafter please follow closely Department's instructions.

Acting.
Polk

861.51/112
    /110

Then on June 8, 1916, Secretary of State Lansing expanded the prohibition and clearly stated that the proposed loans were illegal:

860 Your 563, 565, May 24, & 569 May 25.1 pm Before delivering messages to Vanderlip and Guaranty Trust Company, I must inquire whether they refer to Russian Government loans of any description. If they do, I regret that the Department can not be a party to their transmission, as such action would submit it to justifiable criticism because of participation by this Government in loan transaction by a belligerent for the purpose of carrying on its hostile operations. Such participation is contrary to the accepted rule of international law that neutral Governments should not lend their assistance to the raising of war loans by belligerents.

16. U.S. State Dept. Decimal File, 861.51/111.
17. Handwritten in parentheses.

The last line of the Lansing cable as written, was not transmitted to Petrograd. The line read: "Cannot arrangements be made to send these messages through Russian channels?"

How can we assess these cables and the parties involved?

Clearly the Morgan-Rockefeller interests were not interested in abiding by international law. There is obvious intent in these cables to supply loans to belligerents. There was no hesitation on the part of these firms to use State Department facilities for the negotiations. Further, in spite of protests, the State Department allowed the messages to go through. Finally, and most interesting for subsequent events, Olof Aschberg, the Swedish banker, was a prominent participant and intermediary in the negotiations on behalf of Guaranty Trust. Let us therefore take a closer look at Olof Aschberg.

OLOF ASCHBERG IN NEW YORK, 1916

Olof Aschberg, the "Bolshevik Banker" (or "Bankier der Weltrevolution," as he has been called in the German press), was owner of the Nya Banken, founded 1912 in Stockholm. His codirectors included prominent members of Swedish cooperatives and Swedish socialists, including G. W. Dahl, K. G. Rosling, and C. Gerhard Magnusson.[18] In 1918 Nya Banken was placed on the Allied blacklist for its financial operations in behalf of Germany. In response to the blacklisting, Nya Banken changed its name to Svensk Ekonomiebolaget. The bank remained under the control of Aschberg, and was mainly owned by him. The bank's London agent was the British Bank of North Commerce, whose chairman was Earl Grey, former associate of Cecil Rhodes. Others in Aschberg's interesting circle of business associates included Krassin, who was until the Bolshevik Revolution (when he changed color to emerge as a leading Bolshevik) Russian manager of Siemens-Schukert in Petrograd; Carl Fürstenberg, minister of finance in the first Bolshevik government; and Max May, vice president in charge of foreign operations for Guaranty Trust of New York. Olof Aschberg thought so highly of Max May that a photograph of May is included in Aschberg's book.[19]

18. Olof Aschberg, *En Vandrande Jude Frän Glasbruksgatan* (Stockholm: Albert Bonniers Förlag, n.d.), pp. 98-99, which is included in *Memoarer* (Stockholm: Albert Bonniers Förlag, 1946). See also *Gästboken* (Stockholm: Tidens Förlag, 1955) for further material on Aschberg.
19. Aschberg, p. 123.

In the summer of 1916 Olof Aschberg was in New York representing both Nya Banken and Pierre Bark, the tsarist minister of finance. Aschberg's prime business in New York, according to the *New York Times* (August 4, 1916), was to negotiate a $50 million loan for Russia with an American banking syndicate headed by Stillman's National City Bank. This business was concluded on June 5, 1916; the results were a Russian credit of $50 million in New York at a bank charge of 7½ percent per annum, and a corresponding 150-million-ruble credit for the NCB syndicate in Russia. The New York syndicate then turned around and issued 6½ percent certificates in its own name in the U.S. market to the amount of $50 million. Thus, the NCB syndicate made a profit on the $50 million loan to Russia, floated it on the American market for another profit, and obtained a 150-million-ruble credit in Russia.

During his New York visit on behalf of the tsarist Russian government, Aschberg made some prophetic comments concerning the future for America in Russia:

> The opening for American capital and American initiative, with the awakening brought by the war, will be country-wide when the struggle is over. There are now many Americans in Petrograd, representatives of business firms, keeping in touch with the situation, and as soon as the change comes a huge American trade with Russia should spring up.[20]

OLOF ASCHBERG IN THE BOLSHEVIK REVOLUTION

While this tsarist loan operation was being floated in New York, Nya Banken and Olof Aschberg were funneling funds from the German government to Russian revolutionaries, who would eventually bring down the "Kerensky committee" and establish the Bolshevik regime.

The evidence for Olof Aschberg's intimate connection with financing the Bolshevik Revolution comes from several sources, some of greater value than others. The Nya Banken and Olof Aschberg are prominently cited in the Sisson papers (see chapter three); however, George Kennan has systematically analyzed these papers and shown them to be forged, although they are probably based in part on authentic material. Other evidence originates with Colonel B. V. Nikitine, in charge of counterintelligence in the Kerensky government, and consists of twenty-nine telegrams transmitted from Stockholm

20. *New York Times*, August 4, 1916.

to Petrograd, and vice versa, regarding financing of the Bolsheviks. Three of these telegrams refer to banks—telegrams 10 and 11 refer to Nya Banken, and telegram 14 refers to the Russo-Asiatic Bank in Petrograd. Telegram 10 reads as follows:

> Gisa Fürstenberg Saltsjöbaden. Funds very low cannot assist if really urgent give 500 as last payment pencils huge loss original hopeless instruct Nya Banken cable further 100 thousand Sumenson.

Telegram 11 reads:

> Kozlovsky Sergievskaya 81. First letters received Nya Banken telegraphed cable who Soloman offering local telegraphic agency refers to Bronck Savelievich Avilov.

Fürstenberg was the intermediary between Parvus (Alexander I. Helphand) and the German government. About these transfers, Michael Futrell concludes:

> It was discovered that during the last few months she [Evegeniya Sumenson] had received nearly a million rubles from Fürstenberg through the Nya Banken in Stockholm, and that this money came from German sources.[21]

Telegram 14 of the Nikitine series reads: "Fürstenberg Saltsjöbaden. Number 90 period hundred thousand into Russo-Asiatic Sumenson." The U.S. representative for Russo-Asiatic was MacGregor Grant Company at 120 Broadway, New York City, and the bank was financed by Guaranty Trust in the U.S. and Nya Banken in Sweden.

Another mention of the Nya Banken is in the material "The Charges Against the Bolsheviks," which was published in the Kerensky period. Particularly noteworthy in that material is a document signed by Gregory Alexinsky, a former member of the Second State Duma, in reference to monetary transfers to the Bolsheviks. The document, in part, reads as follows:

> In accordance with the information just received these trusted persons in Stockholm were: the Bolshevik Jacob Fürstenberg, better known under the name of "Hanecki" (Ganetskii), and Parvus (Dr. Helfand); in Petrograd: the Bolshevik attorney, M. U. Kozlovsky, a woman relative of Hanecki—Sumenson, engaged in speculation together with Hanecki, and others. Kozlovsky is the chief receiver of German money, which is transferred from Berlin through the "Disconto-Gesellschaft" to the Stockholm "Via Bank," and thence to the Siberian Bank in Petrograd,

---

21. Michael Futrell, *Northern Underground* (London: Faber and Faber, 1963), p. 162.

where his account at present has a balance of over 2,000,000 rubles. The military censorship has unearthed an uninterrupted exchange of telegrams of a political and financial nature between the German agents and Bolshevik leaders [Stockholm-Petrograd].[22]

Further, there is in the State Dept. files a Green Cipher message from the U.S. embassy in Christiania (named Oslo, 1925), Norway, dated February 21, 1918, that reads: "Am informed that Bolshevik funds are deposited in Nya Banken, Stockholm, Legation Stockholm advised. Schmedeman."[23]

Finally, Michael Futrell, who interviewed Olof Aschberg just before his death, concludes that Bolshevik funds were indeed transferred from Germany through Nya Banken and Jacob Fürstenberg in the guise of payment for goods shipped. According to Futrell, Aschberg confirmed to him that Fürstenberg had a commercial business with Nya Banken and that Fürstenberg had also sent funds to Petrograd. These statements are authenticated in Aschberg's memoirs (see page 70). In sum, Aschberg, through his Nya Banken, was undoubtedly a channel for funds used in the Bolshevik Revolution, and Guaranty Trust was indirectly linked through its association with Aschberg and its interest in MacGregor Grant Co., New York, agent of the Russo-Asiatic Bank, another transfer vehicle.

NYA BANKEN AND GUARANTY TRUST JOIN RUSKOMBANK

Several years later, in the fall of 1922, the Soviets formed their first international bank. It was based on a syndicate that involved the former Russian private bankers and some new investment from German, Swedish, American, and British bankers. Known as the Ruskombank (Foreign Commercial Bank or the Bank of Foreign Commerce), it was headed by Olof Aschberg; its board consisted of tsarist private bankers, representatives of German, Swedish, and American banks, and, of course, representatives of the Soviet Union. The U.S. Stockholm legation reported to Washington on this question and noted, in a reference to Aschberg, that "his reputation is poor. He was referred to in Document 54 of the Sisson documents and

---

22. See Robert Paul Browder and Alexander F. Kerensky, *The Russian Provisional Government, 1917* (Stanford, Calif.: Stanford University Press, 1961), 3: 1365. "Via Bank" is obviously Nya Banken.
23. U.S. State Dept. Decimal File, 861.00/1130.

Dispatch No. 138 of January 4, 1921 from a legation in Copenhagen."[24]

The foreign banking consortium involved in the Ruskombank represented mainly British capital. It included Russo-Asiatic Consolidated Limited, which was one of the largest private creditors of Russia, and which was granted £3 million by the Soviets to compensate for damage to its properties in the Soviet Union by nationalization. The British government itself had already purchased substantial interests in the Russian private banks; according to a State Department report, "The British Government is heavily invested in the consortium in question."[25]

The consortium was granted extensive concessions in Russia and the bank had a share capital of ten million gold rubles. A report in the Danish newspaper *National Titende* stated that "possibilities have been created for cooperation with the Soviet government where this, by political negotiations, would have been impossible."[26] In other words, as the newspaper goes on to say, the politicians had failed to achieve cooperation with the Soviets, but "it may be taken for granted that the capitalistic exploitation of Russia is beginning to assume more definite forms."[27]

In early October 1922 Olof Aschberg met in Berlin with Emil Wittenberg, director of the Nationalbank für Deutschland, and Scheinmann, head of the Russian State Bank. After discussions concerning German involvement in the Ruskombank, the three bankers went to Stockholm and there met with Max May, vice president of the

24. U.S. State Dept. Decimal File, 861.516/129, August 28, 1922. A State Dept. report from Stockholm, dated October 9, 1922 (861.516/137), states in regard to Aschberg, "I met Mr. Aschberg some weeks ago and in the conversation with him he substantially stated all that appeared in this report. He also asked me to inquire whether he could visit the United States and gave as references some of the prominent banks. In connection with this, however, I desire to call the department's attention to Document 54 of the Sisson Documents, and also to many other dispatches which this legation wrote concerning this man during the war, whose reputation and standing is not good. He is undoubtedly working closely in connection with the Soviets, and during the entire war he was in close cooperation with the Germans" (U.S. State Dept. Decimal File, 861.516/137, Stockholm, October 9, 1922. The report was signed by Ira N. Morris).
25. Ibid., 861.516/130, September 13, 1922.
26. Ibid.
27. Ibid.

Guaranty Trust Company. Max May was then designated director of the Foreign Division of the Ruskombank, in addition to Schlesinger, former head of the Moscow Merchant Bank; Kalaschkin, former head of the Junker Bank; and Ternoffsky, former head of the Siberian Bank. The last bank had been partly purchased by the British government in 1918. Professor Gustav Cassell of Sweden agreed to act as adviser to Ruskombank. Cassell was quoted in a Swedish newspaper (*Svenskadagbladet* of October 17, 1922) as follows:

> That a bank has now been started in Russia to take care of purely banking matters is a great step forward, and it seems to me that this bank was established in order to do something to create a new economic life in Russia. What Russia needs is a bank to create internal and external commerce. If there is to be any business between Russia and other countries there must be a bank to handle it. This step forward should be supported in every way by other countries, and when I was asked my advice I stated that I was prepared to give it. I am not in favor of a negative policy and believe that every opportunity should be seized to help in a positive reconstruction. The great question is how to bring the Russian exchange back to normal. It is a complicated question and will necessitate thorough investigation. To solve this problem I am naturally more than willing to take part in the work. To leave Russia to her own resources and her own fate is folly.[28]

The former Siberian Bank building in Petrograd was used as the head office of the Ruskombank, whose objectives were to raise short-term loans in foreign countries, to introduce foreign capital into the Soviet Union, and generally to facilitate Russian overseas trade. It opened on December 1, 1922, in Moscow and employed about 300 persons.

In Sweden Ruskombank was represented by the Svenska Ekonomibolaget of Stockholm, Olof Aschberg's Nya Banken under a new name, and in Germany by the Garantie und Creditbank für Den Osten of Berlin. In the United States the bank was represented by the Guaranty Trust Company of New York. On opening the bank, Olof Aschberg commented:

> The new bank will look after the purchasing of machinery and raw material from England and the United States and it will give guarantees for the completion of contracts. The question of purchases in Sweden has not yet arisen, but it is hoped that such will be the case later on.[29]

28. Ibid., 861.516/140, Stockholm, October 23, 1922.
29. Ibid., 861.516/147, December 8, 1922.

On joining Ruskombank, Max May of Guaranty Trust made a similar statement:

> The United States, being a rich country with well developed industries, does not need to import anything from foreign countries, but . . . it is greatly interested in exporting its products to other countries and considers Russia the most suitable market for that purpose, taking into consideration the vast requirements of Russia in all lines of its economic life.[30]

May stated that the Russian Commercial Bank was "very important" and that it would "largely finance all lines of Russian industries."

From the very beginning the operations of the Ruskombank were restricted by the Soviet foreign-trade monopoly. The bank had difficulties in obtaining advances on Russian goods deposited abroad. Because they were transmitted in the name of Soviet trade delegations, a great deal of Ruskombank funds were locked up in deposits with the Russian State Bank. Finally, in early 1924 the Russian Commercial Bank was fused with the Soviet foreign-trade commissariat, and Olof Aschberg was dismissed from his position at the bank because, it was claimed in Moscow, he had misused bank funds. His original connection with the bank was because of his friendship with Maxim Litvinov. Through this association, so runs a State Department report, Olof Aschberg had access to large sums of money for the purpose of meeting payments on goods ordered by Soviets in Europe:

> These sums apparently were placed in the Ekonomibolaget, a private banking company, owned by Mr. Aschberg. It is now alledged [sic] that a large portion of these funds were employed by Mr. Aschberg for making investments for his personal account and that he is now endeavouring to maintain his position in the bank through his possession of this money. According to my informant Mr. Aschberg has not been the sole one to profit by his operations with the Soviet funds, but has divided the gains with those who are responsible for his appointment in the Russian Commerce Bank, among them being Litvinoff.[31]

Ruskombank then became Vneshtorg, by which it is known today.

We now have to retrace our steps and look at the activities of Aschberg's New York associate, Guaranty Trust Company, during World War I, to lay the foundation for examination of its role in the revolutionary era in Russia.

30. Ibid., 861.516/144, November 18, 1922.
31. Ibid., 861.316/197, Stockholm, March 7, 1924.

GUARANTY TRUST AND GERMAN ESPIONAGE
IN THE UNITED STATES, 1914-1917[32]

During World War I Germany raised considerable funds in New York for espionage and covert operations in North America and South America. It is important to record the flow of these funds because it runs from the same firms—Guaranty Trust and American International Corporation—that were involved in the Bolshevik Revolution and its aftermath. Not to mention the fact (outlined in chapter three) that the German government also financed Lenin's revolutionary activities.

A summary of the loans granted by American banks to German interests in World War I was given to the 1919 Overman Committee of the United States Senate by U.S. Military Intelligence. The summary was based on the deposition of Karl Heynen, who came to the United States in April 1915 to assist Dr. Albert with the commercial and financial affairs of the German government. Heynen's official work was the transportation of goods from the United States to Germany by way of Sweden, Switzerland, and Holland. In fact, he was up to his ears in covert operations.

The major German loans raised in the United States between 1915 and 1918, according to Heynen, were as follows: The first loan, of $400,000, was made about September 1914 by the investment bankers Kuhn, Loeb & Co. Collateral of 25 million marks was deposited with Max M. Warburg in Hamburg, the German affiliate of Kuhn, Loeb & Co. Captain George B. Lester of U.S. Military Intelligence told the Senate that Heynen's reply to the question "Why did you go to Kuhn, Loeb & Co?" was, "Kuhn, Loeb & Co. we considered the natural bankers of the German government and the Reichsbank."

The second loan, of $1.3 million, did not come directly from the United States but was negotiated by John Simon, an agent of the Suedeutsche Disconto-Gesellschaft, to secure funds for making shipments to Germany.

The third loan was from the Chase National Bank (in the Morgan group) in the amount of three million dollars. The fourth loan was from the Mechanics and Metals National Bank in the amount of one million dollars. These loans financed German espionage activi-

---

32. This section is based on the Overman Committee hearings, U.S., Senate, *Brewing and Liquor Interests and German and Bolshevik Propaganda*, Hearings before the Subcommittee on the Judiciary, 65th Cong., 1919, 2:2154-74.

ties in the United States and Mexico. Some funds were traced to Sommerfeld, who was an adviser to Von Rintelen (another German espionage agent) and who was later associated with Hjalmar Schacht and Emil Wittenberg. Sommerfeld was to purchase ammunition for use in Mexico. He had an account with the Guaranty Trust Company and from this payments were made to Western Cartridge Co. of Alton, Illinois, for ammunition that was shipped to El Paso for use in Mexico by Pancho Villa's bandits. About $400,000 was expended on ammunition, Mexican propaganda, and similar activities.

The then German ambassador Count Von Bernstorff has recounted his friendship with Adolph von Pavenstedt, a senior partner of Amsinck & Co., which was controlled and in November 1917 owned by American International Corporation. American International figures prominently in later chapters; its board of directors contained the key names on Wall Street: Rockefeller, Kahn, Stillman, du Pont, Winthrop, etc. According to Von Bernstorff, Von Pavenstedt was "intimately acquainted with all the members of the Embassy."[33] Von Bernstorff himself regarded Von Pavenstedt as one of the most respected, "if not *the* most respected imperial German in New York."[34] Indeed, Von Pavenstedt was "for many years a Chief pay master of the German spy system in this country."[35] In other words, there is no question that Amsinck & Co., controlled by American International Corporation, was intimately associated with the funding of German wartime espionage in the United States. To clinch Von Bernstorff's last statement, there exists a photograph of a check in favor of Amsinck & Co., dated December 8, 1917—just four weeks after the start of the Bolshevik Revolution in Russia—signed Von Papen (another German espionage operator), and having a counterfoil bearing the notation "travelling expenses on Von W [i.e., Von Wedell]." French Strothers,[36] who published the photograph, has stated that this check is evidence that Von Papen "became an accessory after the fact to a crime against American laws"; it also makes Amsinck & Co. subject to a similar charge.

Paul Bolo-Pasha, yet another German espionage agent, and a

33. Count Von Bernstorff, *My Three Years in America* (New York: Scribner's, 1920), p. 261.
34. Ibid.
35. Ibid.
36. French Strothers, *Fighting Germany's Spies* (Garden City, N.Y.: Doubleday, Page, 1918), p. 152.

prominent French financier formerly in the service of the Egyptian government, arrived in New York in March 1916 with a letter of introduction to Von Pavenstedt. Through the latter, Bolo-Pasha met Hugo Schmidt, director of the Deutsche Bank in Berlin and its representative in the United States. One of Bolo-Pasha's projects was to purchase foreign newspapers so as to slant their editorials in favor of Germany. Funds for this program were arranged in Berlin in the form of credit with Guaranty Trust Company, with the credit subsequently made available to Amsinck & Co. Adolph von Pavenstedt, of Amsinck, in turn made the funds available to Bolo-Pasha.

In other words, both Guaranty Trust Company and Amsinck & Co., a subsidiary of American International Corporation, were directly involved in the implementation of German espionage and other activities in the United States. Some links can be established from these firms to each of the major German operators in the U.S.—Dr. Albert, Karl Heynen, Von Rintelen, Von Papan, Count Jacques Minotto (see below), and Paul Bolo-Pasha.

In 1919 the Senate Overman Committee also established that Guaranty Trust had an active role in financing German World War I efforts in an "unneutral" manner. The testimony of the U.S. intelligence officer Becker makes this clear:

> In this mission Hugo Schmidt [of Deutsche Bank] was very largely assisted by certain American banking institutions. It was while we were neutral, but they acted to the detriment of the British interests, and I have considerable data on the activity of the Guaranty Trust Co. in that respect, and would like to know whether the committee wishes me to go into it.
> SENATOR NELSON: That is a branch of the City Bank, is it not?
> MR. BECKER: No.
> SENATOR OVERMAN: If it was inimical to British interests it was unneutral, and I think you had better let it come out.
> SENATOR KING: Was it an ordinary banking transaction?
> MR. BECKER: That would be a matter of opinion. It has to do with camouflaging exchange so as to make it appear to be neutral exchange, when it was really German exchange on London. As a result of those operations in which the Guaranty Trust Co. mainly participated between August 1, 1914, and the time America entered the war, the Deutsche Banke in its branches in South America succeeded in negotiating £4,670,000 of London exchange in war time.
> SENATOR OVERMAN: I think that is competent.[37]

37. U.S., Senate, Overman Committee, 2:2009.

What is really important is not so much that financial assistance was given to Germany, which was only illegal, as that directors of Guaranty Trust were financially assisting the Allies at the same time. In other words, Guaranty Trust was financing both sides of the conflict. This raises the question of morality.

THE GUARANTY TRUST-MINOTTO-CAILLAUX THREADS.[38]

Count Jacques Minotto is a most unlikely but verifiable and persistent thread that links the Bolshevik Revolution in Russia with German banks, German World War I espionage in the United States, the Guaranty Trust Company in New York, the abortive French Bolshevik revolution, and the related Caillaux-Malvy espionage trials in France.

Jacques Minotto was born February 17, 1891, in Berlin, the son of an Austrian father descended from Italian nobility, and a German mother. Young Minotto was educated in Berlin and then entered employment with the Deutsche Bank in Berlin in 1912. Almost immediately Minotto was sent to the United States as assistant to Hugo Schmidt, deputy director of the Deutsche Bank and its New York representative. After a year in New York, Minotto was sent by the Deutsche Bank to London, where he circulated in prominent political and diplomatic circles. At the outbreak of World War I, Minotto returned to the United States and immediately met with the German ambassador Count Von Bernstorff, after which he entered the employ of Guaranty Trust Company in New York. At Guaranty Trust, Minotto was under the direct orders of Max May, director of its foreign department and an associate of Swedish banker Olof Aschberg. Minotto was no minor bank official. The interrogatories of the Caillaux trials in Paris in 1919 established that Minotto worked directly under Max May.[39] On October 25, 1914, Guaranty Trust sent Jacques Minotto to South America to make a report on the political, financial, and commercial situation. As he did in

38. This section is based on the following sources (as well as those cited elsewhere): Jean Bardanne, *Le Colonel Nicolai: espion de genie* (Paris: Editions Siboney, n.d.); Cours de Justice, *Affaire Caillaux, Loustalot et Comby: Procedure Generale Interrogatoires* (Paris, 1919), pp. 349-50, 937-46; Paul Vergnet, *L'Affaire Caillaux* (Paris, 1918), especially the chapter titled "Marx de Mannheim"; Henri Guernut, Emile Kahn, and Camille M. Lemercier, *Etudes documentaires sur L'Affaire Caillaux* (Paris, n.d.), pp. 1012-15; and George Adam, *Treason and Tragedy: An Account of French War Trials* (London: Jonathan Cape, 1929).

39. See p. 70.

London, Washington, and New York, so Minotto moved in the highest diplomatic and political circles here. One purpose of Minotto's mission in Latin America was to establish the mechanism by which Guaranty Trust could be used as an intermediary for the previously mentioned German fund raising on the London money market, which was then denied to Germany because of World War I. Minotto returned to the United States, renewed his association with Count Von Bernstorff and Count Luxberg, and subsequently, in 1916, attempted to obtain a position with U.S. Naval Intelligence. After this he was arrested on charges of pro-German activities. When arrested Minotto was working at the Chicago plant of his father-in-law Louis Swift, of Swift & Co., meatpackers. Swift put up the security for the $50,000 bond required to free Minotto, who was represented by Henry Veeder, the Swift & Co. attorney. Louis Swift was himself arrested for pro-German activities at a later date. As an interesting and not unimportant coincidence, "Major" Harold H. Swift, brother of Louis Swift, was a member of the William Boyce Thompson 1917 Red Cross Mission to Petrograd—that is, one of the group of Wall Street lawyers and businessmen whose intimate connections with the Russian Revolution are to be described later. Helen Swift Neilson, sister of Louis and Harold Swift, was later connected with the pro-Communist Abraham Lincoln Center "Unity." This established a minor link between German banks, American banks, German espionage, and, as we shall see later, the Bolshevik Revolution.[40]

Joseph Caillaux was a famous (sometimes called notorious) French politician. He was also associated with Count Minotto in the latter's Latin America operations for Guaranty Trust, and was later implicated in the famous French espionage cases of 1919, which had Bolshevik connections. In 1911, Caillaux became minister of finance and later in the same year became premier of France. John Louis Malvy became undersecretary of state in the Caillaux government. Several years later Madame Caillaux murdered Gaston Calmette, editor of the prominent Paris newspaper *Figaro*. The prosecution charged that Madame Caillaux murdered Calmette to prevent publication of certain compromising documents. This affair resulted in the departure of Caillaux and his wife from France. The couple went to Latin America and there met with Count Minotto, the agent of

40. This interrelationship is dealt with extensively in the three-volume Overman Committee report of 1919. See bibliography.

the Guaranty Trust Company who was in Latin America to establish intermediaries for German finance. Count Minotto was socially connected with the Caillaux couple in Rio de Janeiro and São Paulo, Brazil, in Montevideo, Uruguay, and in Buenos Aires, Argentina. In other words, Count Minotto was a constant companion of the Caillaux couple while they were in Latin America.[41] On returning to France, Caillaux and his wife stayed at Biarritz as guests of Paul Bolo-Pasha, who was, as we have seen, also a German espionage operator in the United States and France.[42] Later, in July 1915, Count Minotto arrived in France from Italy, met with the Caillaux couple; the same year the Caillaux couple also visited Bolo-Pasha again in Biarritz. In other words, in 1915 and 1916 Caillaux established a continuing social relationship with Count Minotto and Bolo-Pasha, both of whom were German espionage agents in the United States.

Bolo-Pasha's work in France was to gain influence for Germany in the Paris newspapers *Le Temps* and *Figaro*. Bolo-Pasha then went to New York, arriving February 24, 1916. Here he was to negotiate a loan of $2 million—and here he was associated with Von Pavenstedt, the prominent German agent with Amsinck & Co.[43] Severance Johnson, in *The Enemy Within*, has connected Caillaux and Malvy to the 1918 abortive French Bolshevik revolution, and states that if the revolution had succeeded, "Malvy would have been the Trotsky of France had Caillaux been its Lenin."[44] Caillaux and Malvy formed a radical socialist party in France using German funds and were brought to trial for these subversive efforts. The court interrogatories in the 1919 French espionage trials introduce testimony concerning New York bankers and their relationship with these German espionage operators. They also set forth the links between Count Minotto and Caillaux, as well as the relationship of the Guaranty Trust Company to the Deutsche Bank and the cooperation between Hugo Schmidt of Deutsche Bank and Max May of Guaranty Trust Company. The French interrogatory (page 940) has the following extract from the New York deposition of Count Minotto (page 10, and retranslated from the French):

41. See Rudolph Binion, *Defeated Leaders* (New York: Columbia University Press, 1960).
42. George Adam, *Treason and Tragedy: An Account of French War Trials* (London: Jonathan Cape, 1929).
43. Ibid.
44. *The Enemy Within* (London: George Allen & Unwin, 1920).

QUESTION: Under whose orders were you at Guaranty Trust?
REPLY: Under the orders of Mr. Max May.
QUESTION: He was a Vice President?
ANSWER: He was Vice President and Director of the Foreign Department.

Later, in 1922, Max May became a director of the Soviet Ruskombank and represented the interests of Guaranty Trust in that bank. The French interrogatory establishes that Count Minotto, a German espionage agent, was in the employ of Guaranty Trust Company; that Max May was his superior officer; and that Max May was also closely associated with Bolshevik banker Olof Aschberg. In brief: Max May of Guaranty Trust was linked to illegal fund raising and German espionage in the United States during World War I; he was linked indirectly to the Bolshevik Revolution and directly to the establishment of Ruskombank, the first international bank in the Soviet Union.

It is too early to attempt an explanation for this seemingly inconsistent, illegal, and sometimes immoral international activity. In general, there are two plausible explanations: the first, a relentless search for profits; the second—which agrees with the words of Otto Kahn of Kuhn, Loeb & Co. and of American International Corporation in the epigraph to this chapter—the realization of socialist aims, aims which "should, and can, be brought about" by nonsocialist means.

Chapter 5

THE AMERICAN RED CROSS
MISSION IN RUSSIA—1917

Poor Mr. Billings believed he was in charge of a scientific mission for the relief of Russia. . . . He was in reality nothing but a mask—the Red Cross complexion of the mission was nothing but a mask.

Cornelius Kelleher, assistant to William Boyce Thompson (in George F. Kennan, Russia Leaves the War*)*

The Wall Street project in Russia in 1917 used the Red Cross Mission as its operational vehicle. Both Guaranty Trust and National City Bank had representatives in Russia at the time of the revolution. Frederick M. Corse of the National City Bank branch in Petrograd was attached to the American Red Cross Mission, of which a great deal will be said later. Guaranty Trust was represented by Henry Crosby Emery. Emery was temporarily held by the Germans in 1918 and then moved on to represent Guaranty Trust in China.

Up to about 1915 the most influential person in the American Red Cross National Headquarters in Washington, D.C. was Miss Mabel

Boardman. An active and energetic promoter, Miss Boardman had been the moving force behind the Red Cross enterprise, although its endowment came from wealthy and prominent persons including J. P. Morgan, Mrs. E. H. Harriman, Cleveland H. Dodge, and Mrs. Russell Sage. The 1910 fund-raising campaign for $2 million, for example, was successful only because it was supported by these wealthy residents of New York City. In fact, most of the money came from New York City. J. P. Morgan himself contributed $100,000 and seven other contributors in New York City amassed $300,000. Only one person outside New York City contributed over $10,000 and that was William J. Boardman, Miss Boardman's father. Henry P. Davison was chairman of the 1910 New York Fund-Raising Committee and later became chairman of the War Council of the American Red Cross. In other words, in World War I the Red Cross depended heavily on Wall Street, and specifically on the Morgan firm.

The Red Cross was unable to cope with the demands of World War I and in effect was taken over by these New York bankers. According to John Foster Dulles, these businessmen "viewed the American Red Cross as a virtual arm of government, they envisaged making an incalculable contribution to the winning of the war."[1] In so doing they made a mockery of the Red Cross motto: "Neutrality and Humanity."

In exchange for raising funds, Wall Street asked for the Red Cross War Council; and on the recommendation of Cleveland H. Dodge, one of Woodrow Wilson's financial backers, Henry P. Davison, a partner in J. P. Morgan Company, became chairman. The list of administrators of the Red Cross then began to take on the appearance of the New York Directory of Directors: John D. Ryan, president of Anaconda Copper Company (see frontispiece); George W. Hill, president of the American Tobacco Company; Grayson M. P. Murphy, vice president of the Guaranty Trust Company; and Ivy Lee, public relations expert for the Rockefellers. Harry Hopkins, later to achieve fame under President Roosevelt, became assistant to the general manager of the Red Cross in Washington, D.C.

The question of a Red Cross Mission to Russia came before the third meeting of this reconstructed War Council, which was held in the Red Cross Building, Washington, D.C., on Friday, May 29, 1917, at 11:00 A.M. Chairman Davison was deputed to explore the idea

1. John Foster Dulles, *American Red Cross* (New York: Harper, 1950).

with Alexander Legge of the International Harvester Company. Subsequently International Harvester, which had considerable interests in Russia, provided $200,000 to assist financing the Russian mission. At a later meeting it was made known that William Boyce Thompson, director of the Federal Reserve Bank of New York, had "offered to pay the entire expense of the commission"; this offer was accepted in a telegram: "Your desire to pay expenses of commission to Russia is very much appreciated and from our point of view very important."[2]

The members of the mission received no pay. All expenses were paid by William Boyce Thompson and the $200,000 from International Harvester was apparently used in Russia for political subsidies. We know from the files of the U.S. embassy in Petrograd that the U.S. Red Cross gave 4,000 rubles to Prince Lvoff, president of the Council of Ministers, for "relief of revolutionists" and 10,000 rubles in two payments to Kerensky for "relief of political refugees."

AMERICAN RED CROSS MISSION TO RUSSIA, 1917

In August 1917 the American Red Cross Mission to Russia had only a nominal relationship with the American Red Cross, and must truly have been the most unusual Red Cross Mission in history. All expenses, including those of the uniforms—the members were all colonels, majors, captains, or lieutenants—were paid out of the pocket of William Boyce Thompson. One contemporary observer dubbed the all-officer group an "Haytian Army":

> The American Red Cross delegation, about forty Colonels, Majors, Captains and Lieutenants, arrived yesterday. It is headed by Colonel (Doctor) Billings of Chicago, and includes Colonel William B. Thompson and many doctors and civilians, all with military titles; we dubbed the outfit the "Haytian Army" because there were no privates. They have come to fill no clearly defined mission, as far as I can find out, in fact Gov. Francis told me some time ago that he had urged they not be allowed to come, as there were already too many missions from the various allies in Russia. Apparently, this Commission imagined there was urgent call for doctors and nurses in Russia; as a matter of fact there is at present a surplus of medical talent and nurses, native

2. Minutes of the War Council of the American National Red Cross (Washington, D.C., May 1917)

73

and foreign in the country and many half-empty hospitals in the large cities.[3]

The mission actually comprised only twenty-four (not forty), having military rank from lieutenant colonel down to lieutenant, and was supplemented by three orderlies, two motion-picture photographers, and two interpreters, without rank. Only five (out of twenty-four) were doctors; in addition, there were two medical researchers. The mission arrived by train in Petrograd via Siberia in August 1917. The five doctors and orderlies stayed one month, returning to the United States on September 11. Dr. Frank Billings, nominal head of the mission and professor of medicine at the University of Chicago, was reported to be disgusted with the overtly political activities of the majority of the mission. The other medical men were William S. Thayer, professor of medicine at Johns Hopkins University; D. J. McCarthy, Fellow of Phipps Institute for Study and Prevention of Tuberculosis, at Philadelphia; Henry C. Sherman, professor of food chemistry at Columbia University; C. E. A. Winslow, professor of bacteriology and hygiene at Yale Medical School; Wilbur E. Post, professor of medicine at Rush Medical College; Dr. Malcolm Grow, of the Medical Officers Reserve Corps of the U.S. Army; and Orrin Wightman, professor of clinical medicine, New York Polyclinic Hospital. George C. Whipple was listed as professor of sanitary engineering at Harvard University but in fact was partner of the New York firm of Hazen, Whipple & Fuller, engineering consultants. This is significant because Malcolm Pirnie—of whom more later—was listed as an assistant sanitary engineer and employed as an engineer by Hazen, Whipple & Fuller.

The majority of the mission, as seen from the table, was made up of lawyers, financiers, and their assistants, from the New York financial district. The mission was financed by William B. Thompson, described in the official Red Cross circular as "Commissioner and Business Manager; Director United States Federal Bank of New York." Thompson brought along Cornelius Kelleher, described as an attaché to the mission but actually secretary to Thompson and with the same address—14 Wall Street, New York City. Publicity for the mission was handled by Henry S. Brown, of the same address. Thomas Day Thacher was an attorney with Simpson, Thacher & Bartlett, a firm founded by his father, Thomas Thacher, in 1884 and prominently involved in railroad reorganization and mergers. Thom-

3. Gibbs Diary, August 9, 1917. State Historical Society of Wisconsin.

THE 1917 AMERICAN RED CROSS MISSION TO RUSSIA

Members from Wall Street financial community and their affiliations	Medical doctors	Orderlies, interpreters, etc.
Andrews (Liggett & Myers Tobacco)	Billings (doctor)	Brooks (orderly)
Barr (Chase National Bank)	Grow (doctor)	Clark (orderly)
Brown (c/o William B. Thompson)	McCarthy (medical research; doctor)	Rocchia (orderly)
Cochran (McCann Co.)	Post (doctor)	
Kelleher (c/o William B. Thompson)	Sherman (food chemistry)	Travis (movies)
Nicholson (Swift & Co.)	Thayer (doctor)	Wyckoff (movies)
Pirnie (Hazen, Whipple & Fuller)		
Redfield (Stetson, Jennings & Russell)	Wightman (medicine)	Hardy (justice)
Robins (mining promoter)	Winslow (hygiene)	Horn (transportation)
Swift (Swift & Co.)		
Thacher (Simpson, Thacher & Bartlett)		
Thompson (Federal Reserve Bank of N.Y.)		
Wardwell (Stetson, Jennings & Russell)		
Whipple (Hazen, Whipple & Fuller)		
Corse (National City Bank)		
Magnuson (recommended by confidential agent of Colonel Thompson)		

as junior first worked for the family firm, became assistant U.S. attorney under Henry L. Stimson, and returned to the family firm in 1909. The young Thacher was a close friend of Felix Frankfurter and later became assistant to Raymond Robins, also on the Red Cross Mission. In 1925 he was appointed district judge under President Coolidge, became solicitor general under Herbert Hoover, and was a director of the William Boyce Thompson Institute.

Alan Wardwell, also a deputy commissioner and secretary to the chairman, was a lawyer with the law firm of Stetson, Jennings & Russell of 15 Broad Street, New York City, and H. B. Redfield was law secretary to Wardwell. Major Wardwell was the son of William Thomas Wardwell, long-time treasurer of Standard Oil of New Jersey and Standard Oil of New York. The elder Wardwell was one of the signers of the famous Standard Oil trust agreement, a member of the committee to organize Red Cross activities in the Spanish American War, and a director of the Greenwich Savings Bank. His son Alan was a director not only of Greenwich Savings, but also of Bank of New York and Trust Co. and the Georgian Manganese Company (along with W. Averell Harriman, a director of Guaranty Trust). In 1917 Alan Wardwell was affiliated with Stetson, Jennings & Russell and later joined Davis, Polk, Wardwell, Gardner & Read (Frank L. Polk was acting secretary of state during the Bolshevik Revolution period). The Senate Overman Committee noted that Wardwell was favorable to the Soviet regime although Poole, the State Department official on the spot, noted that "Major Wardwell has of all Americans the widest personal knowledge of the terror" (316-23-1449). In the 1920s Wardwell became active with the Russian-American Chamber of Commerce in promoting Soviet trade objectives.

The treasurer of the mission was James W. Andrews, auditor of Liggett & Myers Tobacco Company of St. Louis. Robert I. Barr, another member, was listed as a deputy commissioner; he was a vice president of Chase Securities Company (120 Broadway) and of the Chase National Bank. Listed as being in charge of advertising was William Cochran of 61 Broadway, New York City. Raymond Robins, a mining promoter, was included as a deputy commissioner and described as "a social economist." Finally, the mission included two members of Swift & Company of Union Stockyards, Chicago. The Swifts have been previously mentioned as being connected with German espionage in the United States during World War I.

76

Harold H. Swift, deputy commissioner, was assistant to the vice president of Swift & Company; William G. Nicholson was also with Swift & Company, Union Stockyards.

Two persons were unofficially added to the mission after it arrived in Petrograd: Frederick M. Corse, representative of the National City Bank in Petrograd; and Herbert A. Magnuson, who was "very highly recommended by John W. Finch, the confidential agent in China of Colonel William B. Thompson."[4]

The Pirnie papers, deposited at the Hoover Institution, contain primary material on the mission. Malcolm Pirnie was an engineer employed by the firm of Hazen, Whipple & Fuller, consulting engineers, of 42 Street, New York City. Pirnie was a member of the mission, listed on a manifest as an assistant sanitary engineer. George C. Whipple, a partner in the firm, was also included in the group. The Pirnie papers include an original telegram from William B. Thompson, inviting assistant sanitary engineer Pirnie to meet with him and Henry P. Davison, chairman of the Red Cross War Council and partner in the J. P. Morgan firm, before leaving for Russia. The telegram reads as follows:

WESTERN UNION TELEGRAM New York, June 21, 1917
To Malcolm Pirnie
I should very much like to have you dine with me at the Metropolitan Club, Sixteenth Street and Fifth Avenue New York City at eight o'clock tomorrow Friday evening to meet Mr. H. P. Davison.
W. B. Thompson, 14 Wall Street

The files do not elucidate why Morgan partner Davison and Thompson, director of the Federal Reserve Bank—two of the most prominent financial men in New York—wished to have dinner with an assistant sanitary engineer about to leave for Russia. Neither do the files explain why Davison was subsequently unable to meet Dr. Billings and the commission itself, nor why it was necessary to advise Pirnie of his inability to do so. But we may surmise that the official cover of the mission—Red Cross activities—was of significantly less interest than the Thompson-Pirnie activities, whatever they may have been. We do know that Davison wrote to Dr. Billings on June 25, 1917:

---

4. Billings report to Henry P. Davison, October 22, 1917, American Red Cross Archives.

Dear Doctor Billings:

It is a disappointment to me and to my associates on the War Council not have been able to meet in a body the members of your Commission. . . .

A copy of this letter was also mailed to assistant sanitary engineer Pirnie with a personal letter from Morgan banker Henry P. Davison, which read:

My dear Mr. Pirnie:

You will, I am sure, entirely understand the reason for the letter to Dr. Billings, copy of which is enclosed, and accept it in the spirit in which it is sent. . . .

The purpose of Davison's letter to Dr. Billings was to apologize to the commission and Billings for being unable to meet with them. We may then be justified in supposing that some deeper arrangements were made by Davison and Pirnie concerning the activities of the mission in Russia and that these arrangements were known to Thompson. The probable nature of these activities will be described later.[5]

The American Red Cross Mission (or perhaps we should call it the Wall Street Mission to Russia) also employed three Russian-English interpreters: Captain Ilovaisky, a Russian Bolshevik; Boris Reinstein, a Russian-American, later secretary to Lenin, and the head of Karl Radek's Bureau of International Revolutionary Propaganda, which also employed John Reed and Albert Rhys Williams; and Alexander Gumberg (alias Berg, real name Michael Gruzenberg), who was a brother of Zorin, a Bolshevik minister. Gumberg was also the chief Bolshevik agent in Scandinavia. He later became a confidential assistant to Floyd Odlum of Atlas Corporation in the United States as well as an adviser to Reeve Schley, a vice president of the Chase Bank.

It should be asked in passing: How useful were the translations supplied by these interpreters? On September 13, 1918, H. A. Doolittle, American vice consul at Stockholm, reported to the secretary of state on a conversation with Captain Ilovaisky (who was a "close

5. The Pirnie papers also enable us to fix exactly the dates that members of the mission left Russia. In the case of William B. Thompson, this date is critical to the argument of this book: Thompson left Petrograd for London on December 4, 1917. George F. Kennan states Thompson left Petrograd on November 27, 1917 (*Russia Leaves the War*, p. 1140).

personal friend" of Colonel Robins of the Red Cross Mission) concerning a meeting of the Murman Soviet and the Allies. The question of inviting the Allies to land at Murman was under discussion at the Soviet, with Major Thacher of the Red Cross Mission acting for the Allies. Ilovaisky interpreted Thacher's views for the Soviet. "Ilovaisky spoke at some length in Russian, supposedly translating for Thacher, but in reality for Trotsky . . . ," to the effect that "the United States would never permit such a landing to occur and urging the speedy recognition of the Soviets and their politics."[6] Apparently Thacher suspected he was being mistranslated and expressed his indignation. However, "Ilovaisky immediately telegraphed the substance to Bolshevik headquarters and through their press bureau had it appear in all the papers as emanating from the remarks of Major Thacher and as the general opinion of all truly accredited American representatives."[7]

Ilovaisky recounted to Maddin Summers, U.S. consul general in Moscow, several instances where he (Ilovaisky) and Raymond Robins of the Red Cross Mission had manipulated the Bolshevik press, especially "in regard to the recall of the Ambassador, Mr. Francis." He admitted that they had not been scrupulous, "but had acted according to their ideas of right, regardless of how they might have conflicted with the politics of the accredited American representatives."[8]

This then was the American Red Cross Mission to Russia in 1917.

AMERICAN RED CROSS MISSION TO RUMANIA

In 1917 the American Red Cross also sent a medical assistance mission to Rumania, then fighting the Central Powers as an ally of Russia. A comparison of the American Red Cross Mission to Russia with that sent to Rumania suggests that the Red Cross Mission based in Petrograd had very little official connection with the Red Cross and even less connection with medical assistance. Whereas the Red Cross Mission to Rumania valiantly upheld the Red Cross twin principles of "humanity" and "neutrality," the Red Cross Mission in Petrograd flagrantly abused both.

The American Red Cross Mission to Rumania left the United

---

6. U.S. State Dept. Decimal File, 861.00/3644.
7. Ibid.
8. Ibid.

States in July 1917 and located itself at Jassy. The mission consisted of thirty persons under Chairman Henry W. Anderson, a lawyer from Virginia. Of the thirty, sixteen were either doctors or surgeons. By comparison, out of twenty-nine individuals with the Red Cross Mission to Russia, only three were doctors, although another four members were from universities and specialized in medically related fields. At the most, seven could be classified as doctors with the mission to Russia compared with sixteen with the mission to Rumania. There was about the same number of orderlies and nurses with both missions. The significant comparison, however, is that the Rumanian mission had only two lawyers, one treasurer, and one engineer. The Russian mission had fifteen lawyers and businessmen. None of the Rumanian mission lawyers or doctors came from anywhere near the New York area but all, except one (an "observer" from the Department of Justice in Washington, D.C.), of the lawyers and businessmen with the Russian mission came from that area. Which is to say that more than half the total of the Russian mission came from the New York financial district. In other words, the relative composition of these missions confirms that the mission to Rumania had a legitimate purpose—to practice medicine—while the Russian mission had a nonmedical and strictly political objective. From its personnel, it could be classified as a commercial or financial mission, but from its actions it was a subversive political action group.

PERSONNEL WITH THE AMERICAN RED CROSS MISSIONS TO RUSSIA AND RUMANIA, 1917

	AMERICAN RED CROSS MISSION TO	
Personnel	Russia	Rumania
Medical (doctors and surgeons)	7	16
Orderlies, nurses	7	10
Lawyers and businessmen	15	4
TOTAL	29	30

SOURCES:
American Red Cross, Washington, D.C.
U.S. Department of State, Petrograd embassy, Red Cross file, 1917.

80

The Red Cross Mission to Rumania remained at its post in Jassy for the remainder of 1917 and into 1918. The medical staff of the American Red Cross Mission in Russia—the seven doctors—quit in disgust in August 1917, protested the political activities of Colonel Thompson, and returned to the United States. Consequently, in September 1917, when the Rumanian mission appealed to Petrograd for American doctors and nurses to help out in the near crisis conditions in Jassy, there were no American doctors or nurses in Russia available to go to Rumania.

Whereas the bulk of the mission in Russia occupied its time in internal political maneuvering, the mission in Rumania threw itself into relief work as soon as it arrived. On September 17, 1917, a confidential cable from Henry W. Anderson, chairman of the Rumania mission, to the American ambassador Francis in Petrograd requested immediate and urgent help in the form of $5 million to meet an impending catastrophe in Rumania. Then followed a series of letters, cables, and communications from Anderson to Francis appealing, unsuccessfully, for help.

On September 28, 1917, Vopicka, American minister in Rumania, cabled Francis at length, for relay to Washington, and repeated Anderson's analysis of the Rumanian crisis and the danger of epidemics—and worse—as winter closed in:

Considerable money and heroic measures required prevent far reaching disaster. . . . Useless try handle situation without someone with authority and access to government . . . With proper organization to look after transport receive and distribute supplies.

The hands of Vopicka and Anderson were tied as all Rumanian supplies and financial transactions were handled by the Red Cross Mission in Petrograd—and Thompson and his staff of fifteen Wall Street lawyers and businessmen apparently had matters of greater concern that Rumanian Red Cross affairs. There is no indication in the Petrograd embassy files at the U.S. State Department that Thompson, Robins, or Thacher concerned himself at any time in 1917 or 1918 with the urgent situation in Rumania. Communications from Rumania went to Ambassador Francis or to one of his embassy staff, and occasionally through the consulate in Moscow.

By October 1917 the Rumanian situation reached the crisis point. Vopicka cabled Davison in New York (via Petrograd) on October 5:

Most urgent problem here. . . . Disastrous effect feared. . . . Could you possibly arrange special shipment. . . . Must rush or too late.

Then on November 5 Anderson cabled the Petrograd embassy saying that delays in sending help had already "cost several thousand lives." On November 13 Anderson cabled Ambassador Francis concerning Thompson's lack of interest in Rumanian conditions:

> Requested Thompson furnish details all shipments as received but have not obtained same. . . . Also requested him keep me posted as to transport conditions but received very little information.

Anderson then requested that Ambassador Francis intercede on his behalf in order to have funds for the Rumanian Red Cross handled in a separate account in London, directly under Anderson and removed from the control of Thompson's mission.

THOMPSON IN KERENSKY'S RUSSIA

What then was the Red Cross Mission doing? Thompson certainly acquired a reputation for opulent living in Petrograd, but apparently he undertook only two major projects in Kerensky's Russia: support for an American propaganda program and support for the Russian Liberty Loan. Soon after arriving in Russia Thompson met with Madame Breshko-Breshkovskaya and David Soskice, Kerensky's secretary, and agreed to contribute $2 million to a committee of popular education so that it could "have its own press and . . . engage a staff of lecturers, with cinematograph illustrations" (861.00/1032); this was for the propaganda purpose of urging Russia to continue in the war against Germany. According to Soskice, "a packet of 50,000 rubles" was given to Breshko-Breshkovskaya with the statement, "This is for you to expend according to your best judgment." A further 2,100,000 rubles was deposited into a current bank account. A letter from J. P. Morgan to the State Department (861.51/190) confirms that Morgan cabled 425,000 rubles to Thompson at his request for the Russian Liberty Loan; J. P. also conveyed the interest of the Morgan firm regarding "the wisdom of making an individual subscription through Mr. Thompson" to the Russian Liberty Loan. These sums were transmitted through the National City Bank branch in Petrograd.

THOMPSON GIVES THE BOLSHEVIKS $1 MILLION

Of greater historical significance, however, was the assistance given to the Bolsheviks first by Thompson, then, after December 4, 1917, by Raymond Robins.

Thompson's contribution to the Bolshevik cause was recorded in the contemporary American press. The *Washington Post* of February 2, 1918, carried the following paragraphs:

GIVES BOLSHEVIKI A MILLION

W. B. Thompson, Red Cross Donor, Believes Party Misrepresented.
New York, Feb. 2 (1918). William B. Thompson, who was in Petrograd from July until November last, has made a personal contribution of $1,000,000 to the Bolsheviki for the purpose of spreading their doctrine in Germany and Austria.

Mr. Thompson had an opportunity to study Russian conditions as head of the American Red Cross Mission, expenses of which also were largely defrayed by his personal contributions. He believes that the Bolsheviki constitute the greatest power against Pro-Germanism in Russia and that their propaganda has been undermining the militarist regimes of the General Empires.

Mr. Thompson deprecates American criticism of the Bolsheviki. He believes they have been misrepresented and has made the financial contribution to the cause in the belief that it will be money well spent for the future of Russia as well as for the Allied cause.

Hermann Hagedorn's biography *The Magnate: William Boyce Thompson and His Time (1869-1930)* reproduces a photograph of a cablegram from J. P. Morgan in New York to W. B. Thompson, "Care American Red Cross, Hotel Europe, Petrograd." The cable is date-stamped, showing it was received at Petrograd "8-Dek 1917" (8 December 1917), and reads:

New York Y757/5 24W5 Nil—Your cable second received. We have paid National City Bank one million dollars as instructed—Morgan.

The National City Bank branch in Petrograd had been exempted from the Bolshevik nationalization decree—the only foreign or domestic Russian bank to have been so exempted. Hagedorn says that this million dollars paid into Thompson's NCB account was used for "political purposes."

SOCIALIST MINING PROMOTER RAYMOND ROBINS[9]

William B. Thompson left Russia in early December 1917 to return home. He traveled via London, where, in company with Thomas Lamont of the J. P. Morgan firm, he visited Prime Minister Lloyd George, an episode we pick up in the next chapter. His deputy, Raymond Robins, was left in charge of the Red Cross Mission to Russia. The general impression that Colonel Robins presented in the subsequent months was not overlooked by the press. In the words of the Russian newspaper *Russkoe Slovo,* Robins "on the one

9. Robins is the correct spelling. The name is consistently spelled "Robbins" in the State Department files.

hand represents American labor and on the other hand American capital, which is endeavoring through the Soviets to gain their Russian markets."[10]

Raymond Robins started life as the manager of a Florida phosphate company commissary. From this base he developed a kaolin deposit, then prospected Texas and the Indian territories in the late nineteenth century. Moving north to Alaska, Robins made a fortune in the Klondike gold rush. Then, for no observable reason, he switched to socialism and the reform movement. By 1912 he was an active member of Roosevelt's Progressive Party. He joined the 1917 American Red Cross Mission to Russia as a "social economist."

There is considerable evidence, including Robins' own statements, that his reformist social-good appeals were little more than covers for the acquisition of further power and wealth, reminiscent of Frederick Howe's suggestions in *Confessions of a Monopolist*. For example, in February 1918 Arthur Bullard was in Petrograd with the U.S. Committee on Public Information and engaged in writing a long memorandum for Colonel Edward House. This memorandum was given to Robins by Bullard for comments and criticism before transmission to House in Washington, D.C. Robins' very unsocialistic and imperialistic comments were to the effect that the manuscript was "uncommonly discriminating, far-seeing and well done," but that he had one or two reservations—in particular, that recognition of the Bolsheviks was long overdue, that it should have been effected immediately, and that had the U.S. so recognized the Bolsheviks, "I believe that we would now be in control of the surplus resources of Russia and have control officers at all points on the frontier."[11]

This desire to gain "control of the surplus resources of Russia" was also obvious to Russians. Does this sound like a social reformer in the American Red Cross or a Wall Street mining promoter engaged in the practical exercise of imperialism?

In any event, Robins made no bones about his support for the Bolshevists.[12] Barely three weeks after the Bolshevik phase of the Revolution started, Robins cabled Henry Davison at Red Cross headquarters: "Please urge upon the President the necessity of our continued intercourse with the Bolshevik Government." Interestingly, this cable was in reply to a cable instructing Robins that the "President desires

10. U.S. State Dept. Decimal File, 316-11-1265, March 19, 1918.
11. Bullard ms., U.S. State Dept. Decimal File, 316-11-1265.
12. The *New World Review* (fall 1967, p. 40) comments on Robins, noting that he was "in sympathy with the aims of the Revolution, although a capitalist . . . ."

Limit of Area Controlled by Bolsheviks, January 1918.

the withholding of direct communications by representatives of the United States with the Bolshevik Government."[13] Several State Department reports complained about the partisan nature of Robins' activities. For example, on March 27, 1919, Harris, the American consul at Vladivostok, commented on a long conversation he had had with Robins and protested gross inaccuracies in the latter's reporting. Harris wrote, "Robins stated to me that no German and Austrian prisoners of war had joined the Bolshevik army up to May 1918. Robbins knew this statement was absolutely false." Harris then proceeded to provide the details of evidence available to Robins.[14]

Harris concluded, "Robbins deliberately misstated facts concerning Russia at that time and he has been doing it ever since."

On returning to the United States in 1918, Robins continued his efforts in behalf of the Bolsheviks. When the files of the Soviet Bureau were seized by the Lusk Committee, it was found that Robins had had "considerable correspondence" with Ludwig Martens and other members of the bureau. One of the more interesting documents seized was a letter from Santeri Nuorteva (alias Alexander Nyberg), the first Soviet representative in the U.S., to "Comrade Cahan," editor of the *New York Daily Forward*. The letter called on the party faithful to prepare the way for Raymond Robins:

(To Daily) FORWARD   July 6, 1918
Dear Comrade Cahan:
   It is of the utmost importance that the Socialist press set up a clamor immediately that Col. Raymond Robins, who has just returned from Russia at the head of the Red Cross Mission, should be heard from in a public report to the American people. The armed intervention danger has greatly increased. The reactionists are using the Czecho-Slovak adventure to bring about invasion. Robins has all the facts about this and about the situation in Russia generally. He takes our point of view.
   I am enclosing copy of Call editorial which shows a general line of argument, also some facts about Czecho-Slovaks.

                                                        Fraternally,

   PS&AU   Santeri Nuorteva

THE INTERNATIONAL RED CROSS AND REVOLUTION

Unknown to its administrators, the Red Cross has been used from time to time as a vehicle or cover for revolutionary activities. The

13. Petrograd embassy, Red Cross file.
14. U.S. State Dept. Decimal File, 861.00/4168.

use of Red Cross markings for unauthorized purposes is not uncommon. When Tsar Nicholas was moved from Petrograd to Tobolsk allegedly for his safety (although this direction was towards danger rather than safety), the train carried Japanese Red Cross placards. The State Department files contain examples of revolutionary activity under cover of Red Cross activities. For example, a Russian Red Cross official (Chelgajnov) was arrested in Holland in 1919 for revolutionary acts (316-21-107). During the Hungarian Bolshevik revolution in 1918, led by Bela Kun, Russian members of the Red Cross (or revolutionaries operating as members of the Russian Red Cross) were found in Vienna and Budapest. In 1919 the U.S. ambassador in London cabled Washington startling news; through the British government he had learned that "several Americans who had arrived in this country in the uniform of the Red Cross and who stated that they were Bolsheviks . . . were proceeding through France to Switzerland to spread Bolshevik propaganda." The ambassador noted that about 400 American Red Cross people had arrived in London in November and December 1918; of that number one quarter returned to the United States and "the remainder insisted on proceeding to France." There was a later report on January 15, 1918, to the effect that an editor of a labor newspaper in London had been approached on three different occasions by three different American Red Cross officials who offered to take commissions to Bolsheviks in Germany. The editor had suggested to the U S embassy that it watch American Red Cross personnel. The U.S. State Department took these reports seriously and Polk cabled for names, stating, "If true, I consider it of the greatest importance" (861.00/3602 and /3627).

To summarize: the picture we form of the 1917 American Red Cross Mission to Russia is remote from one of neutral humanitarianism. The mission was in fact a mission of Wall Street financiers to influence and pave the way for control, through either Kerensky or the Bolshevik revolutionaries, of the Russian market and resources. No other explanation will explain the actions of the mission. However, neither Thompson nor Robins was a Bolshevik. Nor was either even a consistent socialist. The writer is inclined to the interpretation that the socialist appeals of each man were covers for more prosaic objectives. Each man was intent upon the commercial; that is, each sought to use the political process in Russia for personal financial ends. Whether the Russian people wanted the Bolsheviks was of no concern. Whether the Bolshevik regime would act against the United States—as it consistently did later—was of no concern. The single overwhelming objective was to gain political and economic influence with the new regime, whatever its ideology. If William Boyce Thompson had acted alone, then his directorship of the Federal Reserve Bank would be inconsequential. However, the fact that his mission was dominated by representatives of Wall Street institutions raises a serious question—in effect, whether the mission was a planned, premeditated operation by a Wall Street syndicate. This the reader will have to judge for himself, as the rest of the story unfolds.

Chapter 6

CONSOLIDATION AND EXPORT OF THE REVOLUTION

Marx's great book *Das Kapital* is at once a monument of reasoning and a storehouse of facts.

Lord Milner, member of the British War Cabinet, 1917, and director of the London Joint Stock Bank

William Boyce Thompson is an unknown name in twentieth-century history, yet Thompson played a crucial role in the Bolshevik Revolution.[1] Indeed, if Thompson had not been in Russia in 1917, subsequent history might have followed a quite different course. Without the financial and, more important, the diplomatic and propaganda assistance given to Trotsky and Lenin by Thompson, Robins, and their New York associates, the Bolsheviks may well have withered away and Russia evolved into a socialist but constitutional society.

Who was William Boyce Thompson? Thompson was a promoter of mining stocks, one of the best in a high-risk business. Before World War I he handled stock-market operations for the Guggenheim copper interests. When the Guggenheims needed quick capital for a stock-market struggle with John D. Rockefeller, it was Thompson

---

1. For a biography see Hermann Hagedorn, *The Magnate: William Boyce Thompson and His Time (1869-1930)* (New York: Reynal & Hitchcock, 1935).

who promoted Yukon Consolidated Goldfields before an unsuspecting public to raise a $3.5 million war chest. Thompson was manager of the Kennecott syndicate, another Guggenheim operation, valued at $200 million. It was Guggenheim Exploration, on the other hand, that took up Thompson's options on the rich Nevada Consolidated Copper Company. About three quarters of the original Guggenheim Exploration Company was controlled by the Guggenheim family, the Whitney family (who owned *Metropolitan* magazine, which employed the Bolshevik John Reed), and John Ryan. In 1916 the Guggenheim interests reorganized into Guggenheim Brothers and brought in William C. Potter, who was formerly with Guggenheim's American Smelting and Refining Company but who was in 1916 first vice president of Guaranty Trust.

Extraordinary skill in raising capital for risky mining promotions earned Thompson a personal fortune and directorships in Inspiration Consolidated Copper Company, Nevada Consolidated Copper Company, and Utah Copper Company—all major domestic copper producers. Copper is, of course, a major material in the manufacture of munitions. Thompson was also director of the Chicago Rock Island & Pacific Railroad, the Magma Arizona Railroad and the Metropolitan Life Insurance Company. And of particular interest for this book, Thompson was "one of the heaviest stockholders in the Chase National Bank." It was Albert H. Wiggin, president of the Chase Bank, who pushed Thompson for a post in the Federal Reserve System; and in 1914 Thompson became the first full-term director of the Federal Reserve Bank of New York—the most important bank in the Federal Reserve System.

By 1917, then, William Boyce Thompson was a financial operator of substantial means, demonstrated ability, with a flair for promotion and implementation of capitalist projects, and with ready access to the centers of political and financial power. This was the same man who first supported Aleksandr Kerensky, and who then became an ardent supporter of the Bolsheviks, bequeathing a surviving symbol of this support—a laudatory pamphlet in Russian, "Pravda o Rossii i Bol'shevikakh."[2]

Before leaving Russia in early December 1917 Thompson handed over the American Red Cross Mission to his deputy Raymond Robins. Robins then organized Russian revolutionaries to implement the Thompson plan for spreading Bolshevik propaganda in Europe

2. Polkovnik' Villiam' Boic' Thompson', "Pravda o Rossii i Bol'shevikakh" (New York: Russian-American Publication Society, 1918).

(see Appendix 3). A French government document confirms this: "It appeared that Colonel Robins . . . was able to send a subversive mission of Russian bolsheviks to Germany to start a revolution there."[3] This mission led to the abortive German Spartacist revolt of 1918. The overall plan also included schemes for dropping Bolshevik literature by airplane or for smuggling it across German lines.

Thompson made preparations in late 1917 to leave Petrograd and sell the Bolshevik Revolution to governments in Europe and to the U.S. With this in mind, Thompson cabled Thomas W. Lamont, a partner in the Morgan firm who was then in Paris with Colonel E. M. House. Lamont recorded the receipt of this cablegram in his biography:

> Just as the House Mission was completing its discussions in Paris in December 1917, I received an arresting cable from my old school and business friend, William Boyce Thompson, who was then in Petrograd in charge of the American Red Cross Mission there.[4]

Lamont journeyed to London and met with Thompson, who had left Petrograd on December 5, traveled via Bergen, Norway, and arrived in London on December 10. The most important achievement of Thompson and Lamont in London was to convince the British War Cabinet—then decidedly anti-Bolshevik—that the Bolshevik regime had come to stay, and that British policy should cease to be anti-Bolshevik, should accept the new realities, and should support Lenin and Trotsky. Thompson and Lamont left London on December 18 and arrived in New York on December 25, 1917. They attempted the same process of conversion in the United States.

A CONSULTATION WITH LLOYD GEORGE

The secret British War Cabinet papers are now available and record the argument used by Thompson to sell the British government on a pro-Bolshevik policy. The prime minister of Great Britain was David Lloyd George. Lloyd George's private and political machinations rivaled those of a Tammany Hall politician—yet in his lifetime and for decades after, biographers were unable, or unwilling, to come to grips with them. In 1970 Donald McCormick's *The Mask of Merlin*

---

3. John Bradley, *Allied Intervention in Russia* (London: Weidenfeld and Nicolson, 1968.)
4. Thomas W. Lamont, *Across World Frontiers* (New York: Harcourt, Brace, 1959), p. 85. See also pp. 94-97 for massive breastbeating over the failure of President Wilson to act promptly to befriend the Soviet regime. Corliss Lamont, his son, became a front-line domestic leftist in the U.S.

Полковникъ Вилліамъ Бойсъ
ТОМПСОНЪ

Правда о Россіи
и Большевикахъ

RUSSIAN-AMERICAN PUBLICATION SOCIETY
44 WHITEHALL STREET
NEW YORK

Cover of Colonel Thompson's pamphlet issued by the Bolsheviks.

lifted the veil of secrecy. McCormick shows that by 1917 David Lloyd George had bogged "too deeply in the mesh of international armaments intrigues to be a free agent" and was beholden to Sir Basil Zaharoff, an international armaments dealer, whose considerable fortune was made by selling arms to both sides in several wars.[5] Zaharoff wielded enormous behind-the-scenes power and, according to McCormick, was consulted on war policies by the Allied leaders. On more than one occasion, reports McCormick, Woodrow Wilson, Lloyd George, and Georges Clemenceau met in Zaharoff's Paris home. McCormick notes that "Allied statesmen and leaders were obliged to consult him before planning any great attack." British intelligence, according to McCormick, "discovered documents which incriminated servants of the Crown as secret agents of Sir Basil Zaharoff *with the knowledge of Lloyd George.*"[6] In 1917 Zaharoff was linked to the Bolsheviks; he sought to divert munitions away from anti-Bolsheviks and had already intervened in behalf of the Bolshevik regime in both London and Paris.

In late 1917, then—at the time Lamont and Thompson arrived in London—Prime Minister Lloyd George was indebted to powerful international armaments interests that were allied to the Bolsheviks and providing assistance to extend Bolshevik power in Russia. The British prime minister who met with William Thompson in 1917 was not then a free agent; Lord Milner was the power behind the scenes and, as the epigraph to this chapter suggests, favorably inclined towards socialism and Karl Marx.

The "secret" War Cabinet papers give the "Prime Minister's account of a conversation with Mr. Thompson, an American returned from Russia,"[7] and the report made by the prime minister to the War Cabinet after meeting with Thompson.[8] The cabinet paper reads as follows:

> The Prime Minister reported a conversation he had had with a Mr. Thompson—an American traveller and a man of considerable means— who had just returned from Russia, and who had given a somewhat different impression of affairs in that country from what was generally

5. Donald McCormick, *The Mask of Merlin* (London: MacDonald, 1963; New York: Holt, Rinehart and Winston, 1964), p. 208. Lloyd George's personal life would certainly leave him open to blackmail.
6. Ibid. McCormick's italics.
7. British War Cabinet papers, no. 302, sec. 2 (Public Records Office, London).
8. The written memorandum that Thompson submitted to Lloyd George and that became the basis for the War Cabinet statement is available from U.S. archival sources and is printed in full in Appendix 3.

believed. The gist of his remarks was to the effect that the Revolution had come to stay; that the Allies had not shown themselves sufficiently sympathetic with the Revolution; and that MM. Trotzki and Lenin were not in German pay, the latter being a fairly distinguished Professor. Mr. Thompson had added that he considered the Allies should conduct in Russia an active propaganda, carried out by some form of Allied Council composed of men especially selected for the purpose; further, that on the whole, he considered, having regard to the character of the de facto Russian Government, the several Allied Governments were not suitably represented in Petrograd. In Mr. Thompson's opinion, it was necessary for the Allies to realise that the Russian army and people were out of the war, and that the Allies would have to choose between Russia as the friendly or a hostile neutral.

The question was discussed as to whether the Allies ought not to change their policy in regard to the de facto Russian Government, the Bolsheviks being stated by Mr. Thompson to be anti-German. In this connection Lord Robert Cecil drew attention to the conditions of the armistice between the German and Russian armies, which provided, inter alia, for trading between the two countries, and for the establishment of a Purchasing Commission in Odessa, the whole arrangement being obviously dictated by the Germans. Lord Robert Cecil expressed the view that the Germans would endeavour to continue the armistice until the Russian army had melted away.

Sir Edward Carson read a communication, signed by M. Trotzki, which had been sent to him by a British subject, the manager of the Russian branch of the Vauxhall Motor Company, who had just returned from Russia [Paper G.T.—3040]. This report indicated that M. Trotzki's policy was, ostensibly at any rate, one of hostility to the organisation of civilised society rather than pro-German. On the other hand, it was suggested that an assumed attitude of this kind was by no means inconsistent with Trotzki's being a German agent, whose object was to ruin Russia in order that Germany might do what she desired in that country.

After hearing Lloyd George's report and supporting arguments, the War Cabinet decided to go along with Thompson and the Bolsheviks. Milner had a former British consul in Russia—Bruce Lockhart—ready and waiting in the wings. Lockhart was briefed and sent to Russia with instructions to work informally with the Soviets.

The thoroughness of Thompson's work in London and the pressure he was able to bring to bear on the situation are suggested by subsequent reports coming into the hands of the War Cabinet, from authentic sources. The reports provide a quite different view of Trotsky and the Bolsheviks from that presented by Thompson, and yet they were ignored by the cabinet. In April 1918 General Jan

Smuts reported to the War Cabinet his talk with General Nieffel, the head of the French Military Mission who had just returned from Russia:

Trotski (sic) . . . was a consummate scoundrel who may not be pro-German, but is thoroughly pro-Trotski and pro-revolutionary and cannot in any way be trusted. His influence is shown by the way he has come to dominate Lockhart, Robins and the French representative. He [Nieffel] counsels great prudence in dealing with Trotski, who he admits is the only really able man in Russia.[9]

Several months later Thomas D. Thacher, Wall Street lawyer and another member of the American Red Cross Mission to Russia, was in London. On April 13, 1918, Thacher wrote to the American ambassador in London to the effect that he had received a request from H. P. Davison, a Morgan partner, "to confer with Lord Northcliffe" concerning the situation in Russia and then to go on to Paris "for other conferences." Lord Northcliffe was ill and Thacher left with yet another Morgan partner, Dwight W. Morrow, a memorandum to be submitted to Northcliffe on his return to London.[10] This memorandum not only made explicit suggestions about Russian policy that supported Thompson's position but even stated that "the fullest assistance should be given to the Soviet government in its efforts to organize a volunteer revolutionary army." The four main proposals in this Thacher report are:

First of all . . . the Allies should discourage Japanese intervention in Siberia.

In the second place, the fullest assistance should be given to the Soviet Government in its efforts to organize a volunteer revolutionary army.

Thirdly, the Allied Governments should give their moral support to the Russian people in their efforts to work out their own political systems free from the domination of any foreign power. . . .

Fourthly, until the time when open conflict shall result between the German Government and the Soviet Government of Russia there will be opportunity for peaceful commercial penetration by German agencies in Russia. So long as there is no open break, it will probably be impossible to entirely prevent such commerce. Steps should, therefore,

9. War Cabinet papers, 24/49/7197 (G.T. 4322) Secret, April 24, 1918.
10. Letter reproduced in full in Appendix 3. It should be noted that we have identified Thomas Lamont, Dwight Morrow, and H. P. Davison as being closely involved in developing policy towards the Bolsheviks. All were partners in the J. P. Morgan firm. Thacher was with the law firm Simpson, Thacher & Bartlett and was a close friend of Felix Frankfurter.

be taken to impede, so far as possible, the transport of grain and raw materials to Germany from Russia.[11]

THOMPSON'S INTENTIONS AND OBJECTIVES

Why would a prominent Wall Street financier, and director of the Federal Reserve Bank, want to organize and assist Bolshevik revolutionaries? Why would not one but several Morgan partners working in concert want to encourage the formation of a Soviet "volunteer revolutionary army"—an army supposedly dedicated to the overthrow of Wall Street, including Thompson, Thomas Lamont, Dwight Morrow, the Morgan firm, and all their associates?

Thompson at least was straightforward about his objectives in Russia: he wanted to keep Russia at war with Germany (yet he argued before the British War Cabinet that Russia was out of the war anyway) and to retain Russia as a market for postwar American enterprise. The December 1917 Thompson memorandum to Lloyd George describes these aims.[12] The memorandum begins, "The Russian situation is lost and Russia lies entirely open to unopposed German exploitation . . . ," and concludes, "I believe that intelligent and courageous work will still prevent Germany from occupying the field to itself and thus exploiting Russia at the expense of the Allies." Consequently, it was German commercial and industrial exploitation of Russia that Thompson feared (this is also reflected in the Thacher memorandum) and that brought Thompson and his New York friends into an alliance with the Bolsheviks. Moreover, this interpretation is reflected in a quasi-jocular statement made by Raymond Robins, Thompson's deputy, to Bruce Lockhart, the British agent:

> You will hear it said that I am the representative of Wall Street; that I am the servant of William B. Thompson to get Altai copper for him; that I have already got 500,000 acres of the best timber land in Russia for myself; that I have already copped off the Trans-Siberian Railway; that they have given me a monopoly of the platinum of Russia; that this explains my working for the soviet . . . . You will hear that talk. Now, I do not think it is true, Commissioner, but let us assume it is true. Let us assume that I am here to capture Russia for Wall Street and American business men. Let us assume that you are a British wolf and I am an American wolf, and that when this war is over we are going to eat each other up for the Russian market; let us do so in perfectly frank, man fashion, but let us assume at the same time that we

11. Complete memorandum is in U.S. State Dept. Decimal File, 316-13-698.
12. See Appendix 3.

96

are fairly intelligent wolves, and that we know that if we do not hunt together in this hour the German wolf will eat us both up, and then let us go to work.[13]

With this in mind let us take a look at Thompson's personal motivations. Thompson was a financier, a promoter, and, although without previous interest in Russia, had personally financed the Red Cross Mission to Russia and used the mission as a vehicle for political maneuvering. From the total picture we can deduce that Thompson's motives were primarily financial and commercial. Specifically, Thompson was interested in the Russian market, and how this market could be influenced, diverted, and captured for postwar exploitation by a Wall Street syndicate, or syndicates. Certainly Thompson viewed Germany as an enemy, but less a political enemy than an economic or a commercial enemy. German industry and German banking were the real enemy. To outwit Germany, Thompson was willing to place seed money on any political power vehicle that would achieve his objective. In other words, Thompson was an American imperialist fighting against German imperialism, and this struggle was shrewdly recognized and exploited by Lenin and Trotsky.

The evidence supports this apolitical approach. In early August 1917, William Boyce Thompson lunched at the U.S. Petrograd embassy with Kerensky, Terestchenko, and the American ambassador Francis. Over lunch Thompson showed his Russian guests a cable he had just sent to the New York office of J. P. Morgan requesting transfer of 425,000 rubles to cover a personal subscription to the new Russian Liberty Loan. Thompson also asked Morgan to "inform my friends I recommend these bonds as the best war investment I know. Will be glad to look after their purchasing here without compensation"; he then offered personally to take up twenty percent of a New York syndicate buying five million rubles of the Russian loan. Not unexpectedly, Kerensky and Terestchenko indicated "great gratification" at support from Wall Street. And Ambassador Francis by cable promptly informed the State Department that the Red Cross commission was "working harmoniously with me," and that it would have an "excellent effect."[14] Other writers have recounted how Thompson attempted to convince the Russian peasants to support Kerensky by investing $1 million of his own

13. U.S., Senate, *Bolshevik Propaganda,* Hearings before a Subcommittee of the Committee on the Judiciary, 65th Cong., 1919, p. 802.
14. U.S. State Dept. Decimal File, 861.51/184.

97

money and U.S. government funds on the same order of magnitude in propaganda activities. Subsequently, the Committee on Civic Education in Free Russia, headed by the revolutionary "Grandmother" Breshkovskaya, with David Soskice (Kerensky's private secretary) as executive, established newspapers, news bureaus, printing plants, and speakers bureaus to promote the appeal—"Fight the kaiser and save the revolution." It is noteworthy that the Thompson-funded Kerensky campaign had the same appeal—"Keep Russia in the war"—as had his financial support of the Bolsheviks. The common link between Thompson's support of Kerensky and his support of Trotsky and Lenin was—"continue the war against Germany" and keep Germany out of Russia.

In brief, behind and below the military, diplomatic, and political aspects of World War I, there was another battle raging, namely, a maneuvering for postwar world economic power by international operators with significant muscle and influence. Thompson was not a Bolshevik; he was not even pro-Bolshevik. Neither was he pro-Kerensky. Nor was he even pro-American. *The overriding motivation was the capturing of the postwar Russian market.* This was a commercial, not an ideological, objective. Ideology could sway revolutionary operators like Kerensky, Trotsky, Lenin et al., but not financiers.

The Lloyd George memorandum demonstrates Thompson's partiality for neither Kerensky nor the Bolsheviks: "After the overthrow of the last Kerensky government we materially aided the dissemination of the Bolshevik literature, distributing it through agents and by aeroplanes to the Germany army."[15] This was written in mid-December 1917, only five weeks after the start of the Bolshevik Revolution, and less than four months after Thompson expressed his support of Kerensky over lunch in the American embassy.

THOMPSON RETURNS TO THE UNITED STATES
Thompson then returned and toured the United States with a public plea for recognition of the Soviets. In a speech to the Rocky Mountain Club of New York in January 1918, Thompson called for assistance for the emerging Bolshevik government and, appealing to an audience composed largely of Westerners, evoked the spirit of the American pioneers:

These men would not have hesitated very long about extending recog-

15. See Appendix 3.

98

nition and giving the fullest help and sympathy to the workingman's government of Russia, because in 1849 and the years following we had out there bolsheviki governments . . . and mighty good governments too. . . . [16]

It strains the imagination to compare the pioneer experience of our Western frontier to the ruthless extermination of political opposition then under way in Russia. To Thompson, promoting this was no doubt looked upon as akin to his promotion of mining stocks in days gone by. As for those in Thompson's audience, we know not what they thought; however, no one raised a challenge. The speaker was a respected director of the Federal Reserve Bank of New York, a self-made millionaire (and that counts for much). And after all, had he not just returned from Russia? But all was not rosy. Thompson's biographer Hermann Hagedorn has written that Wall Street was "stunned," that his friends were "shocked" and "said he had lost his head, had turned Bolshevist himself."[17]

While Wall Street wondered whether he had indeed "turned Bolshevik," Thompson found sympathy among fellow directors on the board of the Federal Reserve Bank of New York. Codirector W. L. Saunders, chairman of Ingersoll-Rand Corporation and a director of the FRB, wrote President Wilson on October 17, 1918, stating that he was "in sympathy with the Soviet form of Government"; at the same time he disclaimed any ulterior motive such as "preparing now to get the trade of the world after the war."[18]

Most interesting of Thompson's fellow directors was George Foster Peabody, deputy chairman of the Federal Reserve Bank of New York and a close friend of socialist Henry George. Peabody had made a fortune in railroad manipulation, as Thompson had made his fortune in the manipulation of copper stocks. Peabody then became active in behalf of government ownership of railroads, and openly adopted socialization.[19] How did Peabody reconcile his private-enterprise success with promotion of government ownership? According to his biographer Louis Ware, "His reasoning told him that it was important for this form of transport to be operated as a public service rather than for the advantage of private interests." This high-sounding do-good reasoning hardly rings true. It would be

16. Inserted by Senator Calder into the *Congressional Record*, January 31, 1918, p. 1409.
17. Hagedorn, op. cit., p. 263.
18. U.S. State Dept. Decimal File, 861.00/3005.
19. Louis Ware, *George Foster Peabody* (Athens: University of Georgia Press, 1951).

more accurate to argue that given the dominant political influence of Peabody and his fellow financiers in Washington, they could by government control of railroads more easily avoid the rigors of competition. Through political influence they could manipulate the police power of the state to achieve what they had been unable, or what was too costly, to achieve under private enterprise. In other words, the police power of the state was a means of maintaining a private monoply. This was exactly as Frederick C. Howe had proposed.[20] The idea of a centrally planned socialist Russia must have appealed to Peabody. Think of it—one gigantic state monopoly! And Thompson, his friend and fellow director, had the inside track with the boys running the operation![21]

THE UNOFFICIAL AMBASSADORS:
ROBINS, LOCKHART, AND SADOUL

The Bolsheviks for their part correctly assessed a lack of sympathy among the Petrograd representatives of the three major Western powers: the United States, Britain and France. The United States was represented by Ambassador Francis, undisguisedly out of sympathy with the revolution. Great Britain was represented by Sir James Buchanan, who had strong ties to the tsarist monarchy and was suspected of having helped along the Kerensky phase of the revolution. France was represented by Ambassador Paleologue, overtly anti-Bolshevik. In early 1918 three additional personages made their appearance; they became *de facto* representatives of these Western countries and edged out the officially recognized representatives.

Raymond Robins took over the Red Cross Mission from W. B. Thompson in early December 1917 but concerned himself more with economic and political matters than obtaining relief and assistance for poverty-stricken Russia. On December 26, 1917, Robins cabled Morgan partner Henry Davison, temporarily the director general of the American Red Cross: "Please urge upon the President the necessity of our continued intercourse with the Bolshevik Government."[22] On January 23, 1918, Robins cabled Thompson, then in New York:

20. See p. 16.
21. If this argument seems too farfetched, the reader should see Gabriel Kolko, *Railroads and Regulation 1877-1916* (New York: W. W. Norton, 1965), which describes how pressures for government control and formation of the Interstate Commerce Commission came from the railroad *owners*, not from farmers and users of railroad services.
22. C. K. Cumming and Walter W. Pettit, *Russian-American Relations, Documents and Papers* (New York: Harcourt, Brace & Howe, 1920), doc. 44.

Soviet Government stronger today than ever before. Its authority and power greatly consolidated by dissolution of Constituent Assembly. . . . Cannot urge too strongly importance of prompt recognition of Bolshevik authority. . . . Sisson approves this text and requests you to show this cable to Creel. Thacher and Wardwell concur.[23]

Later in 1918, on his return to the United States, Robins submitted a report to Secretary of State Robert Lansing containing this opening paragraph: "American economic cooperation with Russia; Russia will welcome American assistance in economic reconstruction."[24]

Robins' persistent efforts in behalf of the Bolshevik cause gave him a certain prestige in the Bolshevik camp, and perhaps even some political influence. The U.S. embassy in London claimed in November 1918 that "Salkind owe[s] his appointment, as Bolshevik Ambassador to Switzerland, to an American . . . no other than Mr. Raymond Robins."[25] About this time reports began filtering into Washington that Robins was himself a Bolshevik; for example, the following from Copenhagen, dated December 3, 1918:

Confidential. According to a statement made by Radek to George de Patpourrie, late Austria Hungarian Consul General at Moscow, Colonel Robbins [*sic*], formerly chief of the American Red Cross Mission to Russia, is at present in Moscow negotiating with the Soviet Government and acts as the intermediary between the Bolsheviki and their friends in the United States. The impression seems to be in some quarters that Colonel Robbins is himself a Bolsheviki while others maintain that he is not but that his activities in Russia have been contrary to the interest of Associated Governments.[26]

Materials in the files of the Soviet Bureau in New York, and seized by the Lusk Committee in 1919, confirm that both Robins and his wife were closely associated with Bolshevik activities in the United States and with the formation of the Soviet Bureau in New York.[27]

The British government established unofficial relations with the Bolshevik regime by sending to Russia a young Russian-speaking agent, Bruce Lockhart. Lockhart was, in effect, Robins' opposite number; but unlike Robins, Lockhart had direct channels to his Foreign Office. Lockhart was not selected by the foreign secretary or the Foreign Office; both were dismayed at the appointment. Ac-

23. Ibid., doc. 54.
24. Ibid., doc. 92.
25. U.S. State Dept. Decimal File, 861.00/3449. But see Kennan, *Russia Leaves the War*, pp. 401-5.
26. Ibid., 861.00/3333.
27. See chapter seven.

cording to Richard Ullman, Lockhart was "selected for his mission by Milner and Lloyd George themselves. . . ." Maxim Litvinov, acting as unofficial Soviet representative in Great Britain, wrote for Lockhart a letter of introduction to Trotsky; in it he called the British agent "a thoroughly honest man who understands our position and sympathizes with us."[28]

We have already noted the pressures on Lloyd George to take a pro-Bolshevik position, especially those from William B. Thompson, and those indirectly from Sir Basil Zaharoff and Lord Milner. Milner was, as the epigraph to this chapter suggests, exceedingly prosocialist. Edward Crankshaw has succinctly outlined Milner's duality.

> Some of the passages [in Milner] on industry and society . . . are passages which any Socialist would be proud to have written. But they were not written by a Socialist. They were written by "the man who made the Boer War." Some of the passages on Imperialism and the white man's burden might have been written by a Tory diehard. They were written by the student of Karl Marx.[29]

According to Lockhart, the socialist bank director Milner was a man who inspired in him "the greatest affection and hero-worship."[30] Lockhart recounts how Milner personally sponsored his Russian appointment, pushed it to cabinet level, and after his appointment talked "almost daily" with Lockhart. While opening the way for recognition of the Bolsheviks, Milner also promoted financial support for their opponents in South Russia and elsewhere, as did Morgan in New York. This dual policy is consistent with the thesis that the *modus operandi* of the politicized internationalists—such as Milner and Thompson—was to place state money on any revolutionary or counterrevolutionary horse that looked a possible winner. The internationalists, of course, claimed any subsequent benefits. The clue is perhaps in Bruce Lockhart's observation that Milner was a man who "believed in the highly organized state."[31]

The French government appointed an even more openly Bolshevik sympathizer, Jacques Sadoul, an old friend of Trotsky.[32]

28. Richard H. Ullman, *Intervention and the War* (Princeton, N.J.: Princeton University Press, 1961), p. 61.
29. Edward Crankshaw, *The Forsaken Idea: A Study of Viscount Milner* (London: Longmans Green, 1952), p. 269.
30. Robert Hamilton Bruce Lockhart, *British Agent* (New York: Putnam's, 1933), p. 119.
31. Ibid., p. 204.
32. See Jacques Sadoul, *Notes sur la revolution bolchevique* (Paris: Editions de la sirene, 1919).

In sum, the Allied governments neutralized their own diplomatic representatives in Petrograd and replaced them with unofficial agents more or less sympathetic to the Bolshevists.

The reports of these unofficial ambassadors were in direct contrast to pleas for help addressed to the West from inside Russia. Maxim Gorky protested the betrayal of revolutionary ideals by the Lenin-Trotsky group, which had imposed the iron grip of a police state in Russia:

> We Russians make up a people that has never yet worked in freedom, that has never yet had a chance to develop all its powers and its talents. And when I think that the revolution gives us the possibility of free work, of a many-sided joy in creating, my heart is filled with great hope and joy, even in these cursed days that are besmirched with blood and alcohol.
>
> There is where begins the line of my decided and irreconcilable separation from the insane actions of the People's Commissaries. I consider Maximalism in ideas very useful for the boundless Russian soul; its task is to develop in this soul great and bold needs, to call forth the so necessary fighting spirit and activity, to promote initiative in this indolent soul and to give it shape and life in general.
>
> But the practical Maximalism of the Anarcho-Communists and visionaries from the Smolny is ruinous for Russia and, above all, for the Russian working class. The People's Commissaries handle Russia like material for an experiment. The Russian people is for them what the Horse is for learned bacteriologists who inoculate the horse with typhus so that the anti-typhus lymph may develop in its blood. Now the Commissaries are trying such a predestined-to-failure experiment upon the Russian people without thinking that the tormented, half-starved horse may die.
>
> The reformers from the Smolny do not worry about Russia. They are cold-bloodedly sacrificing Russia in the name of their dream of the worldwide and European revolution. And just as long as I can, I shall impress this upon the Russian proletarian: "Thou art being led to destruction! Thou art being used as material for an inhuman experiment!"[33]

Also in contrast to the reports of the sympathetic unofficial ambassadors were the reports from the old-line diplomatic representatives. Typical of many messages flowing into Washington in early 1918—particularly after Woodrow Wilson's expression of support for the Bolshevik government—was the following cable from the U. S. legation in Bern, Switzerland:

33. Maxim Gorky, *The New Life*, April 1918.

For Polk. President's message to Consul Moscow not understood here and people are asking why the President expresses support of Bolsheviki, in view of rapine, murder and anarchy of these bands.[34]

Continued support by the Wilson administration for the Bolsheviks led to the resignation of De Witt C. Poole, the capable American chargé d'affaires in Archangel (Russia):

> It is my duty to explain frankly to the department the perplexity into which I have been thrown by the statement of Russian policy adopted by the Peace Conference, January 22, on the motion of the President. The announcement very happily recognizes the revolution and confirms again that entire absence of sympathy for any form of counter revolution which has always been a key note of American policy in Russia, but it contains not one [word] of condemnation for the other enemy of the revolution—the Bolshevik Government.[35]

Thus even in the early days of 1918 the betrayal of the libertarian revolution had been noted by such acute observers as Maxim Gorky and De Witt C. Poole. Poole's resignation shook the State Department, which requested the "utmost reticence regarding your desire to resign" and stated that "it will be necessary to replace you in a natural and normal manner in order to prevent grave and perhaps disastrous effect upon the morale of American troops in the Archangel district which might lead to loss of American lives."[36]

So not only did Allied governments neutralize their own government representatives but the U.S. ignored pleas from within and without Russia to cease support of the Bolsheviks. Influential support of the Soviets came heavily from the New York financial area (little effective support emanated from domestic U.S. revolutionaries). In particular, it came from American International Corporation, a Morgan-controlled firm.

EXPORTING THE REVOLUTION: JACOB H. RUBIN

We are now in a position to compare two cases—not by any means the only such cases—in which American citizens Jacob Rubin and Robert Minor assisted in exporting the revolution to Europe and other parts of Russia.

Jacob H. Rubin was a banker who, in his own words, "helped to form the Soviet Government of Odessa."[37] Rubin was president,

34. U.S. State Dept. Decimal File, 861.00/1305, March 15, 1918.
35. Ibid., 861.00/3804.
36. Ibid.
37. U.S., House, Committee on Foreign Affairs, *Conditions in Russia*, 66th Cong., 3d sess., 1921.

treasurer, and secretary of Rubin Brothers of 19 West 34 Street, New York City. In 1917 he was associated with the Union Bank of Milwaukee and the Provident Loan Society of New York. The trustees of the Provident Loan Society included persons mentioned elsewhere as having connection with the Bolshevik Revolution: P. A. Rockefeller, Mortimer L. Schiff, and James Speyer.

By some process—only vaguely recounted in his book *I Live to Tell*[38]—Rubin was in Odessa in February 1920 and became the subject of a message from Admiral McCully to the State Department (dated February 13, 1920, 861.00/6349). The message was to the effect that Jacob H. Rubin of Union Bank, Milwaukee, was in Odessa and desired to remain with the Bolshevists—"Rubin does not wish to leave, has offered his services to Bolsheviks and apparently sympathizes with them." Rubin later found his way back to the U.S. and gave testimony before the House Committee on Foreign Affairs in 1921:

> I had been with the American Red Cross people at Odessa. I was there when the Red Army took possession of Odessa. At that time I was favorably inclined toward the Soviet Government, because I was a socialist and had been a member of that party for 20 years. I must admit that to a certain extent I helped to form the Soviet Government of Odessa. . . .[39]

While adding that he had been arrested as a spy by the Denikin government of South Russia, we learn little more about Rubin. We do, however, know a great deal more about Robert Minor, who was caught in the act and released by a mechanism reminiscent of Trotsky's release from a Halifax prisoner-of-war camp.

EXPORTING THE REVOLUTION: ROBERT MINOR

Bolshevik propaganda work in Germany,[40] financed and organized by William Boyce Thompson and Raymond Robins, was implemented in the field by American citizens, under the supervision of Trotsky's People's Commissariat for Foreign Affairs:

> One of Trotsky's earliest innovations in the Foreign Office had been to institute a Press Bureau under Karl Radek and a Bureau of Interna-

---

38. Jacob H. Rubin, *I Live to Tell: The Russian Adventures of an American Socialist* (Indianapolis: Bobbs-Merrill, 1934).
39. U.S., House, Committee on Foreign Affairs, op. cit.
40. See George G. Bruntz, *Allied Propaganda and the Collapse of the German Empire in 1918* (Stanford, Calif.: Stanford University Press, 1938), pp. 144-55; see also herein p. 82.

tional Revolutionary Propaganda under Boris Reinstein, among whose assistants were John Reed and Albert Rhys Williams, and the full blast of these power-houses was turned against the Germany army.

A German newspaper, Die Fackel (The Torch), was printed in editions of half a million a day and sent by special train to Central Army Committees in Minsk, Kiev, and other cities, which in turn distributed them to other points along the front.[41]

Robert Minor was an operative in Reinstein's propaganda bureau. Minor's ancestors were prominent in early American history. General Sam Houston, first president of the Republic of Texas, was related to Minor's mother, Routez Houston. Other relatives were Mildred Washington, aunt of George Washington, and General John Minor, campaign manager for Thomas Jefferson. Minor's father was a Virginia lawyer who migrated to Texas. After hard years with few clients, he became a San Antonio judge.

Robert Minor was a talented cartoonist and a socialist. He left Texas to come East. Some of his contributions appeared in *Masses,* a pro-Bolshevik journal. In 1918 Minor was a cartoonist on the staff of the *Philadelphia Public Ledger.* Minor left New York in March 1918 to report the Bolshevik Revolution. While in Russia Minor joined Reinstein's Bureau of International Revolutionary Propaganda (see diagram), along with Philip Price, correspondent of the *Daily Herald* and *Manchester Guardian,* and Jacques Sadoul, the unofficial French ambassador and friend of Trotsky.

Excellent data on the activities of Price, Minor, and Sadoul have survived in the form of a Scotland Yard (London) Secret Special Report, No. 4, entitled, "The Case of Philip Price and Robert Minor," as well as in reports in the files of the State Department, Washington, D.C.[42] According to this Scotland Yard report, Philip Price was in Moscow in mid-1917, before the Bolshevik Revolution, and admitted, "I am up to my neck in the Revolutionary movement." Between the revolution and about the fall of 1918, Price worked with Robert Minor in the Commissariat for Foreign Affairs.

In November 1918 Minor and Price left Russia and went to Germany.[43] Their propaganda products were first used on the Russian Murman front; leaflets were dropped by Bolshevik airplanes

41. John W. Wheeler-Bennett, *The Forgotten Peace* (New York: William Morrow, 1939).
42. There is a copy of this Scotland Yard report in U.S. State Dept. Decimal File, 316-23-1184/9.
43. Joseph North, *Robert Minor: Artist and Crusader* (New York: International Publishers, 1956).

ORGANIZATION OF FOREIGN PROPAGANDA WORK IN 1918

PEOPLE'S COMMISSARIAT FOR FOREIGN AFFAIRS
(Trotsky)

PRESS BUREAU
(Radek)

BUREAU OF INTERNATIONAL REVOLUTIONARY PROPAGANDA
(Reinstein)

Field Operatives
John Reed
Louise Bryant
Albert Rhys Williams
Robert Minor
Philip Price
Jacques Sadoul

amongst British, French, and American troops—according to William Thompson's program.[44] The decision to send Sadoul, Price, and Minor to Germany was made by the Central Executive Committee of the Communist Party. In Germany their activities came to the notice of British, French, and American intelligence. On February 15, 1919, Lieutenant J. Habas of the U.S. Army was sent to Düsseldorf, then under control of a Spartacist revolutionary group; he posed as a deserter from the American army and offered his services to the Spartacists. Habas got to know Philip Price and Robert Minor and suggested that some pamphlets be printed for distribution amongst American troops. The Scotland Yard report relates that Price and Minor had already written several pamphlets for British and American troops, that Price had translated some of Wilhelm Liebknecht's works into English, and that both were working on additional propaganda tracts. Habas reported that Minor and Price said they had worked together in Siberia printing an English-language Bolshevik newspaper for distribution by air among American and British troops.[45]

44. Samples of Minor's propaganda tracts are still in the U.S. State Dept. files. See p. 197-200 on Thompson.
45. See Appendix 3.

On June 8, 1919, Robert Minor was arrested in Paris by the French police and handed over to the American military authorities in Coblenz. Simultaneously, German Spartacists were arrested by the British military authorities in the Cologne area. Subsequently, the Spartacists were convicted on charges of conspiracy to cause mutiny and sedition among Allied forces. Price was arrested but, like Minor, speedily liberated. This hasty release was noted in the State Department:

> Robert Minor has now been released, for reasons that are not quite clear, since the evidence against him appears to have been ample to secure conviction. The release will have an unfortunate effect, for Minor is believed to have been intimately connected with the IWW in America.[46]

The mechanism by which Robert Minor secured his release is recorded in the State Department files. The first relevant document, dated June 12, 1919, is from the U.S. Paris embassy to the secretary of state in Washington, D.C., and marked URGENT AND CONFIDENTIAL.[47] The French Foreign Office informed the embassy that on June 8, Robert Minor, "an American correspondent," had been arrested in Paris and turned over to the general headquarters of the Third American Army in Coblenz. Papers found on Minor appear "to confirm the reports furnished on his activities. It would therefore seem to be established that Minor has entered into relations in Paris with the avowed partisans of Bolshevism." The embassy regarded Minor as a "particularly dangerous man." Inquiries were being made of the American military authorities; the embassy believed this to be a matter within the jurisdiction of the military alone, so that it contemplated no action although instructions would be welcome.

On June 14, Judge R. B. Minor in San Antonio, Texas, telegraphed Frank L. Polk in the State Department:

> Press reports detention my son Robert Minor in Paris for unknown reasons. Please do all possible to protect him I refer to Senators from Texas.
> [sgd.] R. P. Minor, District Judge, San Antonio, Texas[48]

Polk telegraphed Judge Minor that neither the State Department nor the War Department had information on the detention of Robert

46. U.S. State Dept. Decimal File, 316-23-1184.
47. Ibid., 861.00/4680 (316-22-0774).
48. Ibid., 861.00/4685 (/783).

Minor, and that the case was now before the military authorities at Coblenz. Late on June 13 the State Department received a "strictly confidential urgent" message from Paris reporting a statement made by the Office of Military Intelligence (Coblenz) in regard to the detention of Robert Minor: "Minor was arrested in Paris by French authorities upon request of British Military Intelligence and immediately turned over to American headquarters at Coblenz."[49] He was charged with writing and disseminating Bolshevik revolutionary literature, which had been printed in Düsseldorf, amongst British and American troops in the areas they occupied. The military authorities intended to examine the charges against Minor, and if substantiated, to try him by court-martial. If the charges were not substantiated, it was their intention to turn Minor over to the British authorities, "who originally requested that the French hand him over to them."[50] Judge Minor in Texas independently contacted Morris Sheppard, U.S. senator from Texas, and Sheppard contacted Colonel House in Paris. On June 17, 1919, Colonel House sent the following to Senator Sheppard:

> Both the American Ambassador and I are following Robert Minor's case. Am informed that he is detained by American Military authorities at Cologne on serious charges, the exact nature of which it is difficult to discover. Nevertheless, we will take every possible step to insure just consideration for him.[51]

Both Senator Sheppard and Congressman Carlos Bee (14th District, Texas) made their interest known to the State Department. On June 27, 1919, Congressman Bee requested facilities so that Judge Minor could send his son $350 and a message. On July 3 Senator Sheppard wrote Frank Polk, stating that he was "very much interested" in the Robert Minor case, and wondering whether State could ascertain its status, and whether Minor was properly under the jurisdiction of the military authorities. Then on July 8 the Paris embassy cabled Washington: "Confidential. Minor released by American authorities . . . returning to the United States on the first available boat." This sudden release intrigued the State Department, and on August 3 Secretary of State Lansing cabled Paris: "Secret. Referring to previous, am very anxious to obtain reasons for Minor's release by Military authorities."

49. U.S. State Dept. Decimal File, 861.00/4688 (/788).
50. Ibid.
51. Ibid., 316-33-0824.

Originally, U.S. Army authorities had wanted the British to try Robert Minor as "they feared politics might intervene in the United States to prevent a conviction if the prisoner was tried by American court-martial." However, the British government argued that Minor was a United States citizen, that the evidence showed he prepared propaganda against American troops in the first instance, and that, consequently—so the British Chief of Staff suggested—Minor should be tried before an American court. The British Chief of Staff did "consider it of the greatest importance to obtain a conviction if possible."[52]

Documents in the office of the Chief of Staff of the Third Army relate to the internal details of Minor's release.[53] A telegram of June 23, 1919, from Major General Harbord, Chief of Staff of the Third Army (later chairman of the Board of International General Electric, whose executive center, coincidentally, was also at 120 Broadway), to the commanding general, Third Army, stated that Commander in Chief John J. Pershing "directs that you suspend action in the case against Minor pending further orders." There is also a memorandum signed by Brigadier General W. A. Bethel in the office of the judge advocate, dated June 28, 1919, marked "Secret and Confidential," and entitled "Robert Minor, Awaiting Trial by a Military Commission at Headquarters, 3rd Army." The memo reviews the legal case against Minor. Among the points made by Bethel is that the British were obviously reluctant to handle the Minor case because "they fear American opinion in the event of trial by them of an American for a war offense in Europe," even though the offense with which Minor is charged is as serious "as a man can commit." This is a significant statement; Minor, Price, and Sadoul were implementing a program designed by Federal Reserve Bank director Thompson, a fact confirmed by Thompson's own memorandum (see Appendix 3). Was not therefore Thompson (and Robins), to some degree, subject to the same charges?

After interviewing Siegfried, the witness against Minor, and reviewing the evidence, Bethel commented:

> I thoroughly believe Minor to be guilty, but if I was sitting in court, I would not put guilty on the evidence now available—the testimony of one man only and that man acting in the character of a detective and informer.

52. U.S. State Dept. Decimal File, 861.00/4874.
53. Office of Chief of Staff, U.S. Army, National Archives, Washington, D.C.

Bethel goes on to state that it would be known within a week or ten days whether substantial corroboration of Siegfried's testimony was available. If available, "I think Minor should be tried," but "if corroboration cannot be had, I think it would be better to dismiss the case."

This statement by Bethel was relayed in a different form by General Harbord in a telegram of July 5 to General Malin Craig (Chief of Staff, Third Army, Coblenz):

> With reference to the case against Minor, unless other witnesses than Siegfried have been located by this time C in C directs the case be dropped and Minor liberated. Please acknowledge and state action.

The reply from Craig to General Harbord (July 5) records that Minor was liberated in Paris and adds, "This is in accordance with his own wishes and suits our purposes." Craig also adds that other witnesses *had* been obtained.

This exchange of telegrams suggests a degree of haste in dropping the charges against Robert Minor, and haste suggests pressure. There was no significant attempt made to develop evidence. Intervention by Colonel House and General Pershing at the highest levels in Paris and the cablegram from Colonel House to Senator Morris Sheppard give weight to American newspaper reports that both House and President Wilson were responsible for Minor's hasty release without trial.[54]

Minor returned to the United States and, like Thompson and Robins before him, toured the U.S. promoting the wonders of Bolshevik Russia.

By way of summary, we find that Federal Reserve Bank director William Thompson was active in promoting Bolshevik interests in several ways—production of a pamphlet in Russian, financing Bolshevik operations, speeches, organizing (with Robins) a Bolshevik revolutionary mission to Germany (and perhaps France), and with Morgan partner Lamont influencing Lloyd George and the British War Cabinet to effect a change in British policy. Further, Raymond Robins was cited by the French government for organizing Russian Bolsheviks for the German revolution. We know that Robins was undisguisedly working for Soviet interests in Russia and the United States. Finally, we find that Robert Minor, one of the revolutionary

---

54. U.S., Senate, *Congressional Record*, October 1919, pp. 6430, 6664-66, 7353-54; and *New York Times*, October 11, 1919. See also *Sacramento Bee*, July 17, 1919.

propagandists used in Thompson's program, was released under circumstances suggesting intervention from the highest levels of the U.S. government.

Obviously, this is but a fraction of a much wider picture. These are hardly accidental or random events. They constitute a coherent, continuing pattern over several years. They suggest powerful influence at the summit levels of several governments.

Chapter 7

THE BOLSHEVIKS
RETURN TO NEW YORK

Martens is very much in the limelight. There appears to be no doubt about his connection with the Guarantee [sic] Trust Company, Though it is surprising that so large and influential an enterprise should have dealings with a Bolshevik concern.

Scotland Yard Intelligence Report, London, 1919[1]

Following on the initial successes of the revolution, the Soviets wasted little time in attempting through former U.S. residents to establish diplomatic relations with and propaganda outlets in the United States. In June 1918 the American consul in Harbin cabled Washington:

Albert R. Williams, bearer Department passport 52,913 May 15, 1917 proceeding United States to establish information bureau for Soviet Government for which he has written authority. Shall I visa?[2]

Washington denied the visa and so Williams was unsuccessful in his attempt to establish an information bureau here. Williams was followed by Alexander Nyberg (alias Santeri Nuorteva), a former Finnish immigrant to the United States in January 1912, who became the first operative Soviet representative in the United States.

1. Copy in U.S. State Dept. Decimal File, 316-22-656.
2. Ibid., 861.00/1970.

113

Nyberg was an active propagandist. In fact, in 1919 he was, according to J. Edgar Hoover (in a letter to the U.S. Committee on Foreign Affairs), "the forerunner of LCAK Martens and with Gregory Weinstein the most active individual of official Bolshevik propaganda in the United States."[3]

Nyberg was none too successful as a diplomatic representative or, ultimately, as a propagandist. The State Department files record an interview with Nyberg by the counselors' office, dated January 29, 1919. Nyberg was accompanied by H. Kellogg, described as "an American citizen, graduate of Harvard," and, more surprisingly, by a Mr. McFarland, an attorney for the Hearst organization. The State Department records show that Nyberg made "many misstatements in regard to the attitude to the Bolshevik Government" and claimed that Peters, the Lett terrorist police chief in Petrograd, was merely a "kind-hearted poet." Nyberg requested the department to cable Lenin, "on the theory that it might be helpful in bringing about the conference proposed by the Allies at Paris."[4] The proposed message, a rambling appeal to Lenin to gain international acceptance by appearing at the Paris Conference, was not sent.[5]

A RAID ON THE SOVIET BUREAU IN NEW YORK

Alexander Nyberg (Nuorteva) was then let go and replaced by the Soviet Bureau, which was established in early 1919 in the World Tower Building, 110 West 40 Street, New York City. The bureau was headed by a German citizen, Ludwig C. A. K. Martens, who is usually billed as the first ambassador of the Soviet Union in the United States, and who, up to that time, had been vice president of Weinberg & Posner, an engineering firm located at 120 Broadway, New York City. Why the "ambassador" and his offices were located in New York rather than in Washington, D.C. was not explained; it does suggest that trade rather than diplomacy was its primary objective. In any event, the bureau promptly issued a call for Russian trade with the United States. Industry had collapsed and Russia direly needed machinery, railway goods, clothing, chemicals, drugs—indeed, everything utilized by a modern civilization. In exchange the Soviets offered gold and raw materials. The Soviet Bureau then proceeded to arrange contracts with American firms,

3. U.S., House, Committee on Foreign Affairs, *Conditions in Russia*, 66th Cong., 3d sess., 1921, p. 78.
4. U.S. State Dept. Decimal File, 316-19-1120.
5. Ibid.

ignoring the facts of the embargo and nonrecognition. At the same time it was providing financial support for the emerging Communist Party U.S.A.[6]

On May 7, 1919, the State Department slapped down business intervention in behalf of the bureau (noted elsewhere),[7] and repudiated Ludwig Martens, the Soviet Bureau, and the Bolshevik government of Russia. This official rebuttal did not deter the eager order-hunters in American industry. When the Soviet Bureau offices were raided on June 12, 1919, by representatives of the Lusk Committee of the state of New York, files of letters to and from American businessmen, representing almost a thousand firms, were unearthed. The British Home Office Directorate of Intelligence "Special Report No. 5 (Secret)," issued from Scotland Yard, London, July 14, 1919, and written by Basil H. Thompson, was based on this seized material; the report noted:

> . . . Every effort was made from the first by Martens and his associates to arouse the interest of American capitalists and there are grounds for believing that the Bureau has received financial support from some Russian export firms, as well as from the Guarantee [sic] Trust Company, although this firm has denied the allegation that it is financing Martens' organisation.[8]

It was noted by Thompson that the monthly rent of the Soviet Bureau offices was $300 and the office salaries came to about $4,000. Martens' funds to pay these bills came partly from Soviet couriers—such as John Reed and Michael Gruzenberg who brought diamonds from Russia for sale in the U.S., and partly from American business firms, including the Guaranty Trust Company of New York. The British reports summarized the files seized by the Lusk investigators from the bureau offices, and this summary is worth quoting in full:

> (1) There was an intrigue afoot about the time the President first went to France to get the Administration to use Nuorteva as an intermediary with the Russian Soviet Government, with a view to bring about its recognition by America. Endeavour was made to bring Colonel House into it, and there is a long and interesting letter to Frederick C. Howe, on whose support and sympathy Nuorteva appeared to rely. There are other records connecting Howe with Martens and Nuorteva.

6. See Benjamin Gitlow, U.S., House, *Un-American Propaganda Activities* (Washington, 1939), vols. 7-8, p. 4539.
7. See p. 119.
8. Copy in U.S. State Dept. Decimal File, 316-22-656. Confirmation of Guaranty Trust involvement comes in later intelligence reports.

(2) There is a file of correspondence with Eugene Debs.

(3) A letter from Amos Pinchot to William Kent of the U.S. Tariff Commission in an envelope addressed to Senator Lenroot, introduces Evans Clark "now in the Bureau of the Russian Soviet Republic." "He wants to talk to you about the recognition of Kolchak and the raising of the blockade, etc."

(4) A report to Felix Frankfurter, dated 27th May, 1919 speaks of the virulent campaign vilifying the Russian Government.

(5) There is considerable correspondence between a Colonel and Mrs. Raymond Robbins [sic] and Nuorteva, both in 1918 and 1919. In July 1918 Mrs. Robbins asked Nuorteva for articles for "Life and Labour," the organ of the National Women's Trade League. In February and March, 1919, Nuorteva tried, through Robbins, to get invited to give evidence before the Overman Committee. He also wanted Robbins to denounce the Sisson documents.

(6) In a letter from the Jansen Cloth Products Company, New York, to Nuorteva, dated March 30th, 1918, E. Werner Knudsen says that he understands that Nuorteva intends to make arrangements for the export of food-stuffs through Finland and he offers his services. We have a file on Knudsen, who passed information to and from Germany by way of Mexico with regard to British shipping.[9]

Ludwig Martens, the intelligence report continued, was in touch with all the leaders of "the left" in the United States, including John Reed, Ludwig Lore, and Harry J. Boland, the Irish rebel. A vigorous campaign against Aleksandr Kolchak in Siberia had been organized by Martens. The report concludes:

> [Martens'] organization is a powerful weapon for supporting the Bolshevik cause in the United States and . . . he is in close touch with the promoters of political unrest throughout the whole American continent.

The Scotland Yard list of personnel employed by the Soviet Bureau in New York coincides quite closely with a similar list in the Lusk Committee files in Albany, New York, which are today open for public inspection.[10] There is one essential difference between the

9. On Frederick C. Howe see pp. 16, 177, for an early statement of the manner in which financiers use society and its problems for their own ends; on Felix Frankfurter, later Supreme Court justice, see Appendix 3 for an early Frankfurter letter to Nuorteva; on Raymond Robins see p. 100.

10. The Lusk Committee list of personnel in the Soviet Bureau is printed in Appendix 3. The list includes Kenneth Durant, aide to Colonel House; Dudley Field Malone, appointed by President Wilson as collector of customs for the Port of New York; and Morris Hillquit, the financial intermediary between New York banker Eugene Boissevain on the one hand, and John Reed and Soviet agent Michael Gruzenberg on the other.

two lists: the British analysis included the name "Julius Hammer" whereas Hammer was omitted from the Lusk Committee report.[11] The British report characterizes Julius Hammer as follows:

> In Julius Hammer, Martens has a real Bolshevik and ardent Left Wing adherent, who came not long ago from Russia. He was one of the organizers of the Left Wing movement in New York, and speaks at meetings on the same platform with such Left Wing leaders as Reed, Hourwich, Lore and Larkin.

There also exists other evidence of Hammer's work in behalf of the Soviets. A letter from National City Bank, New York, to the U.S. Treasury Department stated that documents received by the bank from Martens were "witnessed by a Dr. Julius Hammer for the Acting Director of the Financial Department" of the Soviet Bureau.[12]

The Hammer family has had close ties with Russia and the Soviet regime from 1917 to the present. Armand Hammer is today able to acquire the most lucrative of Soviet contracts. Jacob, grandfather of Armand Hammer, and Julius were born in Russia. Armand, Harry, and Victor, sons of Julius, were born in the United States and are U.S. citizens. Victor was a well-known artist; his son—also named Armand—and granddaughter are Soviet citizens and reside in the Soviet Union. Armand Hammer is chairman of Occidental Petroleum Corporation and has a son, Julian, who is director of advertising and publications for Occidental Petroleum.

Julius Hammer was a prominent member and financier of the left wing of the Socialist Party. At its 1919 convention Hammer served with Bertram D. Wolfe and Benjamin Gitlow on the steering committee that gave birth to the Communist Party of the U.S.

In 1920 Julius Hammer was given a sentence of three-and-one-half to fifteen years in Sing Sing for criminal abortion. Lenin suggested—with justification—that Julius was "imprisoned on the charge of practicing illegal abortions but in fact because of communism."[13] Other U.S. Communist Party members were sentenced to jail for sedition or deported to the Soviet Union. Soviet representatives in the United States made strenuous but unsuccessful efforts to have Julius and his fellow party members released.

Another prominent member of the Soviet Bureau was the assistant secretary, Kenneth Durant, a former aide to Colonel House. In 1920

11. Julius Hammer was the father of Armand Hammer, who today is chairman of the Occidental Petroleum Corp. of Los Angeles.
12. See Appendix 3.
13. V. I. Lenin, *Polnoe Sobranie Sochinenii,* 5th ed. (Moscow, 1958), 53:267.

Durant was identified as a Soviet courier. Appendix 3 reproduces a letter to Kenneth Durant that was seized by the U.S. Department of Justice in 1920 and that describes Durant's close relationship with the Soviet hierarchy. It was inserted into the record of a House committee's hearings in 1920, with the following commentary:

> MR. NEWTON: It is a matter of interest to this committee to know what was the nature of that letter, and I have a copy of the letter that I want inserted in the record in connection with the witness' testimony.
> MR. MASON: That letter has never been shown to the witness. He said that he never saw the letter, and had asked to see it, and that the department had refused to show it to him. We would not put any witness on the stand and ask him to testify to a letter without seeing it.
> MR. NEWTON: The witness testified that he has such a letter, and he testified that they found it in his coat in the trunk, I believe. That letter was addressed to a Mr. Kenneth Durant, and that letter had within it another envelope which was likewise sealed. They were opened by the Government officials and a photostatic copy made. The letter, I may say, is signed by a man by the name of "Bill." It refers specifically to soviet moneys on deposit in Christiania, Norway, a portion of which they want turned over here to officials of the soviet government in this country.[14]

Kenneth Durant, who acted as Soviet courier in the transfer of funds, was treasurer for the Soviet Bureau and press secretary and publisher of *Soviet Russia*, the official organ of the Soviet Bureau. Durant came from a well-to-do Philadelphia family. He spent most of his life in the service of the Soviets, first in charge of publicity work at the Soviet Bureau then from 1923 to 1944 as manager of the Soviet *Tass* bureau in the United States. J. Edgar Hoover described Durant as "at all times . . . particularly active in the interests of Martens and of the Soviet government."[15]

Felix Frankfurter—later justice of the Supreme Court—was also prominent in the Soviet Bureau files. A letter from Frankfurter to Soviet agent Nuorteva is reproduced in Appendix 3 and suggests that Frankfurter had some influence with the bureau.

In brief, the Soviet Bureau could not have been established without influential assistance from within the United States. Part of this assistance came from specific influential appointments to the Soviet Bureau staff and part came from business firms outside the bureau, firms that were reluctant to make their support publicly known.

14. U.S., House, Committee on Foreign Affairs, *Conditions in Russia*, 66th Cong., 3d sess., 1921, p. 75. "Bill" was William Bobroff, Soviet agent.
15. Ibid., p. 78.

118

CORPORATE ALLIES FOR THE SOVIET BUREAU

On February 1, 1920, the front page of the *New York Times* carried a boxed notation stating that Martens was to be arrested and deported to Russia. At the same time Martens was being sought as a witness to appear before a subcommittee of the Senate Foreign Relations Committee investigating Soviet activity in the United States. After lying low for a few days Martens appeared before the committee, claimed diplomatic privilege, and refused to give up "official" papers in his possession. Then after a flurry of publicity, Martens "relented," handed over his papers, and admitted to revolutionary activities in the United States with the ultimate aim of overthrowing the capitalist system.

Martens boasted to the news media and Congress that big corporations, the Chicago packers among them, were aiding the Soviets:

> According to Martens, instead of carrying on propaganda among the radicals and the proletariat he has addressed most of his efforts to winning to the side of Russia the big business and manufacturing interests of this country, the packers, the United States Steel Corporation, the Standard Oil Company and other big concerns engaged in international trade. Martens asserted that most of the big business houses of the country were aiding him in his effort to get the government to recognize the Soviet government.[16]

This claim was expanded by A. A. Heller, commercial attaché at the Soviet Bureau:

> "Among the people helping us to get recognition from the State Department are the big Chicago packers, Armour, Swift, Nelson Morris and Cudahy. . . . Among the other firms are . . . the American Steel Export Company, the Lehigh Machine Company, the Adrian Knitting Company, the International Harvester Company, the Aluminum Goods Manufacturing Company, the Aluminum Company of America, the American Car and Foundry Export Company, M.C.D. Borden & Sons."[17]

The *New York Times* followed up these claims and reported comments of the firms named. "I have never heard of this man [Martens] before in my life," declared G. F. Swift, Jr., in charge of the export department of Swift & Co. "Most certainly I am sure that we have never had any dealings with him of any kind."[18] The *Times* added that O. H. Swift, the only other member of the firm that

16. *New York Times,* November 17, 1919.
17. Ibid.
18. Ibid.

119

could be contacted, "also denied any knowledge whatever of Martens or his bureau in New York." The Swift statement was evasive at best. When the Lusk Committee investigators seized the Soviet Bureau files, they found correspondence between the bureau and almost all the firms named by Martens and Heller. The "list of firms that offered to do business with Russian Soviet Bureau," compiled from these files, included an entry (page 16), "Swift and Company, Union Stock Yards, Chicago, Ill." In other words, Swift *had* been in communication with Martens despite its denial to the *New York Times.*

The *New York Times* contacted United States Steel and reported, "Judge Elbert H. Gary said last night that there was no foundation for the statement with the Soviet representative here had had any dealings with the United States Steel Corporation." This is technically correct. The United States Steel Corporation is not listed in the Soviet files, but the list *does* contain (page 16) an affiliate, "United States Steel Products Co., 30 Church Street, New York City."

The Lusk Committee list records the following about other firms mentioned by Martens and Heller: Standard Oil—not listed. Armour & Co., meatpackers—listed as "Armour Leather" and "Armour & Co. Union Stock Yards, Chicago." Morris Co., meatpackers, is listed on page 13. Cudahy—listed on page 6. American Steel Export Co.— listed on page 2 as located at the Woolworth Building; it had offered to trade with the USSR. Lehigh Machine Co.—not listed. Adrian Knitting Co.—listed on page 1. International Harvester Co.— listed on page 11. Aluminum Goods Manufacturing Co.—listed on page 1. Aluminum Company of America—not listed. American Car and Foundry Export—the closest listing is "American Car Co.—Philadelphia." M.C.D. Borden & Sons—listed as located at 90 Worth Street, on page 4.

Then on Saturday, June 21, 1919, Santeri Nuorteva (Alexander Nyberg) confirmed in a press interview the role of International Harvester:

Q [by *New York Times* reporter]: What is your business?
A: Purchasing director for Soviet Russia.
Q: What did you do to accomplish this?
A: Addressed myself to American manufacturers.
Q: Name them.
A: International Harvester Corporation is among them.
Q: Whom did you see?
A: Mr. Koenig.

Q: Did you go to see him?

A: Yes.

Q: Give more names.

A: I went to see so many, about 500 people and I can't remember all the names. We have files in the office disclosing them.[19]

In brief, the claims by Heller and Martens relating to their widespread contacts among certain U.S. firms[20] were substantiated by the office files of the Soviet Bureau. On the other hand, for their own good reasons, these firms appeared unwilling to confirm their activities.

EUROPEAN BANKERS AID THE BOLSHEVIKS

In addition to Guaranty Trust and the private banker Boissevain in New York, some European bankers gave direct help to maintain and expand the Bolshevik hold on Russia. A 1918 State Department report from our Stockholm embassy details these financial transfers. The department commended its author, stating that his "reports on conditions in Russia, the spread of Bolshevism in Europe, and financial questions . . . have proved most helpful to the Department. Department is much gratified by your capable handling of the legation's business."[21] According to this report, one of these "Bolshevik bankers" acting in behalf of the emerging Soviet regime was Dmitri Rubenstein, of the former Russo-French bank in Petrograd. Rubenstein, an associate of the notorious Grigori Rasputin, had been jailed in prerevolutionary Petrograd in connection with the sale of the Second Russian Life Insurance Company. The American manager and director of the Second Russian Life Insurance Company was John MacGregor Grant, who was located at 120 Broadway, New York City. Grant was also the New York representative of Putiloff's Banque Russo-Asiatique. In August 1918 Grant was (for unknown reasons) listed on the Military Intelligence Bureau "suspect list."[22] This may have occurred because Olof Aschberg in early 1918 reported opening a foreign credit in Petrograd "with the John MacGregor Grant Co., export concern, which it [Aschberg] finances in Sweden and which is financed in America by the Guarantee [sic] Trust Co."[23] After the revolution Dmitri

19. *New York Times*, June 21, 1919.

20. See p. 119.

21. U.S. State Dept. Decimal File, 861.51/411, November 23, 1918.

22. Ibid., 316-125-1212.

23. U.S., Department of State, *Foreign Relations of the United States: 1918, Russia*, 1:373.

Rubenstein moved to Stockholm and became financial agent for the Bolsheviks. The State Department noted that while Rubenstein was "not a Bolshevik, he has been unscrupulous in money making, and it is suspected that he may be making the contemplated visit to America in Bolshevik interest and for Bolshevik pay."[24]

Another Stockholm "Bolshevik banker" was Abram Givatovzo, brother-in-law of Trotsky and Lev Kamenev. The State Department report asserted that while Givatovzo pretended to be "very anti-Bolshevik," he had in fact received "large sums" of money from the Bolsheviks by courier for financing revolutionary operations. Givatovzo was part of a syndicate that included Denisoff of the former Siberian bank, Kamenka of the Asoff Don Bank, and Davidoff of the Bank of Foreign Commerce. This syndicate sold the assets of the former Siberian Bank to the British government.

Yet another tsarist private banker, Gregory Lessine, handled Bolshevik business through the firm of Dardel and Hagborg. Other "Bolshevik bankers" named in the report are Stifter and Jakob Berline, who previously controlled, through his wife, the Petrograd Nelkens Bank. Isidor Kon was used by these bankers as an agent.

The most interesting of these Europe-based bankers operating in behalf of the Bolsheviks was Gregory Benenson, formerly chairman in Petrograd of the Russian and English Bank—a bank which included on its board of directors Lord Balfour (secretary of state for foreign affairs in England) and Sir I. M. H. Amory, as well as S. H. Cripps and H. Guedalla. Benenson traveled to Petrograd after the revolution, then on to Stockholm. He came, said one State Department official, "bringing to my knowledge ten million rubles with him as he offered them to me at a high price for the use of our Embassy Archangel." Benenson had an arrangement with the Bolsheviks to exchange sixty million rubles for £1.5 million sterling.

In January 1919 the private bankers in Copenhagen that were associated with Bolshevik institutions became alarmed by rumors that the Danish political police had marked the Soviet legation and those persons in contact with the Bolsheviks for expulsion from Denmark. These bankers and the legation hastily attempted to remove their funds from Danish banks—in particular, seven million rubles from the Revisionsbanken.[25] Also, confidential documents were hidden in the offices of the Martin Larsen Insurance Company.

24. U.S. State Dept. Decimal File, 861.00/4878, July 21, 1919.
25. Ibid., 316-21-115/21.

Consequently, we can identify a pattern of assistance by capitalist bankers for the Soviet Union. Some of these were American bankers, some were tsarist bankers who were exiled and living in Europe, and some were European bankers. Their common objective was profit, not ideology.

The questionable aspects of the work of these "Bolshevik bankers," as they were called, arises from the framework of contemporary events in Russia. In 1919 French, British, and American troops were fighting Soviet troops in the Archangel region. In one clash in April 1919, for example, American casualties were one officer, five men killed, and nine missing.[26] Indeed, at one point in 1919 General Tasker H. Bliss, the U.S. commander in Archangel, affirmed the British statement that "Allied troops in the Murmansk and Archangel districts were in danger of extermination unless they were speedily reinforced."[27] Reinforcements were then on the way under the command of Brigadier General W. P. Richardson.

In brief, while Guaranty Trust and first-rank American firms were assisting the formation of the Soviet Bureau in New York, American troops were in conflict with Soviet troops in North Russia. Moreover, these conflicts were daily reported in the *New York Times,* presumably read by these bankers and businessmen. Further, as we shall see in chapter ten, the financial circles that were supporting the Soviet Bureau in New York also formed in New York the "United Americans"—a virulently anti-Communist organization predicting bloody revolution, mass starvation, and panic in the streets of New York.

26. *New York Times,* April 5, 1919.
27. Ibid.

Chapter 8

120 BROADWAY, NEW YORK CITY

William B. Thompson, who was in Petrograd from July until November last, has made a personal contribution of $1,000,000 to the Bolsheviki for the purpose of spreading their doctrine in Germany and Austria. . . .

Washington Post, February 2, 1918

While collecting material for this book a single location and address in the Wall Street area came to the fore—120 Broadway, New York City. Conceivably, this book could have been written incorporating only persons, firms, and organizations located at 120 Broadway in the year 1917. Although this research method would have been forced and unnatural, it would have excluded only a relatively small segment of the story.

The original building at 120 Broadway was destroyed by fire before World War I. Subsequently the site was sold to the Equitable Office Building Corporation, organized by General T. Coleman du Pont, president of du Pont de Nemours Powder Company.[1] A new building was completed in 1915 and the Equitable Life Assurance

1. By a quirk the papers of incorporation for the Equitable Office Building were drawn up by Dwight W. Morrow, later a Morgan partner, but then a member of the law firm of Simpson, Thacher & Bartlett. The Thacher firm contributed two members to the 1917 American Red Cross Mission to Russia (see chapter five).

Company moved back to its old site.[2] In passing we should note an interesting interlock in Equitable history. In 1916 the cashier of the Berlin Equitable Life office was William Schacht, the father of Hjalmar Horace Greeley Schacht—later to become Hitler's banker, and financial genie. William Schacht was an American citizen, worked thirty years for Equitable in Germany, and owned a Berlin house known as "Equitable Villa." Before joining Hitler, young Hjalmar Schacht served as a member of the Workers and Soldiers Council (a soviet) of Zehlendorf; this he left in 1918 to join the board of the Nationalbank für Deutschland. His codirector at DONAT was Emil Wittenberg, who, with Max May of Guaranty Trust Company of New York, was a director of the first Soviet international bank, Ruskombank.

In any event, the building at 120 Broadway was in 1917 known as the Equitable Life Building. A large building, although by no means the largest office building in New York City, it occupies a one-block area at Broadway and Pine, and has thirty-four floors. The Bankers Club was located on the thirty-fourth floor. The tenant list in 1917 in effect reflected American involvement in the Bolshevik Revolution and its aftermath. For example, the headquarters of the No. 2 District of the Federal Reserve System—the New York area—by far the most important of the Federal Reserve districts, was located at 120 Broadway. The offices of several individual directors of the Federal Reserve Bank of New York and, most important, the American International Corporation were also at 120 Broadway. By way of contrast, Ludwig Martens, appointed by the Soviets as the first Bolshevik "ambassador" to the United States and head of the Soviet Bureau, was in 1917 the vice president of Weinberg & Posner—and also had offices at 120 Broadway.*

Is this concentration an accident? Does the geographical contiguity have any significance? Before attempting to suggest an answer, we have to switch our frame of reference and abandon the left-right spectrum of political analysis.

With an almost unanimous lack of perception the academic world has described and analyzed international political relations in the context of an unrelenting conflict between capitalism and communism, and rigid adherence to this Marxian formula has distorted

2. R. Carlyle Buley, *The Equitable Life Assurance Society of the United States* (New York: Appleton-Century-Crofts, n.d.).

* The John MacGregor Grant Co., agent for the Russo-Asiatic Bank (involved in financing the Bolsheviks), was at 120 Broadway—and financed by Guaranty Trust Company.

modern history. Tossed out from time to time are odd remarks to the effect that the polarity is indeed spurious, but these are quickly dispatched to limbo. For example, Carroll Quigley, professor of international relations at Georgetown University, made the following comment on the House of Morgan:

> More than fifty years ago the Morgan firm decided to infiltrate the Left-wing political movements in the United States. This was relatively easy to do, since these groups were starved for funds and eager for a voice to reach the people. Wall Street supplied both. The purpose was not to destroy, dominate or take over . . .[3]

Professor Quigley's comment, apparently based on confidential documentation, has all the ingredients of an historical bombshell if it can be supported. We suggest that the Morgan firm infiltrated not only the domestic left, as noted by Quigley, but also the foreign left—that is, the Bolshevik movement and the Third International. Even further, through friends in the U.S. State Department, Morgan and allied financial interests, particularly the Rockefeller family, have exerted a powerful influence on U.S.-Russian relations from World War I to the present. The evidence presented in this chapter will suggest that two of the operational vehicles for infiltrating or influencing foreign revolutionary movements were located at 120 Broadway: the first, the Federal Reserve Bank of New York, heavily laced with Morgan appointees; the second, the Morgan-controlled American International Corporation. Further, there was an important interlock between the Federal Reserve Bank of New York and the American International Corporation—C. A. Stone, the president of American International, was also a director of the Federal Reserve Bank.

The tentative hypothesis then is that this unusual concentration at a single address was a reflection of purposeful actions by specific firms and persons and that these actions and events cannot be analyzed within the usual spectrum of left-right political antagonism.

AMERICAN INTERNATIONAL CORPORATION

The American International Corporation (AIC) was organized in New York on November 22, 1915, by the J. P. Morgan interests, with major participation by Stillman's National City Bank and the Rockefeller interests. The general office of AIC was at 120 Broad-

3. Carroll Quigley, *Tragedy and Hope* (New York: Macmillan, 1966), p. 938. Quigley was writing in 1965, so this places the start of the infiltration at about 1915, a date consistent with the evidence here presented.

way. The company's charter authorized it to engage in any kind of business, except banking and public utilities, in any country in the world. The stated purpose of the corporation was to develop domestic and foreign enterprises, to extend American activities abroad, and to promote the interests of American and foreign bankers, business and engineering.

Frank A. Vanderlip has described in his memoirs how American International was formed and the excitement created on Wall Street over its business potential.[4] The original idea was generated by a discussion between Stone & Webster—the international railroad contractors who "were convinced there was not much more railroad building to be done in the United States"—and Jim Perkins and Frank A. Vanderlip of National City Bank (NCB).[5] The original capital authorization was $50 million and the board of directors represented the leading lights of the New York financial world. Vanderlip records that he wrote as follows to NCB president Stillman, enthusing over the enormous potential for American International Corporation:

James A. Farrell and Albert Wiggin have been invited [to be on the board] but had to consult their committees before accepting. I also have in mind asking Henry Walters and Myron T. Herrick. Mr. Herrick is objected to by Mr. Rockefeller quite strongly but Mr. Stone wants him and I feel strongly that he would be particularly desirable in France. The whole thing has gone along with a smoothness that has been gratifying and the reception of it has been marked by an enthusiasm which has been surprising to me even though I was so strongly convinced we were on the right track.

I saw James J. Hill today, for example. He said at first that he could not possibly think of extending his responsibilities, but after I had finished telling him what we expected to do, he said he would be glad to go on the board, would take a large amount of stock and particularly wanted a substantial interest in the City Bank and commissioned me to buy him the stock at the market.

I talked with Ogden Armour about the matter today for the first time. He sat in perfect silence while I went through the story, and, without asking a single question, he said he would go on the board and wanted $500,000 stock.

Mr. Coffin [of General Electric] is another man who is retiring from everything, but has become so enthusiastic over this that he was willing to go on the board, and offers the most active cooperation.

4. Frank A. Vanderlip, *From Farm Boy to Financier* (New York: A. Appleton-Century, 1935).
5. Ibid., p. 267.

I felt very good over getting Sabin. The Guaranty Trust is altogether the most active competitor we have in the field and it is of great value to get them into the fold in this way. They have been particularly enthusiastic at Kuhn, Loeb's. They want to take up to $2,500,000. There was really quite a little competition to see who should get on the board, but as I had happened to talk with Kahn and had invited him first, it was decided he should go on. He is perhaps the most enthusiastic of any one. They want half a million stock for Sir Ernest Castle* to whom they have cabled the plan and they have back from him approval of it.

I explained the whole matter to the Board [of the City Bank] Tuesday and got nothing but favorable comments.[6]

Everybody coveted the AIC stock. Joe Grace (of W. R. Grace & Co.) wanted $600,000 in addition to his interest in National City Bank. Ambrose Monell wanted $500,000. George Baker wanted $250,000. And "William Rockefeller tried, vainly, to get me to put him down for $5,000,000 of the common."[7]

By 1916 AIC investments overseas amounted to more than $23 million and in 1917 to more than $27 million. The company established representation in London, Paris, Buenos Aires, and Peking as well as in Petrograd, Russia. Less than two years after its formation AIC was operating on a substantial scale in Australia, Argentina, Uruguay, Paraguay, Colombia, Brazil, Chile, China, Japan, India, Ceylon, Italy, Switzerland, France, Spain, Cuba, Mexico, and other countries in Central America.

American International owned several subsidiary companies outright, had substantial interests in yet other companies, and operated still other firms in the United States and abroad. The Allied Machinery Company of America was founded in February 1916 and the entire share capital taken up by American International Corporation. The vice president of American International Corporation was Frederick Holbrook, an engineer and formerly head of the Holbrook Cabot & Rollins Corporation. In January 1917 the Grace Russian Company was formed, the joint owners being W. R. Grace & Co. and the San Galli Trading Company of Petrograd. American International Corporation had a substantial investment in the Grace Russian Company and through Holbrook an interlocking director-

* Sir Ernest Cassel, prominent British financier.
6. Ibid., pp. 268-69. It should be noted that several names mentioned by Vanderlip turn up elsewhere in this book: Rockefeller, Armour, Guaranty Trust, and (Otto) Kahn all had some connection more or less with the Bolshevik Revolution and its aftermath.
7. Ibid., p. 269.

ship. AIC also invested in United Fruit Company, which was involved in Central American revolutions in the 1920s. The American International Shipbuilding Corporation was wholly owned by AIC and signed substantial contracts for war vessels with the Emergency Fleet Corporation: one contract called for fifty vessels, followed by another contract for forty vessels, followed by yet another contract for sixty cargo vessels. American International Shipbuilding was the largest single recipient of contracts awarded by the U.S. government Emergency Fleet Corporation. Another company operated by AIC was G. Amsinck & Co., Inc. of New York; control of the company was acquired in November 1917. Amsinck was the source of financing for German espionage in the United States (see page 66). In November 1917 the American International Corporation formed and wholly owned the Symington Forge Corporation, a major government contractor for shell forgings. Consequently, American International Corporation had significant interest in war contracts within the United States and overseas. It had, in a word, a vested interest in the continuance of World War I.

The directors of American International and some of their associations were (in 1917):

J. OGDEN ARMOUR Meatpacker, of Armour & Company, Chicago; director of the National City Bank of New York; and mentioned by A. A. Heller in connection with the Soviet Bureau (see p. 119).

GEORGE JOHNSON BALDWIN Of Stone & Webster, 120 Broadway. During World War I Baldwin was chairman of the board of American International Shipbuilding, senior vice president of American International Corporation, director of G. Amsinck (Von Pavenstedt of Amsinck was a German espionage paymaster in the U.S., see page 65), and a trustee of the Carnegie Foundation, which financed the Marburg Plan for international socialism to be controlled behind the scenes by world finance (see page 174-6).

C. A. COFFIN Chairman of General Electric (executive office: 120 Broadway), chairman of cooperation committee of the American Red Cross.

W. E. COREY (14 Wall Street) Director of American Bank Note Company, Mechanics and Metals Bank, Midvale Steel and Ordnance, and International Nickel Company; later director of National City Bank.

ROBERT DOLLAR San Francisco shipping magnate, who attempted in behalf of the Soviets to import tsarist gold rubles into U.S. in 1920, in contravention of U.S. regulations.

PIERRE S. DU PONT Of the du Pont family.

PHILIP A. S. FRANKLIN Director of National City Bank.

J. P. GRACE Director of National City Bank.

R. F. HERRICK Director, New York Life Insurance; former president of the American Bankers Association; trustee of Carnegie Foundation.

OTTO H. KAHN Partner in Kuhn, Loeb. Kahn's father came to America in 1948, "having taken part in the unsuccessful German revolution of that year." According to J. H. Thomas (British socialist, financed by the Soviets), "Otto Kahn's face is towards the light."

H. W. PRITCHETT Trustee of Carnegie Foundation.

PERCY A. ROCKEFELLER Son of John D. Rockefeller; married to Isabel, daughter of J. A. Stillman of National City Bank.

JOHN D. RYAN Director of copper-mining companies, National City Bank, and Mechanics and Metals Bank. (See frontispiece to this book.)

W. L. SAUNDERS Director the Federal Reserve Bank of New York, 120 Broadway, and chairman of Ingersoll-Rand. According to the *National Cyclopaedia* (26:81): "Throughout the war he was one of the President's most trusted advisers." See page 15 for his views on the Soviets.

J. A. STILLMAN President of National City Bank, after his father (J. Stillman, chairman of NCB) died in March 1918.

C. A. STONE Director (1920-22) of Federal Reserve Bank of New York, 120 Broadway; chairman of Stone & Webster, 120 Broadway; president (1916-23) of American International Corporation, 120 Broadway.

T. N. VAIL President of National City Bank of Troy, New York.

F. A. VANDERLIP President of National City Bank.

E. S. WEBSTER Of Stone & Webster, 120 Broadway.

A. H. WIGGIN Director of Federal Reserve Bank of New York in the early 1930s.

BECKMAN WINTHROPE Director of National City Bank.

WILLIAM WOODWARD Director of Federal Reserve Bank of New York, 120 Broadway, and Hanover National Bank.

The interlock of the twenty-two directors of American International Corporation with other institutions is significant. The National City Bank had no fewer than ten directors on the board of AIC; Stillman of NCB was at that time an intermediary between the Rockefeller and Morgan interests, and both the Morgan and the Rockefeller interests were represented directly on AIC. Kuhn, Loeb and the du Ponts each had one director. Stone & Webster had three directors. No fewer than four directors of AIC (Saunders, Stone, Wiggin, Woodward) either were directors of or were later to join the Federal Reserve Bank of New York. We have noted in an earlier chapter that William Boyce Thompson, who contributed funds and his considerable prestige to the Bolshevik Revolution, was also a director of the Federal Reserve Bank of New York—the directorate of the FRB of New York comprised only nine members.

THE INFLUENCE OF AMERICAN INTERNATIONAL ON THE REVOLUTION

Having identified the directors of AIC we now have to identify their revolutionary influence.

As the Bolshevik Revolution took hold in central Russia, Secretary of State Robert Lansing requested the views of American International Corporation on the policy to be pursued towards the Soviet regime. On January 16, 1918—barely two months after the takeover in Petrograd and Moscow, and before a fraction of Russia had come under Bolshevik control—William Franklin Sands, executive secretary of American International Corporation, submitted the requested memorandum on the Russian political situation to Secretary Lansing. Sands covering letter, headed 120 Broadway, began:

To the Honourable   January 16, 1918
    Secretary of State
        Washington D.C.
Sir
I have the honor to enclose herewith the memorandum which you requested me to make for you on my view of the political situation in Russia.
    I have separated it into three parts; an explanation of the historical causes of the Revolution, told as briefly as possible; a suggestion as to policy and a recital of the various branches of American activity at work now in Russia. . . . [8]

Although the Bolsheviks had only precarious control in Russia—and indeed were to come near to losing even this in the spring of 1918—Sands wrote that already (January 1918) the United States had delayed too long in recognizing "Trotzky." He added, "Whatever ground may have been lost, should be regained now, even at the cost of a slight personal triumph for Trotzky."[9]

8. U.S. State Dept. Decimal File, 861.00/961.
9. Sands memorandum to Lansing, p. 9.

132

Firms located at, or near, 120 Broadway:
American International Corp 120 Broadway
National City Bank 55 Wall Street
Bankers Trust Co Bldg 14 Wall Street
New York Stock Exchange 13 Wall Street/12 Broad
Morgan Building corner Wall & Broad
Federal Reserve Bank of NY 120 Broadway
Equitable Building 120 Broadway
Bankers Club 120 Broadway
Simpson, Thacher & Bartlett 62 Cedar St
William Boyce Thompson 14 Wall Street
Hazen, Whipple & Fuller 42nd Street Building
Chase National Bank 57 Broadway
McCann Co 61 Broadway
Stetson, Jennings & Russell 15 Broad Street
Guggenheim Exploration 120 Broadway
Weinberg & Posner 120 Broadway
Soviet Bureau 110 West 40th Street
John MacGregor Grant Co 120 Broadway
Stone & Webster 120 Broadway
General Electric Co 120 Broadway
Morris Plan of NY 120 Broadway
Sinclair Gulf Corp 120 Broadway
Guaranty Securities 120 Broadway
Guaranty Trust 140 Broadway

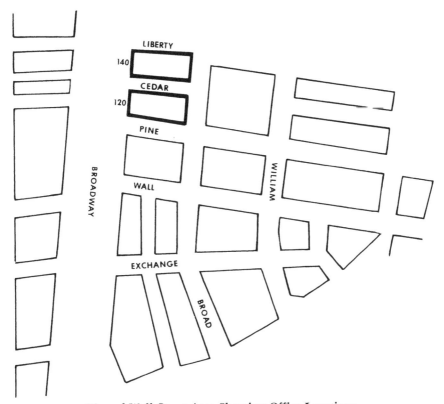

Map of Wall Street Area Showing Office Locations

Sands then elaborates the manner in which the U.S. could make up for lost time, parallels the Bolshevik Revolution to "our own revolution," and concludes: "I have every reason to believe that the Administration plans for Russia will receive all possible support from Congress, and the hearty endorsement of public opinion in the United States."

In brief, Sands, as executive secretary of a corporation whose directors were the most prestigious on Wall Street, provided an emphatic endorsement of the Bolsheviks and the Bolshevik Revolution, and within a matter of weeks after the revolution started. And as a director of the Federal Reserve Bank of New York, Sands had just contributed $1 million to the Bolsheviks—such endorsement of the Bolsheviks by banking interests is at least consistent.

Moreover, William Sands of American International was a man with truly uncommon connections and influence in the State Department.

Sands' career had alternated between the State Department and Wall Street. In the late nineteenth and early twentieth century he held various U.S. diplomatic posts. In 1910 he left the department to join the banking firm of James Speyer to negotiate an Ecuadorian loan, and for the next two years represented the Central Aguirre Sugar Company in Puerto Rico. In 1916 he was in Russia on "Red Cross work"—actually a two-man "Special Mission" with Basil Miles—and returned to join the American International Corporation in New York.[10]

In early 1918 Sands became the known and intended recipient of certain Russian "secret treaties." If the State Department files are to be believed, it appears that Sands was also a courier, and that he had some prior access to official documents—prior, that is, to U.S. government officials. On January 14, 1918, just two days before Sands wrote his memo on policy towards the Bolsheviks, Secretary Lansing caused the following cable to be sent in Green Cipher

10. William Franklin Sands wrote several books, including *Undiplomatic Memoirs* (New York: McGraw-Hill, 1930), a biography covering the years to 1904. Later he wrote *Our Jungle Diplomacy* (Chapel Hill: University of North Carolina Press, 1944), an unremarkable treatise on imperialism in Latin America. The latter work is notable only for a minor point on page 102: the willingness to blame a particularly unsavory imperialistic adventure on Adolf Stahl, a New York banker, while pointing out quite unnecessarily that Stahl was of "German-Jewish origin." In August 1918 he published an article, "Salvaging Russia," in *Asia*, to explain support of the Bolshevik regime.

to the American legation in Stockholm: "Important official papers for Sands to bring here were left at Legation. Have you forwarded them? Lansing." The reply of January 16 from Morris in Stockholm reads: "Your 460 January 14, 5 pm. Said documents forwarded Department in pouch number 34 on December 28th." To these documents is attached another memo, signed "BM" (Basil Miles, an associate of Sands): "Mr. Phillips. They failed to give Sands 1st installment of secret treaties wh. [which] he brought from Petrograd to Stockholm."[11]

Putting aside the question why a private citizen would be carrying Russian secret treaties and the question of the content of such secret treaties (probably an early version of the so-called Sisson Documents), we can at least deduce that the AIC executive secretary traveled from Petrograd to Stockholm in late 1917 and must indeed have been a privileged and influential citizen to have access to secret treaties.[12]

A few months later, on July 1, 1918, Sands wrote to Treasury Secretary McAdoo suggesting a commission for "economic assistance to Russia." He urged that since it would be difficult for a government commission to "provide the machinery" for any such assistance, "it seems, therefore, necessary to call in the financial, commercial and manufacturing interest of the United States to provide such machinery under the control of the Chief Commissioner or whatever official is selected by the President for this purpose."[13] In other words, Sands obviously intended that any commercial exploitation of Bolshevik Russia was going to include 120 Broadway.

THE FEDERAL RESERVE BANK OF NEW YORK

The certification of incorporation of the Federal Reserve Bank of New York was filed May 18, 1914. It provided for three Class A directors representing member banks in the district, three Class B directors representing commerce, agriculture, and industry, and three Class C directors representing the Federal Reserve Board. The original directors were elected in 1914; they proceeded to generate an energetic program. In the first year of organization the Federal Reserve Bank of New York held no fewer than 50 meetings.

11. All the above in U.S. State Dept. Decimal File, 861.00/969.
12. The author cannot forbear comparing the treatment of academic researchers. In 1973, for example, the writer was still denied access to some State Department files *dated 1919*.
13. U.S. State Dept. Decimal File, 861.51/333.

From our viewpoint what is interesting is the association between, on the one hand, the directors of the Federal Reserve Bank (in the New York district) and of American International Corporation, and, on the other, the emerging Soviet Russia.

In 1917 the three Class A directors were Franklin D. Locke, William Woodward, and Robert H. Treman. William Woodward was a director of American International Corporation (120 Broadway) and of the Rockefeller-controlled Hanover National Bank. Neither Locke nor Treman enters our story. The three Class B directors in 1917 were William Boyce Thompson, Henry R. Towne, and Leslie R. Palmer. We have already noted William B. Thompson's substantial cash contribution to the Bolshevik cause. Henry R. Towne was chairman of the board of directors of the Morris Plan of New York, located at 120 Broadway; his seat was later taken by Charles A. Stone of American International Corporation (120 Broadway) and of Stone & Webster (120 Broadway). Leslie R. Palmer does not come into our story. The three Class C directors were Pierre Jay, W. L. Saunders, and George Foster Peabody. Nothing is known about Pierre Jay, except that his office was at 120 Broadway and he appeared to be significant only as the owner of Brearley School, Ltd. William Lawrence Saunders was also a director of American International Corporation; he openly avowed, as we have seen, pro-Bolshevik sympathies, disclosing them in a letter to President Woodrow Wilson (see page 15). George Foster Peabody was an active socialist (see page 99-100).

In brief, of the nine directors of the Federal Reserve Bank of New York, four were physically located at 120 Broadway and two were then connected with American International Corporation. And at least four members of AIC's board were at one time or another directors of the FRB of New York. We could term all of this significant, but regard it not necessarily as a dominant interest.

AMERICAN-RUSSIAN INDUSTRIAL SYNDICATE INC.

William Franklin Sands' proposal for an economic commission to Russia was not adopted. Instead, a private vehicle was put together to exploit Russian markets and the earlier support given the Bolsheviks. A group of industrialists from 120 Broadway formed the American-Russian Industrial Syndicate Inc. to develop and foster these opportunities. The financial backing for the new firm came from the Guggenheim Brothers, 120 Broadway, previously associated with William Boyce Thompson (Guggenheim controlled

136

American Smelting and Refining, and the Kennecott and Utah copper companies); from Harry F. Sinclair, president of Sinclair Gulf Corp., also 120 Broadway; and from James G. White of J. G. White Engineering Corp. of 43 Exchange Place—the address of the American-Russian Industrial Syndicate.

In the fall of 1919 the U.S. embassy in London cabled Washington about Messrs. Lubovitch and Rossi "representing American-Russian Industrial Syndicate Incorporated. . . . What is the reputation and the attitude of the Department toward the syndicate and the individuals?"[14]

To this cable State Department officer Basil Miles, a former assoicate of Sands, replied:

> . . . Gentlemen mentioned together with their corporation are of good standing being backed financially by the White, Sinclair and Guggenheim interests for the purpose of opening up business relations with Russia.[15]

So we may conclude that Wall Street interests had quite definite ideas of the manner in which the new Russian market was to be exploited. The assistance and advice proffered in behalf of the Bolsheviks by interested parties in Washington and elsewhere were not to remain unrewarded.

JOHN REED: ESTABLISHMENT REVOLUTIONARY

Quite apart from American International's influence in the State Department is its intimate relationship—which AIC itself called "control"—with a known Bolshevik: John Reed. Reed was a prolific, widely read author of the World War I era who contributed to the Bolshevik-oriented *Masses*[16] and to the Morgan-controlled journal *Metropolitan*. Reed's book on the Bolshevik Revolution, *Ten Days That Shook the World,* sports an introduction by Nikolai Lenin, and became Reed's best-known and most widely read literary effort. Today the book reads like a superficial commentary on current events, is interspersed with Bolshevik proclamations and decrees, and is permeated with that mystic fervor the Bolsheviks know will arouse foreign sympathizers. After the revolution Reed became an

---

14. U.S. State Dept. Decimal File, 861.516/84, September 2, 1919.
15. Ibid.
16. Other contributors to the *Masses* mentioned in this book were journalist Robert Minor, chairman of the U.S. Public Information Committee; George Creel; Carl Sandburg, poet-historian; and Boardman Robinson, an artist.

American member of the executive committee of the Third International. He died of typhus in Russia in 1920.

The crucial issue that presents itself here is not Reed's known pro-Bolshevik tenor and activities, but how Reed who had the entire confidence of Lenin ("Here is a book I should like to see published in millions of copies and translated into all languages," commented Lenin in *Ten Days*), who was a member of the Third International, and who possessed a Military Revolutionary Committee pass (No. 955, issued November 16, 1917) giving him entry into the Smolny Institute (the revolutionary headquarters) at any time as the representative of the "American Socialist press," was also—despite these things—a puppet under the "control" of the Morgan financial interests through the American International Corporation. Documentary evidence exists for this seeming conflict (see below and Appendix 3).

Let's fill in the background. Articles for the *Metropolitan* and the *Masses* gave John Reed a wide audience for reporting the Mexican and the Russian Bolshevik revolutions. Reed's biographer Granville Hicks has suggested, in *John Reed,* that "he was . . . the spokesman of the Bolsheviks in the United States." On the other hand, Reed's financial support from 1913 to 1918 came heavily from the *Metropolitan*—owned by Harry Payne Whitney, a director of the Guaranty Trust, an institution cited in every chapter of this book—and also from the New York private banker and merchant Eugene Boissevain, who channeled funds to Reed both directly and through the pro-Bolshevik *Masses.* In other words, John Reed's financial support came from two supposedly competing elements in the political spectrum. These funds were for writing and may be classified as: payments from *Metropolitan* from 1913 onwards for articles; payments from *Masses* from 1913 onwards, which income at least in part originated with Eugene Boissevain. A third category should be mentioned: Reed received some minor and apparently unconnected payments from Red Cross commissioner Raymond Robins in Petrograd. Presumably he also received smaller sums for articles written for other journals, and book royalties; but no evidence has been found giving the amounts of such payments.

JOHN REED AND THE *METROPOLITAN* MAGAZINE

The *Metropolitan* supported contemporary establishment causes including, for example, war preparedness. The magazine was owned by Harry Payne Whitney (1872-1930), who founded the Navy League and was partner in the J. P. Morgan firm. In the late 1890s Whitney became a director of American Smelting and Refining and of Guggenheim Exploration. Upon his father's death in 1908, he became a director of numerous other companies, including Guaranty Trust Company. Reed began writing for Whitney's *Metropolitan* in July 1913 and contributed a half-dozen articles on the Mexican revolutions: "With Villa in Mexico," "The Causes Behind Mexico's Revolution," "If We Enter Mexico," "With Villa on the March," etc. Reed's sympathies were with revolutionist Pancho Villa. You will recall the link (see page 65) between Guaranty Trust and Villa's ammunition supplies.

In any event, *Metropolitan* was Reed's main source of income. In the words of biographer Granville Hicks, "Money meant primarily work for the *Metropolitan* and incidentally articles and stories for other paying magazines." But employment by *Metropolitan* did not inhibit Reed from writing articles critical of the Morgan and Rockefeller interests. One such piece, "At the Throat of the Republic" (*Masses*, July 1916), traced the relationship between munitions industries, the national security-preparedness lobby, the interlocking directorates of the Morgan-Rockefeller interest, "and showed that they dominated both the preparedness societies and the newly formed American International Corporation, organized for the exploitation of backward countries."[17]

In 1915 John Reed was arrested in Russia by tsarist authorities, and the *Metropolitan* intervened with the State Department in Reed's behalf. On June 21, 1915, H. J. Whigham wrote Secretary of State Robert Lansing informing him that John Reed and Boardman Robinson (also arrested and also a contributor to the *Masses*) were in Russia "with commission from the *Metropolitan* magazine to write articles and to make illustrations in the Eastern field of the War." Whigham pointed out that neither had "any desire or authority from us to interfere with the operations of any belligerent powers that be." Whigham's letter continues:

> If Mr. Reed carried letters of introduction from Bucharest to people in Galicia of an anti-Russian frame of mind I am sure that it was done innocently with the simple intention of meeting as many people as possible. . . .

Whigham points out to Secretary Lansing that John Reed was known at the White House and had given "some assistance" to the

---

17. Granville Hicks, *John Reed, 1887-1920* (New York: Macmillan, 1936), p. 215.

administration on Mexican affairs; he concludes: "We have the highest regard for Reed's great qualities as a writer and thinker and we are very anxious as regards his safety."[18] The Whigham letter is not, let it be noted, from an establishment journal in support of a Bolshevik writer; it is from an establishment journal in support of a Bolshevik writer for the *Masses* and similar revolutionary sheets, a writer who was also the author of trenchant attacks ("The Involuntary Ethics of Big Business: A Fable for Pessimists," for example) on the same Morgan interests that owned *Metropolitan*.

The evidence of finance by the private banker Boissevain is incontrovertible. On February 23, 1918, the American legation at Christiania, Norway, sent a cable to Washington in behalf of John Reed for delivery to Socialist Party leader Morris Hillquit. The cable stated in part: "Tell Boissevain must draw on him but carefully." A cryptic note by Basil Miles in the State Department files, dated April 3, 1918, states, "If Reed is coming home he might as well have money. I understand alternatives are ejection by Norway or polite return. If this so latter seems preferable." This protective note is followed by a cable dated April 1, 1918, and again from the American legation at Christiania: "John Reed urgently request Eugene Boissevain, 29 Williams Street, New York, telegraph care legation $300.00."[19] This cable was relayed to Eugene Boissevain by the State Department on April 3, 1918.

Reed apparently received his funds and arrived safely back in the United States. The next document in the State Department files is a letter to William Franklin Sands from John Reed, dated June 4, 1918, and written from Croton-on-Hudson, New York. In the letter Reed asserts that he has drawn up a memorandum for the State Department, and appeals to Sands to use his influence to get release of the boxes of papers brought back from Russia. Reed concludes, "Forgive me for bothering you, but I don't know where else to turn, and I can't afford another trip to Washington." Subsequently, Frank Polk, acting secretary of state, received a letter from Sands regarding the release of John Reed's papers. Sands' letter, dated June 5, 1918, from 120 Broadway, is here reproduced in full; it makes quite explicit statements about control of Reed:

18. U.S. State Dept. Decimal File, 860d.1121 R 25/4.
19. Ibid., 360d.1121/R25/18. According to Granville Hicks in *John Reed*, "*Masses* could not pay his [Reed's] expenses. Finally, friends of the magazine, notably Eugene Boissevain, raised the money" (p. 249).

120 BROADWAY
NEW YORK

June fifth, 1918

My dear Mr. Polk:

I take the liberty of enclosing to you an appeal from John ("Jack") Reed to help him, if possible, to secure the release of the papers which he brought into the country with him from Russia.

I had a conversation with Mr. Reed when he first arrived, in which he sketched certain attempts by the Soviet Government to initiate constructive development, and expressed the desire to place whatever observations he had made or information he had obtained through his connection with Leon Trotzky, at the disposal of our Government. I suggested that he write a memorandum on this subject for you, and promised to telephone to Washington to ask you to give him an interview for this purpose. He brought home with him a mass of papers which were taken from him for examination, and on this subject also he wished to speak to someone in authority, in order to voluntarily offer any information they might contain to the Government, and to ask for the release of those which he needed for his newspaper and magazine work.

I do not believe that Mr. Reed is either a "Bolshevik" or a "dangerous anarchist," as I have heard him described. He is a sensational journalist, without doubt, but that is all. He is not trying to embarrass our Government, and for this reason refused the "protection" which I understand was offered to him by Trotzky, when he returned to New York to face the indictment against him in the "Masses" trial. He is liked by the Petrograd Bolsheviki, however, and, therefore, anything which our police may do which looks like "persecution" will be resented in Petrograd, which I believe to be undesirable because unnecessary. *He can be handled and controlled much better by other means than through the police.*

I have not seen the memorandum he gave to Mr. Bullitt—*I wanted him to let me see it first and perhaps to edit it,* but he had not the opportunity to do so.

I hope that you will not consider me to be intrusive in this matter or meddling with matters which do not concern me. I believe it to be wise not to offend the Bolshevik leaders *unless and until it may become necessary to do so—if it should become necessary*—and it is unwise to look on every one as a suspicious or even dangerous character, who has had friendly relations with the Bolsheviki in Russia. *I think it better policy to attempt to use such people for our own purposes in*

141

developing our policy toward Russia, if it is possible to do so. The lecture which Reed was prevented by the police from delivering in Philadelphia (he lost his head, came into conflict with the police and was arrested) is the only lecture on Russia which I would have paid to hear, if I had not already seen his notes on the subject. It covered a subject which we might quite possibly find to be a point of contact with the Soviet Government, from which to begin constructive work!

Can we not use him, instead of embittering him and making him an enemy? He is not well balanced, but he is, unless I am very much mistaken, *susceptible to discreet guidance and might be quite useful.*

Sincerely yours,
William Franklin Sands

The Honourable
  Frank Lyon Polk
    Counselor for the Department of State
      Washington, D.C.

WFS:AO
Enclosure[20]

The significance of this document is the hard revelation of direct intervention by an officer (executive secretary) of American International Corporation in behalf of a known Bolshevik. Ponder a few of Sands' statements about Reed: "He can be handled and controlled much better by other means than through the police"; and, "Can we not use him, instead of embittering him and making him an enemy? . . . he is, unless I am very much mistaken, susceptible to discreet guidance and might be quite useful." Quite obviously, the American International Corporation viewed John Reed as an agent or a potential agent who could be, and probably had already been, brought under its control. The fact that Sands was in a position to request editing a memorandum by Reed (for Bullitt) suggests some degree of control had already been established.

Then note Sands' potentially hostile attitude towards—and barely veiled intent to provoke—the Bolsheviks: "I believe it to be wise not to offend the Bolshevik leaders unless and *until it may become necessary to do so*—if it should become necessary . . ." (italics added).

20. U.S. State Dept. Decimal File, 360.D.1121.R/20/22½, /R25 (John Reed). The letter was transferred by Mr. Polk to the State Department archives on May 2, 1935. All italics added.

This is an extraordinary letter in behalf of a Soviet agent from a private U.S. citizen whose counsel the State Department had sought, and continued to seek.

A later memorandum, March 19, 1920, in the State files reported the arrest of John Reed by the Finnish authorities at Abo, and Reed's possession of English, American and German passports. Reed, traveling under the alias of Casgormlich, carried diamonds, a large sum of money, Soviet propaganda literature, and film. On April 21, 1920, the American legation at Helsingfors cabled the State Department:

> Am forwarding by the next pouch certified copies of letters from Emma Goldman, Trotsky, Lenin and Sirola found in Reed's possession. Foreign Office has promised to furnish complete record of the Court proceedings.

Once again Sands intervened: "I knew Mr. Reed personally."[21] And, as in 1915, *Metropolitan* magazine also came to Reed's aid. H. J. Whigham wrote on April 15, 1920, to Bainbridge Colby in the State Department: "Have heard John Reed in danger of being executed in Finland. Hope the State Dept. can take immediate steps to see that he gets proper trial. Urgently request prompt action."[22] This was in addition to an April 13, 1920 telegram from Harry Hopkins, who was destined for fame under President Roosevelt:

> Understand State Dept. has information Jack Reed arrested Finland, will be executed. As one of his friends and yours and on his wife's behalf urge you take prompt action prevent execution and secure release. Feel sure can rely your immediate and effective intervention.[23]

John Reed was subsequently released by the Finnish authorities.

This paradoxical account on intervention in behalf of a Soviet agent can have several explanations. One hypothesis that fits other evidence concerning Wall Street and the Bolshevik Revolution is that John Reed was in effect an agent of the Morgan interests— perhaps only half aware of his double role—that his anticapitalist writing maintained the valuable myth that *all* capitalists are in perpetual warfare with all socialist revolutionaries. Carroll Quigley, as we have already noted, reported that the Morgan interests finan-

---

21. Ibid., 360d.1121 R 25/72.
22. Ibid.
23. This was addressed to Bainbridge Colby, ibid., 360d.1121 R 25/30. Another letter, dated April 14, 1920, and addressed to the secretary of state from 100 Broadway, New York, was from W. Bourke Cochrane; it also pleaded for the release of John Reed.

cially supported domestic revolutionary organizations and anticapitalist writings.[24] And we have presented in this chapter irrefutable documentary evidence that the Morgan interests were also effecting control of a Soviet agent, interceding on his behalf and, more important, generally intervening in behalf of Soviet interests with the U.S. government. These activities centered at a single address: 120 Broadway, New York City.

24. Quigley, op. cit.

Chapter 9

GUARANTY TRUST
GOES TO RUSSIA

> **Soviet Government desire Guarantee [*sic*] Trust Company to become fiscal agent in United States for all Soviet operations and contemplates American purchase Eestibank with a view to complete linking of Soviet fortunes with American financial interests.**
>
> *William H. Coombs, reporting to the U.S. embassy in London, June 1, 1920 (U.S. State Dept. Decimal File, 861.51/752). ("Eestibank" was an Estonian bank)*

In 1918 the Soviets faced a bewildering array of internal and external problems. They occupied a mere fraction of Russia. To subdue the remainder, they needed foreign arms, imported food, outside financial support, diplomatic recognition, and—above all—foreign trade. To gain diplomatic recognition and foreign trade, the Soviets first needed representation abroad, and representation in turn required financing through gold or foreign currencies. As we have already seen, the first step was to establish the Soviet Bureau in New York under Ludwig Martens. At the same time, efforts were made to transfer funds to the United States and Europe for purchases of needed goods. Then influence was exerted in the U.S. to gain recognition or to obtain the export licenses needed to ship goods to Russia.

New York bankers and lawyers provided significant—in some cases, critical—assistance for each of these tasks. When Professor George V. Lomonossoff, the Russian technical expert in the Soviet Bureau, needed to transfer funds from the chief Soviet agent in Scandinavia, a prominant Wall Street attorney came to his assistance—using official State Department channels and the acting secretary of state as an intermediary. When gold had to be transferred to the United States, it was American International Corporation, Kuhn, Loeb & Co., and Guaranty Trust that requested the facilities and used their influence in Washington to smooth the way. And when it came to recognition, we find American firms pleading with Congress and with the public to endorse the Soviet regime.

Lest the reader should deduce—too hastily—from these assertions that Wall Street was indeed tinged with Red, or that Red flags were flying in the street (see frontispiece), we also in a later chapter present evidence that the J. P. Morgan firm financed Admiral Kolchak in Siberia. Aleksandr Kolchak was fighting the Bolsheviks, to install his own brand of authoritarian rule. The firm also contributed to the anti-Communist United Americans organization.

WALL STREET COMES TO THE AID OF PROFESSOR LOMONOSSOFF

The case of Professor Lomonossoff is a detailed case history of Wall Street assistance to the early Soviet regime. In late 1918 George V. Lomonossoff, member of the Soviet Bureau in New York and later first Soviet commissar of railroads, found himself stranded in the United States without funds. At this time Bolshevik funds were denied entry into the United States; indeed, there was no official recognition of the regime at all. Lomonossoff was the subject of a letter of October 24, 1918, from the U.S. Department of Justice to the Department of State.[1] The letter referred to Lomonossoff's Bolshevik attributes and pro-Bolshevik speeches. The investigator concluded, "Prof. Lomonossoff is not a Bolshevik although his speeches constitute unequivocal support for the Bolshevik cause." Yet Lomonossoff was able to pull strings at the highest levels of the administration to have $25,000 transferred from the Soviet Union through a Soviet espionage agent in Scandinavia (who was himself later to become confidential assistant to Reeve

1. U.S. State Dept. Decimal File, 861.00/3094.

Schley, a vice president of Chase Bank). All this with the assistance of a member of a prominent Wall Street firm of attorneys![2]

The evidence is presented in detail because the details themselves point up the close relationship between certain interests that up to now have been thought of as bitter enemies. The first indication of Lomonossoff's problem is a letter dated January 7, 1919, from Thomas L. Chadbourne of Chadbourne, Babbitt & Wall of 14 Wall Street (same Address as William Boyce Thompson's) to Frank Polk, acting secretary of state. Note the friendly salutation and casual reference to Michael Gruzenberg, alias Alexander Gumberg, chief Soviet agent in Scandinavia and later Lomonossoff's assistant:

Dear Frank: You were kind enough to say that if I could inform you of the status of the $25,000 item of personal funds belonging to Mr. & Mrs. Lomonossoff you would set in motion the machinery necessary to obtain it here for them.

I have communicated with Mr. Lomonossoff with respect to it, and he tells me that Mr. Michael Gruzenberg, who went to Russia for Mr. Lomonossoff prior to the difficulties between Ambassador Bakhmeteff and Mr. Lomonossoff, transmitted the information to him respecting this money through three Russians who recently arrived from Sweden, and Mr. Lomonossoff believes that the money is held at the Russian embassy in Stockholm, Milmskilnad Gaten 37. If inquiry from the State Department should develop this to be not the place where the money is on deposit, then the Russian embassy in Stockholm can give the exact address of Mr. Gruzenberg, who can give the proper information respecting it. Mr. Lomonossoff does not receive letters from Mr. Gruzenberg, although he is informed that they have been written: nor have any of his letters to Mr. Gruzenberg been delivered, he is also informed. For this reason it is impossible to be more definite than I have been, but I hope something can be done to relieve his and his wife's embarrassment for lack of funds, and it only needs a little help to secure this money which belongs to them to aid them on this side of the water.

Thanking you in advance for anything you can do, I beg to remain, as ever,

Yours sincerely,

Thomas L. Chadbourne.

2. This section is from U.S., Senate, *Russian Propaganda*, hearings before a subcommittee of the Committee on Foreign Relations, 66th Cong., 2d sess., 1920.

In 1919, at the time this letter was written, Chadbourne was a dollar-a-year man in Washington, counsel and director of the U.S. War Trade Board, and a director of the U.S. Russian Bureau Inc., an official front company of the U.S. government. Previously, in 1915, Chadbourne organized Midvale Steel and Ordnance to take advantage of war business. In 1916 he became chairman of the Democratic Finance Committee and later a director of Wright Aeronautical and of Mack Trucks.

The reason Lomonossoff was not receiving letters from Gruzenberg is that they were, in all probability, being intercepted by one of several governments taking a keen interest in the latter's activities.

On January 11, 1919, Frank Polk cabled the American legation in Stockholm:

> Department is in receipt of information that $25,000, personal funds of . . . . Kindly inquire of the Russian Legation informally and personally if such funds are held thus. Ascertain, if not, address of Mr. Michael Gruzenberg, reported to be in possession of information on this subject. Department not concerned officially, merely undertaking inquiries on behalf of a former Russian official in this country.
>
> Polk, Acting

Polk appears in this letter to be unaware of Lomonossoff's Bolshevik connections, and refers to him as "a former Russian official in this country." Be that as it may, within three days Polk received a reply from Morris at the U.S. Legation in Stockholm:

> January 14, 3 p.m. 3492. Your January 12, 3 p.m., No. 1443.
>
> Sum of $25,000 of former president of Russian commission of ways of communication in United States not known to Russian legation; neither can address of Mr. Michael Gruzenberg be obtained.
>
> Morris

Apparently Frank Polk then wrote to Chadbourne (the letter is not included in the source) and indicated that State could find neither Lomonossoff nor Michael Gruzenberg. Chadbourne replied on January 21, 1919:

> Dear Frank: Many thanks for your letter of January 17. I understand that there are two Russian legations in Sweden, one being the soviet and the other the Kerensky, and I presume your inquiry was directed to the soviet legation as that was the address I gave you in my letter, namely, Milmskilnad Gaten 37, Stockholm.

Michael Gruzenberg's address is, Holmenkollen Sanitarium, Christiania, Norway, and I think the soviet legation could find out all about the funds through Gruzenberg if they will communicate with him.

Thanking you for taking this trouble and assuring you of my deep appreciation, I remain,

Sincerely yours,

Thomas L. Chadbourne

We should note that a Wall Street lawyer had the address of Gruzenberg, chief Bolshevik agent in Scandinavia, at a time when the acting secretary of state and the U.S. Stockholm legation had no record of the address; nor could the legation track it down. Chadbourne also presumed that the Soviets were the official government of Russia, although that government was not recognized by the United States, and Chadbourne's official government position on the War Trade Board would require him to know that.

Frank Polk then cabled the American legation at Christiania, Norway, with the address of Michael Gruzenberg. It is not known whether Polk knew he was passing on the address of an espionage agent, but his message was as follows:

To American Legation, Christiania. January 25, 1919. It is reported that Michael Gruzenberg is at Holmenkollen Sanitarium. Is it possible for you to locate him and inquire if he has any knowledge respecting disposition of $25,000 fund belonging to former president of Russian mission of ways of communication in the United States, Professor Lomonossoff.

Polk, Acting

The U.S. representative (Schmedeman) at Christiania knew Gruzenberg well. Indeed, the name had figured in reports from Schmedeman to Washington concerning Gruzenberg's pro-Soviet activities in Norway. Schmedeman replied:

January 29, 8 p.m. 1543. Important. Your January 25, telegram No. 650.

Before departing to-day for Russia, Michael Gruzenberg informed our naval attache that when in Russia some few months ago he had received, at Lomonossoff's request, $25,000 from the Russian Railway Experimental Institute, of which Prof. Lomonossoff was president. Gruzenberg claims that to-day he cabled attorney for Lomonossoff in New York, Morris Hillquitt [sic], that he, Gruzenberg, is in possession of the money, and before forwarding it is awaiting further instructions from the United States, requesting in the cablegram that

Lomonossoff be furnished with living expenses for himself and family by Hillquitt pending the receipt of the money.[3]

As Minister Morris was traveling to Stockholm on the same train as Gruzenberg, the latter stated that he would advise further with Morris in reference to this subject.

Schmedeman

The U.S. minister traveled with Gruzenberg to Stockholm where he received the following cable from Polk:

It is reported by legation at Christiania that Michael Gruzenberg has for Prof. G. Lomonossoff, the . . . sum of $25,000, received from Russian Railway Experimental Institute. If you can do so without being involved with Bolshevik authorities, department will be glad for you to facilitate transfer of this money to Prof. Lomonossoff in this country. Kindly reply.

Polk, Acting

This cable produced results, for on February 5, 1919, Frank Polk wrote to Chadbourne about a "dangerous bolshevik agitator," Gruzenberg:

My Dear Tom: I have a telegram from Christiania indicating that Michael Gruzenberg has the $25,000 of Prof. Lomonossoff, and received it from the Russian Railway Experimental Institute, and that he had cabled Morris Hillquitt [sic], at New York, to furnish Prof. Lomonossoff money for living expenses until the fund in question can be transmitted to him. As Gruzenberg has just been deported from Norway as a dangerous bolshevik agitator, he may have had difficulties in telegraphing from that country. I understand he has now gone to Christiania, and while it is somewhat out of the department's line of action, I shall be glad, if you wish, to see if I can have Mr. Gruzenberg remit the money to Prof. Lomonossoff from Stockholm, and am telegraphing our minister there to find out if that can be done.

Very sincerely, yours,
Frank L. Polk

The telegram from Christiania referred to in Polk's letter reads as follows:

February 3, 6 p.m., 3580. Important. Referring department's January 12, No. 1443, $10,000 has now been deposited in Stockholm to my order to be forwarded to Prof. Lomonossoff by Michael Gruzenberg, one of the former representatives of the bolsheviks in Norway. I informed him before accepting this money that I would communicate with you and inquire if it is your wish that this money be forwarded

3. Morris Hillquit was the intermediary between New York banker Eugene Boissevain and John Reed in Petrograd.

to Lomonossoff. Therefore I request instructions as to my course of action.

Morris

Subsequently Morris, in Stockholm, requested disposal instructions for a $10,000 draft deposited in a Stockholm bank. His phrase "[this] has been my only connection with the affair" suggests that Morris was aware that the Soviets could, and probably would, claim this as an officially expedited monetary transfer, since this action *implied* approval by the U.S. of such monetary transfers. Up to this time the Soviets had been required to smuggle money into the U.S.

Four p.m. February 12, 3610, Routine.
With reference to my February 3, 6 p.m., No. 3580, and your February 8, 7 p.m., No. 1501. It is not clear to me whether it is your wish for me to transfer through you the $10,000 referred to Prof. Lomonossoff. Being advised by Gruzenberg that he had deposited this money to the order of Lomonossoff in a Stockholm bank and has advised the bank that this draft could be sent to America through me, provided I so ordered, has been my only connection with the affair. Kindly wire instructions.

Morris

Then follows a series of letters on the transfer of the $10,000 from A/B Nordisk Resebureau to Thomas L. Chadbourne at 520 Park Avenue, New York City, through the medium of the State Department. The first letter contains instructions from Polk, on the mechanics of the transfer; the second, from Morris to Polk, contains $10,000; the third, from Morris to A/B Nordisk Resebureau, requesting a draft; the fourth is a reply from the bank with a check; and the fifth is the acknowledgment.

Your February 12, 4 p.m., No. 3610.
Money may be transmitted direct to Thomas L. Chadbourne, 520 Park Avenue, New York City,

Polk, Acting

* * * * *

Dispatch, No. 1600, March 6, 1919:
The Honorable the Secretary of State,
   Washington
Sir: Referring to my telegram, No. 3610 of February 12, and to the department's reply, No. 1524 of February 19 in regard to the sum of $10,000 for Professor Lomonossoff, I have the honor herewith to in-

close copy of a letter which I addressed on February 25 to A. B. Nordisk Resebureau, the bankers with whom this money was deposited; a copy of the reply of A. B. Nordisk Resebureau, dated February 26; and a copy of my letter to the A. B. Nordisk Resebureau, dated February 27.

It will be seen from this correspondence that the bank was desirous of having this money forwarded to Professor Lomonossoff. I explained to them, however, as will be seen from my letter of February 27, that I had received authorization to forward it directly to Mr. Thomas L. Chadbourne, 520 Park Avenue, New York City. I also inclose herewith an envelope addressed to Mr. Chadbourne, in which are inclosed a letter to him, together with a check on the National City Bank of New York for $10,000.

I have the honor to be, sir,
Your obedient servant,
Ira N. Morris

*　*　*　*　*

A. B. Nordisk Reserbureau,
  No. 4 Vestra Tradgardsgatan, Stockholm.
Gentlemen: Upon receipt of your letter of January 30, stating that you had received $10,000 to be paid out to Prof. G. V. Lomonossoff, upon my request, I immediately telegraphed to my Government asking whether they wished this money forwarded to Prof. Lomonossoff. I am to-day in receipt of a reply authorizing me to forward the money direct to Mr. Thomas L. Chadbourne, payable to Prof. Lomonossoff. I shall be glad to forward it as instructed by my Government.

I am, gentlemen,
Very truly, yours,
Ira N. Morris

*　*　*　*　*

Mr. I. N. Morris,
  American Minister, Stockholm
Dear Sir: We beg to acknowledge the receipt of your favor of yesterday regarding payment of dollars 10,000—to Professor G. V. Lomonossoff, and we hereby have the pleasure to inclose a check for said amount to the order of Professor G. V. Lomonossoff, which we understand that you are kindly forwarding to this gentleman. We shall be glad to have your receipt for same, and beg to remain,

Yours, respectfully,
A. B. Nordisk Reserbureau
E. Molin

*　*　*　*　*

A. B. Nordisk Resebureau.
Stockholm

Gentlemen: I beg to acknowledge receipt of your letter of February 26, inclosing a check for $10,000 payable to Professor G. V. Lomonossoff. As I advised you in my letter of February 25, I have been authorized to forward this check to Mr. Thomas L. Chadbourne, 520 Park Avenue, New York City, and I shall forward it to this gentleman within the next few days, unless you indicate a wish to the contrary.

Very truly, yours,
Ira N. Morris

Then follow an internal State Department memorandum and Chadbourne's acknowledgment:

Mr. Phillips to Mr. Chadbourne, April 3, 1919.
Sir: Referring to previous correspondence regarding a remittance of ten thousand dollars from A. B. Norsdisk Resebureau to Professor G. V. Lomonossoff, which you requested to be transmitted through the American Legation at Stockholm, the department informs you that it is in receipt of a dispatch from the American minister at Stockholm dated March 6, 1919, covering the enclosed letter addressed to you, together with a check for the amount referred to, drawn to the order to Professor Lomonossoff.

I am, sir, your obedient servant
William Phillips,
Acting Secretary of State.

Inclosure: Sealed letter addressed Mr. Thomas L. Chadbourne, inclosed with 1,600 from Sweden.

* * * * *

Reply of Mr. Chadbourne, April 5, 1919.
Sir: I beg to acknowledge receipt of your letter of April 3, enclosing letter addressed to me, containing check for $10,000 drawn to the order of Professor Lomonossoff, which check I have to-day delivered.

I beg to remain, with great respect,
Very truly, yours,
Thomas L. Chadbourne

Subsequently the Stockholm legation enquired concerning Lomonossoff's address in the U.S. and was informed by the State Department that "as far as the department is aware Professor George V. Lomonossoff can be reached in care of Mr. Thomas L. Chadbourne, 520 Park Avenue, New York City."

It is evident that the State Department, for the reason either of personal friendship between Polk and Chadbourne or of political influence, felt it had to go along and act as bagman for a Bolshevik agent—just ejected from Norway. But why would a prestigious establishment law firm be so intimately interested in the health and welfare of a Bolshevik emissary? Perhaps a contemporary State Department report gives the clue:

> Martens, the Bolshevik representative, and Professor Lomonossoff are banking on the fact that Bullitt and his party will make a favorable report to the Mission and the President regarding conditions in Soviet Russia and that on the basis of this report the Government of the United States will favor dealing with the Soviet Government as proposed by Martens. March 29, 1919.[4]

THE STAGE IS SET FOR COMMERCIAL EXPLOITATION OF RUSSIA

It was commercial exploitation of Russia that excited Wall Street, and Wall Street had lost no time in preparing its program. On May 1, 1918—an auspicious date for Red revolutionaries—the American League to Aid and Cooperate with Russia was established, and its program approved in a conference held in the Senate Office Building, Washington, D.C. The officers and executive committee of the league represented some superficially dissimilar factions. Its president was Dr. Frank J. Goodnow, president of Johns Hopkins University. Vice presidents were the ever active William Boyce Thompson, Oscar S. Straus, James Duncan, and Frederick C. Howe, who wrote *Confessions of a Monopolist*, the rule book by which monopolists could control society. The Treasurer was George P. Whalen, vice president of Vacuum Oil Company. Congress was represented by Senator William Edgar Borah and Senator John Sharp Williams, of the Senate Foreign Relations Committee; Senator William N. Calder; and Senator Robert L. Owen, chairman of the Banking and Currency Committee. House members were Henry R. Cooper and Henry D. Flood, chairman of the House Foreign Affairs Committee. American business was represented by Henry Ford; Charles A. Coffin, chairman of the board of General Electric Company; and M. A. Oudin, then foreign manager of General Electric. George P. Whalen represented Vacuum Oil Company, and Daniel Willard was president of the Baltimore & Ohio Railroad. The more overtly revolutionary element was represented by Mrs. Raymond Robins, whose name was later found to be prominent in the Soviet Bureau files and in the Lusk Committee hearings; Henry L. Slobodin, described as a "prominent patriotic socialist"; and Lincoln Steffens, a domestic Communist of note.

4. U.S. State Dept. Decimal File, 861.00/4214a.

In other words, this was a hybrid executive committee; it represented domestic revolutionary elements, the Congress of the United States, and financial interests prominently involved with Russian affairs.

Approved by the executive committee was a program that emphasized the establishment of an official Russian division in the U.S. government "directed by strong men." This division would enlist the aid of universities, scientific organizations, and other institutions to study the "Russian question," would coordinate and unite organizations within the United States "for the safeguarding of Russia," would arrange for a "special intelligence committee for the investigation of the Russian matter," and, generally, would itself study and investigate what was deemed to be the "Russian question." The executive committee then passed a resolution supporting President Woodrow Wilson's message to the Soviet congress in Moscow and the league affirmed its own support for the new Soviet Russia.

A few weeks later, on May 20, 1918, Frank J. Goodnow and Herbert A. Carpenter, representing the league, called upon Assistant Secretary of State William Phillips and impressed upon him the necessity for establishing an "official Russian Division of the Government to coordinate all Russian matters. They asked me [wrote Phillips] whether they should take this matter up with the President."[5]

Phillips reported this directly to the secretary of state and on the next day wrote Charles R. Crane in New York City requesting his views on the American League to Aid and Cooperate with Russia. Phillips besought Crane, "I really want your advice as to how we should treat the league . . . . We do not want to stir up trouble by refusing to cooperate with them. On the other hand it is a queer committee and I don't quite 'get it.'"[6]

In early June there arrived at the State Department a letter from William Franklin Sands of American International Corporation for Secretary of State Robert Lansing. Sands proposed that the United States appoint an administrator in Russia rather than a commission, and opined that "the suggestion of an allied military force in Russia at the present moment seems to me to be a very dangerous one."[7] Sands emphasized the possibility of trade with Russia and that this possibility could be advanced "by a well chosen administrator enjoying the full confidence of the government"; he indicated that

5. Ibid., 861.00/1938.
6. Ibid.
7. Ibid., 861.00/2003.

"Mr. Hoover" might fit the role.[8] The letter was passed to Phillips by Basil Miles, a former associate of Sands, with the expression, "I think the Secretary would find it worthwhile to look through."

In early June the War Trade Board, subordinate to the State Department, passed a resolution, and a committee of the board comprising Thomas L. Chadbourne (Professor Lomonossoff's contact), Clarence M. Woolley, and John Foster Dulles submitted a memorandum to the Department of State, urging consideration of ways and means "to bring about closer and more friendly commercial relations between the United States and Russia." The board recommended a mission to Russia and reopened the question whether this should result from an invitation from the Soviet government.

Then on June 10, M. A. Oudin, foreign manager of General Electric Company, expressed his views on Russia and clearly favored a "constructive plan for the economic assistance" of Russia.[9] In August 1918 Cyrus M. McCormick of International Harvester wrote to Basil Miles at the State Department and praised the President's program for Russia, which McCormick thought would be "a golden opportunity."[10]

Consequently, we find in mid-1918 a concerted effort by a segment of American business—obviously prepared to open up trade—to take advantage of its own preferred position regarding the Soviets.

GERMANY AND THE UNITED STATES STRUGGLE FOR RUSSIAN BUSINESS

In 1918 such assistance to the embryonic Bolshevik regime was justified on the grounds of defeating Germany and inhibiting German exploitation of Russia. This was the argument used by W. B. Thompson and Raymond Robins in sending Bolshevik revolutionaries and propaganda teams into Germany in 1918. The argument was also employed by Thompson in 1917 when conferring with Prime Minister Lloyd George about obtaining British support for the emerging Bolshevik regime. In June 1918 Ambassador Francis and his staff returned from Russia and urged President Wilson "to recognize and aid the Soviet government of Russia."[11] These reports made by the embassy staff to the State Department were leaked to

8. Ibid.
9. Ibid., 861.00/2002.
10. Ibid.
11. Ibid., M 316-18-1306.

156

the press and widely printed. Above all, it was claimed that delay in recognizing the Soviet Union would aid Germany "and helps the German plan to foster reaction and counter-revolution."[12] Exaggerated statistics were cited to support the proposal—for example, that the Soviet government represented ninety percent of the Russian people "and the other ten percent is the former propertied and governing class . . . . Naturally they are displeased."[13] A former American official was quoted as saying, "If we do nothing—that is, if we just let things drift—we help weaken the Russian Soviet Government. And that plays Germany's game."[14] So, it was recommended that "a commission armed with credit and good business advice could help much."

Meanwhile, inside Russia the economic situation had become critical and the inevitability of an embrace with capitalism dawned on the Communist Party and its planners. Lenin crystallized this awareness before the Tenth Congress of the Russian Communist Party:

> Without the assistance of capital it will be impossible for us to retain proletarian power in an incredibly ruined country in which the peasantry, also ruined, constitutes the overwhelming majority—and, of course, for this assistance capital will squeeze hundreds per cent out of us. This is what we have to understand. Hence, either this type of economic relations or nothing . . . . [15]

Then Leon Trotsky was quoted as saying, "What we need here is an organizer like Bernard M. Baruch."[16]

Soviet awareness of its impending economic doom suggests that American and German business was attracted by the opportunity of exploiting the Russian market for needed goods; the Germans, in fact, made an early start in 1918. The first deals made by the Soviet Bureau in New York indicate that earlier American financial and moral support of the Bolsheviks was paying off in the form of contracts.

The largest order in 1919-20 was contracted to Morris & Co., Chicago meatpackers, for fifty million pounds of food products, valued at approximately $10 million. The Morris meatpacking family was related to the Swift family. Helen Swift, later connected

12. Ibid.
13. Ibid.
14. Ibid.
15. V. I. Lenin, Report to the Tenth Congress of the Russian Communist Party (Bolshevik), March 15, 1921.
16. William Reswick, *I Dreamt Revolution* (Chicago: Henry Regnery, 1952), p. 78.

CONTRACTS MADE IN 1919 BY THE SOVIET BUREAU WITH U.S. FIRMS

Date of Contract	Firm	Goods Sold	Value
July 7, 1919	Milwaukee Shaper Co.*	Machinery	$ 45,071
July 30, 1919	Kempsmith Mfg. Co.*	Machinery	97,470
May 10, 1919	F. Mayer Boot & Shoe*	Boots	1,201,250
August 1919	Steel Sole Shoe & Co.*	Boots	58,750
July 23, 1919	Eline Berlow, N.Y.	Boots	3,000,000
July 24, 1919	Fischmann & Co.	Clothing	3,000,000
September 29, 1919	Weinberg & Posner	Machinery	3,000,000
October 27, 1919	LeHigh Machine Co.	Printing presses	4,500,000
January 22, 1920	Morris & Co. Chicago	50 million pounds of food products	10,000,000

*Later handled through Bobroff Foreign Trade and Engineering Co., Milwaukee.

SOURCE: U.S., Senate, *Russian Propaganda,* hearings before a subcommittee of the Committee on Foreign Relations, 66th Cong., 2d sess., 1920, p. 71.

with the Abraham Lincoln Center "Unity," was married to Edward Morris (of the meatpacking firm) and was also the brother of Harold H. Swift, a "major" in the 1917 Thompson Red Cross Mission to Russia.

Ludwig Martens was formerly vice president of Weinberg & Posner, located at 120 Broadway, New York City, and this firm was given a $3 million order.

SOVIET GOLD AND AMERICAN BANKS

Gold was the only practical means by which the Soviet Union could pay for its foreign purchases and the international bankers were quite willing to facilitate Soviet gold shipments. Russian gold exports, primarily imperial gold coins, started in early 1920, to Norway and Sweden. These were transshipped to Holland and Germany for other world destinations, including the United States.

In August 1920, a shipment of Russian gold coins was received at the Den Norske Handelsbank in Norway as a guarantee for payment of 3,000 tons of coal by Niels Juul and Company in the U.S. in behalf of the Soviet government. These coins were transferred to the Norges Bank for safekeeping. The coins were examined and weighed, were found to have been minted before the outbreak of war in 1914, and were therefore genuine imperial Russian coins.[17]

Shortly after this initial episode, the Robert Dollar Company of San Francisco received gold bars, valued at thirty-nine million Swedish kroner, in its Stockholm account; the gold "bore the stamp of the old Czar Government of Russia." The Dollar Company agent in Stockholm applied to the American Express Company for facilities to ship the gold to the United States. American Express refused to handle the shipment. Robert Dollar, it should be noted, was a director of American International Company; thus AIC was linked to the first attempt at shipping gold direct to America.[18]

Simultaneously it was reported that three ships had left Reval on the Baltic Sea with Soviet gold destined for the U.S. The S.S. *Gauthod* loaded 216 boxes of gold under the supervision of Professor Lomonossoff—now returning to the United States. The S.S. *Carl Line* loaded 216 boxes of gold under the supervision of three Russian agents. The S.S. *Ruheleva* was laden with 108 boxes of gold. Each box contained three poods of gold valued at sixty thousand gold rubles each. This was followed by a shipment on the S.S. *Wheeling Mold.*

Kuhn, Loeb & Company, apparently acting in behalf of Guaranty Trust Company, then inquired of the State Department concerning the official attitude towards the receipt of Soviet gold. In a report the department expressed concern because if acceptance was refused, then "the gold [would] probably come back on the hands of the War Department, causing thereby direct governmental responsibility

17. U.S. State Dept. Decimal File, 861.51/815.
18. Ibid., 861.51/836.

159

and increased embarrassment."[19] The report, written by Merle Smith in conference with Kelley and Gilbert, argues that unless the possessor has definite knowledge as to imperfect title, it would be impossible to refuse acceptance. It was anticipated that the U.S. would be requested to melt the gold in the assay office, and it was thereupon decided to telegraph Kuhn, Loeb & Company that no restrictions would be imposed on the importation of Soviet gold into the United States.

The gold arrived at the New York Assay Office and was deposited not by Kuhn, Loeb & Company—but by Guaranty Trust Company of New York City. Guaranty Trust then inquired of the Federal Reserve Board, which in turn inquired of the U.S. Treasury, concerning acceptance and payment. The superintendent of the New York Assay Office informed the Treasury that the approximately seven million dollars of gold had no identifying marks and that "the bars deposited have already been melted in United States mint bars." The Treasury suggested that the Federal Reserve Board determine whether Guaranty Trust Company had acted "for its own account, or the account of another in presenting the gold," and particularly "whether or not any transfer of credit or exchange transaction has resulted from the importation or deposit of the gold."[20]

On November 10, 1920, A. Breton, a vice president of the Guaranty Trust, wrote to Assistant Secretary Gilbert of the Treasury Department complaining that Guaranty had not received from the assay office the usual immediate advance against deposits of "yellow metal left with them for reduction." The letter states that Guaranty Trust had received satisfactory assurances that the bars were the product of melting French and Belgium coins, although it had purchased the metal in Holland. The letter requested that the Treasury expedite payment for the gold. In reply the Treasury argued that it "does not purchase gold tendered to the United States mint or assay offices which is known or suspected to be of Soviet origin," and in view of known Soviet sales of gold in Holland, the gold submitted by Guaranty Trust Company was held to be a "doubtful case, with suggestions of Soviet origin." It suggested that the Guaranty Trust Company could withdraw the gold from the assay office at any time it wished or could "present such further evidence to the Treasury, the Federal Reserve Bank of New York or the Department of State

19. Ibid., 861.51/837, October 4, 1920.
20. Ibid., 861.51/837, October 24, 1920.

as may be necessary to clear the gold of any suspicion of Soviet origin."[21]

There is no file record concerning final disposition of this case but presumably the Guaranty Trust Company was paid for the shipment. Obviously this gold deposit was to implement the mid-1920 fiscal agreement between Guaranty Trust and the Soviet government under which the company became the Soviet agent in the United States (see epigraph to this chapter).

It was determined at a later date that Soviet gold was also being sent to the Swedish mint. The Swedish mint "melts Russian gold, assays it and affixes the Swedish mint stamp at the request of Swedish banks or other Swedish subjects owing the gold."[22] And at the same time Olof Aschberg, head of Svenska Ekonomie A/B (the Soviet intermediary and affiliate of Guaranty Trust), was offering "unlimited quantities of Russian gold" through Swedish banks.[23]

In brief, we can tie American International Corporation, the influential Professor Lomonossoff, Guaranty Trust, and Olof Aschberg (whom we've previously identified) to the first attempts to import Soviet gold into the United States.

MAX MAY OF GUARANTY TRUST
BECOMES DIRECTOR OF RUSKOMBANK

Guaranty Trust's interest in Soviet Russia was renewed in 1920 in the form of a letter from Henry C. Emery, assistant manager of the Foreign Department of Guaranty Trust, to De Witt C. Poole in the State Department. The letter was dated January 21, 1920, just a few weeks before Allen Walker, the manager of the Foreign Department, became active in forming the virulent anti-Soviet organization United Americans (see page 165). Emery posed numerous questions about the legal basis of the Soviet government and banking in Russia and inquired whether the Soviet government was the de facto government in Russia.[24] "Revolt before 1922 planned by Reds," claimed United Americans in 1920, but Guaranty Trust had started negotiations with these same Reds and was acting as the Soviet agent in the U.S. in mid-1920.

In January 1922 Secretary of Commerce Herbert Hoover, inter-

21. Ibid., 861.51/853, November 11, 1920.
22. Ibid., 316-119, 1132.
23. Ibid., 316-119-785. This report has more data on transfers of Russian gold through other countries and intermediaries. See also 316-119-846.
24. Ibid., 861.516/86.

ceded with the State Department in behalf of a Guaranty Trust scheme to set up exchange relations with the "New State Bank at Moscow." This scheme, wrote Herbert Hoover, "would not be objectionable if a stipulation were made that all monies coming into their possession should be used for the purchase of civilian commodities in the United States"; and after asserting that such relations appeared to be in line with general policy, Hoover added, "It might be advantageous to have these transactions organized in such a manner that we know what the movement is instead of disintegrated operations now current."[25] Of course, such "disintegrated operations" are consistent with the operations of a free market, but this approach Herbert Hoover rejected in favor of channeling the exchange through specified and controllable sources in New York. Secretary of State Charles E. Hughes expressed dislike of the Hoover-Guaranty Trust scheme, which he thought could be regarded as de facto recognition of the Soviets while the foreign credits acquired might be used to the disadvantage of the United States.[26] A noncommittal reply was sent by State to Guaranty Trust. However, Guaranty went ahead (with Herbert Hoover's support),[27] participated in formation of the first Soviet international bank, and Max May of Guaranty Trust became head of the foreign department of the new Ruskombank.[28]

25. Ibid., 861.516/111.
26. Ibid.
27. Ibid., 861.516/176.
28. See p. 161 herein.

Chapter 10

J. P. MORGAN GIVES A LITTLE HELP TO THE OTHER SIDE

I would not sit down to lunch with a Morgan—except possibly to learn something of his motives and attitudes.

William E. Dodd, Ambassador Dodd's Diary, 1933-1938

So far our story has revolved around a single major financial house—Guaranty Trust Company, the largest trust company in the United States and controlled by the J. P. Morgan firm. Guaranty Trust used Olof Aschberg, the Bolshevik banker, as its intermediary in Russia before and after the revolution. Guaranty was a backer of Ludwig Martens and his Soviet Bureau, the first Soviet representatives in the United States. And in mid-1920 Guaranty was the Soviet fiscal agent in the U.S.; the first shipments of Soviet gold to the United States also traced back to Guaranty Trust.

There is a startling reverse side to this pro-Bolshevik activity—Guaranty Trust was a founder of United Americans, a virulent anti-Soviet organization which noisily threatened Red invasion by 1922, claimed that $20 million of Soviet funds were on the way to fund Red revolution, and forecast panic in the streets and mass starvation in New York City. This duplicity raises, of course, serious questions about the intentions of Guaranty Trust and its directors. Dealing with the Soviets, even backing them, can be explained by apolitical greed or simply profit motive. On the other hand, spreading propaganda designed to create fear and panic while at the same time encouraging the conditions that give rise to the fear and panic is a considerably more serious problem. It suggests utter moral depravity. Let's first look more closely at the anti-Communist United Americans.

UNITED AMERICANS FORMED TO FIGHT COMMUNISM[1]

In 1920 the organization United Americans was founded. It was limited to citizens of the United States and planned for five million members, "whose sole purpose would be to combat the teachings of the socialists, communists, I.W.W., Russian organizations and radical farmers societies."

In other words, United Americans was to fight all those institutions and groups believed to be anticapitalist.

The officers of the preliminary organization established to build up United Americans were Allen Walker of the Guaranty Trust Company; Daniel Willard, president of the Baltimore & Ohio Railroad; H. H. Westinghouse, of Westinghouse Air Brake Company; and Otto H. Kahn, of Kuhn, Loeb & Company and American International Corporation. These Wall Streeters were backed up by assorted university presidents and Newton W. Gilbert (former governor of the Philippines). Obviously, United Americans was, at first glance, exactly the kind of organization that establishment capitalists would be expected to finance and join. Its formation should have brought no great surprise.

On the other hand, as we have already seen, these financiers were also deeply involved in *supporting* the new Soviet regime in Russia—although this support was behind the scenes, recorded only in government files, and not to be made public for 50 years. As part of United Americans, Walker, Willard, Westinghouse, and Kahn were playing a double game. Otto H. Kahn, a founder of the anti-Communist organization, was reported by the British socialist J. H. Thomas as having his "face towards the light." Kahn wrote the preface to Thomas's book. In 1924 Otto Kahn addressed the League for Industrial Democracy and professed common objectives with this activist socialist group (see page 49). The Baltimore & Ohio Railroad (Willard's employer) was active in the development of Russia during the 1920s. Westinghouse in 1920, the year United Americans was founded, was operating a plant in Russia that had been exempted from nationalization. And the role of Guaranty Trust has already been minutely described.

1. *New York Times,* June 21, 1919.

164

UNITED AMERICANS REVEALS
"STARTLING DISCLOSURES" ON REDS

In March 1920 the *New York Times* headlined an extensive, detailed scare story about Red invasion of the United States within two years, an invasion which was to be financed by $20 million of Soviet funds "obtained by the murder and robbery of the Russian nobility."[2]

United Americans had, it was revealed, made a survey of "radical activities" in the United States, and had done so in its role as an organization formed to "preserve the Constitution of the United States with the representative form of government and the right of individual possession which the Constitution provides."

Further, the survey, it was proclaimed, had the backing of the executive board, "including Otto H. Kahn, Allen Walker of the Guaranty Trust Company, Daniel Willard," and others. The survey asserted that

> the radical leaders are confident of effecting a revolution within two years, that the start is to be made in New York City with a general strike, that Red leaders have predicted much bloodshed and that the Russian Soviet Government has contributed $20,000,000 to the American radical movement.

The Soviet gold shipments to Guaranty Trust in mid-1920 (540 boxes of three poods each) were worth roughly $15,000,000 (at $20 a troy ounce), and other gold shipments through Robert Dollar and Olof Aschberg brought the total very close to $20 million. The information about Soviet gold for the radical movement was called "thoroughly reliable" and was "being turned over to the Government." The Reds, it was asserted, planned to starve New York into submission within four days:

> Meanwhile the Reds count on a financial panic within the next few weeks to help their cause along. A panic would cause distress among the workingmen and thus render them more susceptible to revolution doctrine.

The United Americans' report grossly overstated the number of radicals in the United States, at first tossing around figures like two or five million and then settling for precisely 3,465,000 members in four radical organizations. The report concluded by emphasizing the possibility of bloodshed and quoted "Skaczewski, President of the International Publishing Association, otherwise the Communist Par-

2. Ibid., March 28, 1920.

165

ty, [who] boasted that the time was coming soon when the Communists would destroy utterly the present form of society."

In brief, United Americans published a report without substantiating evidence, designed to scare the man in the street into panic. The significant point of course is that this is the same group that was responsible for protecting and subsidizing, indeed assisting, the Soviets so they could undertake these same plans.

CONCLUSIONS CONCERNING UNITED AMERICANS

Is this a case of the right hand not knowing what the left hand was doing? Probably not. We are talking about heads of companies, eminently successful companies at that. So United Americans was probably a ruse to divert public—and official—attention from the subterranean efforts being made to gain entry to the Russian market.

United Americans is the only documented example known to this writer of an organization assisting the Soviet regime and also in the forefront of opposition to the Soviets. This is by no means an inconsistent course of action, and further research should at least focus on the following aspects:

(a) Are there other examples of double-dealing by influential groups generally known as the establishment?

(b) Can these examples be extended into other areas? For example, is there evidence that labor troubles have been instigated by these groups?

(c) What is the ultimate purpose of these pincer tactics? Can they be related to the Marxian axiom: thesis versus antithesis yields synthesis? It is a puzzle why the Marxist movement would attack capitalism head-on if its objective was a Communist world and if it truly accepted the dialectic. If the objective is a Communist world—that is, if communism is the desired synthesis—and capitalism is the thesis, then something apart from capitalism or communism has to be antithesis. Could therefore capitalism be the thesis and communism the antithesis, with the objective of the revolutionary groups and their backers being a synthesizing of these two systems into some world system yet undescribed?

MORGAN AND ROCKEFELLER AID KOLCHAK

Concurrently with these efforts to aid the Soviet Bureau and United Americans, the J. P. Morgan firm, which controlled Guaranty Trust, was providing financial assistance for one of the Bolshevik's primary opponents, Admiral Aleksandr Kolchak in Siberia. On June 23, 1919,

Congressman Mason introduced House Resolution 132 instructing the State Department "to make inquiry as to all and singular as to the truth of . . . press reports" charging that Russian bondholders had used their influence to bring about the "retention of American troops in Russia" in order to ensure continued payment of interest on Russian bonds. According to a file memorandum by Basil Miles, an associate of William F. Sands, Congressman Mason charged that certain banks were attempting to secure recognition of Admiral Kolchak in Siberia to get payment on former Russian bonds.

Then in August 1919 the secretary of state, Robert Lansing, received from the Rockefeller-influenced National City Bank of New York a letter requesting official comment on a proposed loan of $5 million to Admiral Kolchak; and from J. P. Morgan & Co. and other bankers another letter requesting the views of the department concerning an additional proposed £10 million sterling loan to Kolchak by a consortium of British and American bankers.[3]

Secretary Lansing informed the bankers that the U.S. had not recognized Kolchak and, although prepared to render him assistance, "the Department did not feel it could assume the responsibility of encouraging such negotiations but that, nevertheless, there seemed to be no objection to the loan provided the bankers deemed it advisable to make it."[4]

Subsequently, on September 30, Lansing informed the American consul general at Omsk that the "loan has since gone through in regular course"[5] Two fifths was taken up by British banks and three fifths by American banks. Two thirds of the total was to be spent in Britain and the United States and the remaining one third wherever the Kolchak Government wished. The loan was secured by Russian gold (Kolchak's) that was shipped to San Francisco. The timing of the previously described Soviet exports of gold suggests that cooperation with the Soviets on gold sales was determined on the heels of the Kolchak gold-loan agreement.

The Soviet gold sales and the Kolchak loan also suggest that Carroll Quigley's statement that Morgan interests infiltrated the domestic left applied also to overseas revolutionary *and* counterrevolutionary movements. Summer 1919 was a time of Soviet military reverses in the Crimea and the Ukraine and this black picture may have induced British and American bankers to mend their fences with the

3. U.S. State Dept. Decimal File, 861.51/649.
4. Ibid., 861.51/675.
5. Ibid., 861.51/656.

anti-Bolshevik forces. The obvious rationale would be to have a foot in all camps, and so be in a favorable position to negotiate for concessions and business after the revolution or counterrevolution had succeeded and a new government stabilized. As the outcome of any conflict cannot be seen at the start, the idea is to place sizable bets on all the horses in the revolutionary race. Thus assistance was given on the one hand to the Soviets and on the other to Kolchak—while the British government was supporting Denikin in the Ukraine and the French government went to the aid of the Poles.

In autumn 1919 the Berlin newspaper *Berliner Zeitung am Mittak* (October 8 and 9) accused the Morgan firm of financing the West Russian government and the Russian-German forces in the Baltic fighting the Bolsheviks—both allied to Kolchak. The Morgan firm strenuously denied the charge: "This firm has had no discussion, or meeting, with the West Russian Government or with anyone pretending to represent it, at any time."[6] But if the financing charge was inaccurate there is evidence of collaboration. Documents found by Latvian government intelligence among the papers of Colonel Bermondt, commander of the Western Volunteer Army, confirm "the relations claimed existing between Kolchak's London Agent and the German industrial ring which was back of Bermondt."[7]

In other words, we know that J. P. Morgan, London, and New York bankers financed Kolchak. There is also evidence that connects Kolchak and his army with other anti-Bolshevik armies. And there seems to be little question that German industrial and banking circles were financing the all-Russian anti-Bolshevik army in the Baltic. Obviously bankers' funds have no national flag.

6. Ibid., 861.51/767—a letter from J. P. Morgan to Department of State, November 11, 1919. The financing itself was a hoax (see AP report in State Department files following the Morgan letter).
7. Ibid., 861.51/6172 and /6361.

CHAPTER 11

THE ALLIANCE OF
BANKERS AND REVOLUTION

The name Rockefeller does not connote a revolutionary, and my life situation has fostered a careful and cautious attitude that verges on conservatism. I am not given to errant causes . . .

John D. Rockefeller III, The Second American Revolution *(New York: Harper & Row, 1973)*

THE EVIDENCE PRESENTED: A SYNOPSIS

Evidence already published by George Katkov, Stefan Possony, and Michael Futrell has established that the return to Russia of Lenin and his party of exiled Bolsheviks, followed a few weeks later by a party of Mensheviks, was financed and organized by the German government.[1] The necessary funds were transferred in part through the Nya Banken in Stockholm, owned by Olof Aschberg, and the dual German objectives were: (a) removal of Russia from the war, and (b) control of the postwar Russian market.[2]

---

1. Michael Futrell, *Northern Underground* (London: Faber and Faber, 1963); Stefan Possony, *Lenin: The Compulsive Revolutionary* (London: George Allen & Unwin, 1966); and George Katkov, "German Foreign Office Documents on Financial Support to the Bolsheviks in 1917," *International Affairs* 32 (Royal Institute of International Affairs, 1956).
2. Ibid., especially Katkov.

We have now gone beyond this evidence to establish a continuing working relationship between Bolshevik banker Olof Aschberg and the Morgan-controlled Guaranty Trust Company in New York before, during, and after the Russian Revolution. In tsarist times Aschberg was the Morgan agent in Russia and negotiator for Russian loans in the United States; during 1917 Aschberg was financial intermediary for the revolutionaries; and after the revolution Aschberg became head of Ruskombank, the first Soviet international bank, while Max May, a vice president of the Morgan-controlled Guaranty Trust, became director and chief of the Ruskombank foreign department. We have presented documentary evidence of a continuing working relationship between the Guaranty Trust Company and the Bolsheviks. The directors of Guaranty Trust in 1917 are listed in Appendix 1.

Moreover, there is evidence of transfers of funds from Wall Street bankers to international revolutionary activities. For example, there is the statement (substantiated by a cablegram) by William Boyce Thompson—a director of the Federal Reserve Bank of New York, a large stockholder in the Rockefeller-controlled Chase Bank, and a financial associate of the Guggenheims and the Morgans—that he (Thompson) contributed $1 million to the Bolshevik Revolution for propaganda purposes. Another example is John Reed, the American member of the Third International executive committee who was financed and supported by Eugene Boissevain, a private New York banker, and who was employed by Harry Payne Whitney's *Metropolitan* magazine. Whitney was at that time a director of Guaranty Trust. We also established that Ludwig Martens, the first Soviet "ambassador" to the United States, was (according to British Intelligence chief Sir Basil Thompson) backed by funds from Guaranty Trust Company. In tracing Trotsky's funding in the U.S. we arrived at German sources, yet to be identified, in New York. And though we do not know the precise German sources of Trotsky's funds, we *do* know that Von Pavenstedt, the chief German espionage paymaster in the U.S., was also senior partner of Amsinck & Co. Amsinck was owned by the ever-present American International Corporation—also controlled by the J. P. Morgan firm.

Further, Wall Street firms including Guaranty Trust were involved with Carranza's and Villa's wartime revolutionary activities in Mexico. We also identified documentary evidence concerning a Wall Street syndicate's financing of the 1912 Sun Yat-sen revolution in China, a revolution that is today hailed by the Chinese Communists as the precursor of Mao's revolution in China. Charles B.

Hill, New York attorney negotiating with Sun Yat-sen in behalf of this syndicate, was a director of three Westinghouse subsidiaries, and we have found that Charles R. Crane of Westinghouse in Russia was involved in the Russian Revolution.

Quite apart from finance, we identified other, and possibly more significant, evidence of Wall Street involvement in the Bolshevik cause. The American Red Cross Mission to Russia was a private venture of William B. Thompson, who publicly proffered partisan support to the Bolsheviks. British War Cabinet papers now available record that British policy was diverted towards the Lenin-Trotsky regime by the personal intervention of Thompson with Lloyd George in December 1917. We have reproduced statements by director Thompson and deputy chairman William Lawrence Saunders, both of the Federal Reserve Bank of New York, strongly favoring the Bolshevists. John Reed not only was financed from Wall Street, but had consistent support for his activities, even to the extent of intervention with the State Department from William Franklin Sands, executive secretary of American International Corporation. In the sedition case of Robert Minor there are strong indications and some circumstantial evidence that Colonel Edward House intervened to have Minor released. The significance of the Minor case is that William B. Thompson's program for Bolshevik revolution in Germany was the very program Minor was implementing when arrested in Germany.

Some international agents, for example Alexander Gumberg, worked for Wall Street *and* the Bolsheviks. In 1917 Gumberg was the representative of a U.S. firm in Petrograd, worked for Thompson's American Red Cross Mission, became chief Bolshevik agent in Scandinavia until he was deported from Norway, then became confidential assistant to Reeve Schley of Chase Bank in New York and later to Floyd Odlum of Atlas Corporation.

This activity in behalf of the Bolsheviks originated in large part from a single address: 120 Broadway, New York City. The evidence for this observation is outlined but no conclusive reason is given for the unusual concentration of activity at a single address, except to state that it appears to be the foreign counterpart of Carroll Quigley's claim that J. P. Morgan infiltrated the domestic left. Morgan also infiltrated the international left.

The Federal Reserve Bank of New York was at 120 Broadway. The vehicle for this pro-Bolshevik activity was American International Corporation—at 120 Broadway. AIC views on the Bolshevik regime were requested by Secretary of State Robert Lansing only a few weeks after the revolution began, and Sands, executive secretary of AIC, could barely restrain his enthusiasm for the Bolshevik cause. Ludwig Martens, the Soviet's first ambassador, had been vice president of Weinberg & Posner, which was also located at 120 Broadway. Guaranty Trust Company was next door at 140 Broadway but Guaranty Securities Co. was at 120 Broadway. In 1917 Hunt, Hill & Betts was at 120 Broadway, and Charles B. Hill of this firm was the negotiator in the Sun Yat-sen dealings. John MacGregor Grant Co., which was financed by Olof Aschberg in Sweden and Guaranty Trust in the United States, and which was on the Military Intelligence black list, was at 120 Broadway. The Guggenheims and the executive heart of General Electric (also interested in American International) were at 120 Broadway. We find it therefore hardly surprising that the Bankers Club was also at 120 Broadway, on the top floor (the thirty-fourth).

It is significant that support for the Bolsheviks did not cease with consolidation of the revolution; therefore, this support cannot be wholly explained in terms of the war with Germany. The American-Russian syndicate formed in 1918 to obtain concessions in Russia was backed by the White, Guggenheim, and Sinclair interests. Directors of companies controlled by these three financiers included Thomas W. Lamont (Guaranty Trust), William Boyce Thompson (Federal Reserve Bank), and John Reed's employer Harry Payne Whitney (Guaranty Trust). This strongly suggests that the syndicate was formed to cash in on earlier support for the Bolshevik cause in the revolutionary period. And then we found that Guaranty Trust financially backed the Soviet Bureau in New York in 1919.

The first really concrete signal that previous political and financial support was paying off came in 1923 when the Soviets formed their first international bank, Ruskombank. Morgan associate Olof Aschberg became nominal head of this Soviet bank; Max May, a vice president of Guaranty Trust, became a director of Ruskombank, and the Ruskombank promptly appointed Guaranty Trust Company its U.S. agent.

THE EXPLANATION FOR THE UNHOLY ALLIANCE

What motive explains this coalition of capitalists and Bolsheviks?

Russia was then—and is today—the largest untapped market in the world. Moreover, Russia, then and now, constituted the greatest potential competitive threat to American industrial and financial supremacy. (A glance at a world map is sufficient to spotlight the geographical difference between the vast land mass of Russia and the smaller United States.) Wall Street must have cold shivers when it visualizes Russia as a second super American industrial giant.

But why allow Russia to become a competitor and a challenge to U.S. supremacy? In the late nineteenth century, Morgan, Rockefeller, and Guggenheim had demonstrated their monopolistic proclivities. In *Railroads and Regulation 1877-1916* Gabriel Kolko has demonstrated how the railroad owners, not the farmers, wanted state control of railroads in order to preserve their monopoly and abolish competition. So the simplest explanation of our evidence is that a syndicate of Wall Street financiers enlarged their monopoly ambitions and broadened horizons on a global scale. *The gigantic Russian market was to be converted into a captive market and a technical colony to be exploited by a few high-powered American financiers and the corporations under their control.* What the Interstate Commerce Commission and the Federal Trade Commission under the thumb of American industry could achieve for that industry at home, a planned socialist government could achieve for it abroad—given suitable support and inducements from Wall Street and Washington, D.C.

Finally, lest this explanation seem too radical, remember that it was Trotsky who appointed tsarist generals to consolidate the Red Army; that it was Trotsky who appealed for American officers to control revolutionary Russia and intervene in behalf of the Soviets; that it was Trotsky who squashed first the libertarian element in the Russian Revolution and then the workers and peasants; and that recorded history *totally* ignores the 700,000-man Green Army composed of ex-Bolsheviks, angered at betrayal of the revolution, who fought the Whites *and* the Reds. In other words, we are suggesting that the Bolshevik Revolution was an alliance of statists: statist revolutionaries and statist financiers aligned against the genuine revolutionary libertarian elements in Russia.[3]

The question now in the readers' minds must be, were these bankers also secret Bolsheviks? No, of course not. The financiers were without ideology. It would be a gross misinterpretation to assume that assistance for the Bolshevists was ideologically motivated, in any narrow sense. The financiers were *power*-motivated and therefore assisted *any* political vehicle that would give them an entrée to power: Trotsky, Lenin, the tsar, Kolchak, Denikin—all

---

3. See also Voline (V. M. Eichenbaum), *Nineteen-Seventeen: The Russian Revolution Betrayed* (New York: Libertarian Book Club, n.d.).

received aid, more or less. All, that is, but those who wanted a truly free individualist society.

Neither was aid restricted to statist Bolsheviks and statist counter-Bolsheviks. John P. Diggins, in *Mussolini and Fascism: The View from America*,[4] has noted in regard to Thomas Lamont of Guaranty Trust that

> Of all American business leaders, the one who most vigorously patron-ized the cause of Fascism was Thomas W. Lamont. Head of the power-ful J. P. Morgan banking network, Lamont served as something of a business consultant for the government of Fascist Italy.

Lamont secured a $100 million loan for Mussolini in 1926 at a particularly crucial time for the Italian dictator. We might remem-ber too that the director of Guaranty Trust was the father of Cor-liss Lamont, a domestic Communist. This evenhanded approach to the twin totalitarian systems, communism and fascism, was not confined to the Lamont family. For example, Otto Kahn, director of American International Corporation and of Kuhn, Leob & Co., felt sure that "American capital invested in Italy will find safety, encouragement, opportunity and reward."[5] This is the same Otto Kahn who lectured the socialist League of Industrial Democracy in 1924 that *its* objectives were *his* objectives.[6] They differed only—according to Otto Kahn—over the means of achieving these objec-tives.

Ivy Lee, Rockefeller's public relations man, made similar pro-nouncements, and was responsible for selling the Soviet regime to the gullible American public in the late 1920s. We also have ob-served that Basil Miles, in charge of the Russian desk at the State Department and a former associate of William Franklin Sands, was decidedly helpful to the businessmen promoting Bolshevik causes; but in 1923 the same Miles authored a profascist article, "Italy's Black Shirts and Business."[7] "Success of the Fascists is an expres-sion of Italy's youth," wrote Miles while glorifying the fascist movement and applauding its esteem for American business.

THE MARBURG PLAN

The Marburg Plan, financed by Andrew Carnegie's ample heritage, was produced in the early years of the twentieth century. It sug-gests premeditation for this kind of superficial schizophrenia, which

4. Princeton, N.J.: Princeton University Press, 1972.
5. Ibid., p. 149.
6. See p. 49.
7. *Nation's Business*, February 1923, pp. 22-23.

174

in fact masks an integrated program of power acquisition: "What then if Carnegie and his unlimited wealth, the international financiers and the Socialists could be organized in a movement to compel the formation of a league to enforce peace."[8]

The governments of the world, according to the Marburg Plan, were to be socialized while the ultimate power would remain in the hands of the international financiers "to control its councils and enforce peace [and so] provide a specific for all the political ills of mankind."[9]

This idea was knit with other elements with similar objectives. Lord Milner in England provides the transatlantic example of banking interests recognizing the virtues and possibilities of Marxism. Milner was a banker, influential in British wartime policy, and pro-Marxist.[10] In New York the socialist "X" club was founded in 1903. It counted among its members not only the Communist Lincoln Steffens, the socialist William English Walling, and the Communist banker Morris Hillquit, but also John Dewey, James T. Shotwell, Charles Edward Russell, and Rufus Weeks (vice president of New York Life Insurance Company). The annual meeting of the Economic Club in the Astor Hotel, New York, witnessed socialist speakers. In 1908, when A. Barton Hepburn, president of Chase National Bank, was president of the Economic Club, the main speaker was the aforementioned Morris Hillquit, who "had abundant opportunity to preach socialism to a gathering which represented wealth and financial interests."[11]

From these unlikely seeds grew the modern internationalist movement, which included not only the financiers Carnegie, Paul Warburg, Otto Kahn, Bernard Baruch, and Herbert Hoover, but also the Carnegie Foundation and its progeny *International Conciliation*. The trustees of Carnegie were, as we have seen, prominent on the board of American International Corporation. In 1910 Carnegie donated $10 million to found the Carnegie Endowment for International Peace, and among those on the board of trustees were Elihu Root (Root Mission to Russia, 1917), Cleveland H. Dodge (a financial backer of President Wilson), George W. Perkins (Morgan partner), G. J. Balch (AIC and Amsinck), R. F. Herrick (AIC), H. W. Pritchett (AIC), and other Wall Street luminaries. Woodrow Wilson

8. Jennings C. Wise, *Woodrow Wilson: Disciple of Revolution* (New York: Paisley Press, 1938), p. 45.
9. Ibid., p. 46.
10. See p. 89.
11. Morris Hillquit, *Loose Leaves from a Busy Life* (New York: Macmillan, 1934), p. 81.

came under the powerful influence of—and indeed was financially indebted to—this group of internationalists. As Jennings C. Wise has written, "Historians must never forget that Woodrow Wilson . . . made it possible for Leon Trotsky to enter Russia with an American passport."[12]

But Leon Trotsky also declared himself an internationalist. We have remarked with some interest his high-level internationalist connections, or at least friends, in Canada. Trotsky then was not pro-Russian, or pro-Allied, or pro-German, as many have tried to make him out to be. Trotsky was *for* world revolution, *for* world dictatorship; he was, in one word, an internationalist.[13] Bolshevists and bankers have then this significant common ground—internationalism. Revolution and international finance are not at all inconsistent if the result of revolution is to establish more centralized authority. International finance prefers to deal with central governments. The last thing the banking community wants is laissez-faire economy and decentralized power because these would disperse power.

This, therefore, is an explanation that fits the evidence. This handful of bankers and promoters was not Bolshevik, or Communist, or socialist, or Democrat, or even American. Above all else these men wanted markets, preferably captive international markets—and a monopoly of the captive world market as the ultimate goal. They wanted markets that could be exploited monopolistically without fear of competition from Russians, Germans, or anyone else—including American businessmen outside the charmed circle. This closed group was apolitical and amoral. In 1917, it had a single-minded objective—a captive market in Russia, all presented under, and intellectually protected by, the shelter of a league to enforce the peace.

Wall Street did indeed achieve its goal. American firms controlled by this syndicate were later to go on and build the Soviet Union, and today are well on their way to bringing the Soviet military-industrial complex into the age of the computer.

Today the objective is still alive and well. John D. Rockefeller expounds it in his book *The Second American Revolution*—which sports a five-pointed star on the title page.[14] The book contains a naked plea for humanism, that is, a plea that our first priority is to

12. Wise, op. cit., p. 647.
13. Leon Trotsky, *The Bolsheviki and World Peace* (New York: Boni & Liveright, 1918).
14. In May 1973 Chase Manhattan Bank (chairman, David Rockefeller) opened its Moscow office at 1 Karl Marx Square. Moscow. The New York office is at 1 Chase Manhattan Plaza.

work for others. In other words, a plea for collectivism. Humanism is collectivism. It is notable that the Rockefellers, who have promoted this humanistic idea for a century, have not turned their OWN property over to others. Presumably it is implicit in their recommendation that *we* all work *for* the Rockefellers. Rockefeller's book promotes collectivism under the guises of "cautious conservatism" and "the public good." It is in effect a plea for the continuation of the earlier Morgan-Rockefeller support of collectivist enterprises and mass subversion of individual rights.

In brief, the public good has been, and is today, used as a device and an excuse for self-aggrandizement by an elitist circle that pleads for world peace and human decency. But so long as the reader looks at world history in terms of an inexorable Marxian conflict between capitalism and communism, the objectives of such an alliance between international finance and international revolution remain elusive. So will the ludicrousness of promotion of the public good by plunderers. If these alliances still elude the reader, then he should ponder the obvious fact that these same international interests and promoters are always willing to determine what *other* people should do, but are signally unwilling to be first in line to give up their own wealth and power. Their mouths are open, their pockets are closed.

This technique, used by the monopolists to gouge society, was set forth in the early twentieth century by Frederick C. Howe in *The Confessions of a Monopolist*.[15] First, says Howe, politics is a necessary part of business. To control industries it is necessary to control Congress and the regulators and thus make society go to work for you, the monopolist. So, according to Howe, the two principles of a successful monopolist are, "First, let Society work for you; and second, make a business of politics."[16] These, wrote Howe, are the basic "rules of big business."

Is there any evidence that this magnificently sweeping objective was also known to Congress and the academic world? Certainly the possibility was known and known publicly. For example, witness the testimony of Albert Rhys Williams, an astute commentator on the revolution, before the Senate Overman Committee:

> . . . it is probably true that under the soviet government industrial life will perhaps be much slower in development than under the usual capitalistic system. But why should a great industrial country like America desire the creation and consequent competition of another great

15. Chicago: Public Publishing, n.d.
16. Ibid.

177

industrial rival? Are not the interests of America in this regard in line with the slow tempo of development which soviet Russia projects for herself?

SENATOR WOLCOTT: Then your argument is that it would be to the interest of America to have Russia repressed?

MR. WILLIAMS: Not repressed . . . .

SENATOR WOLCOTT: You say. Why should America desire Russia to become an industrial competitor with her?

MR. WILLIAMS: This is speaking from a capitalistic standpoint. The whole interest of America is not, I think, to have another great industrial rival, like Germany, England, France, and Italy, thrown on the market in competition. I think another government over there besides the Soviet government would perhaps increase the tempo or rate of development of Russia, and we would have another rival. Of course, this is arguing from a capitalistic standpoint.

SENATOR WOLCOTT: So you are presenting an argument here which you think might appeal to the American people, your point being this, that if we recognize the Soviet government of Russia as it is constituted we will be recognizing a government that can not compete with us in industry for a great many years?

MR. WILLIAMS: That is a fact.

SENATOR WOLCOTT: That is an argument that under the Soviet government Russia is in no position, for a great many years at least, to approach America industrially?

MR. WILLIAMS: Absolutely.[17]

And in that forthright statement by Albert Rhys Williams is the basic clue to the revisionist interpretation of Russian history over the past half century.

Wall Street, or rather the Morgan-Rockefeller complex represented at 120 Broadway and 14 Wall Street, had something very close to Williams' argument in mind. Wall Street went to bat in Washington for the Bolsheviks. It succeeded. The Soviet totalitarian regime survived. In the 1930s foreign firms, mostly of the Morgan-Rockefeller group, built the five-year plans. They have continued to build Russia, economically and militarily.[18] On the other hand, Wall Street presumably did not foresee the Korean War and the Vietnam

17. U.S., Senate, *Bolshevik Propaganda,* hearings before a subcommittee of the Committee on the Judiciary, 65th Cong., pp. 679-80. See also herein p. 107 for the role of Williams in Radek's Press Bureau.
18. See Antony C. Sutton, *Western Technology and Soviet Economic Development,* 3 vols. (Stanford, Calif.: Hoover Institution, 1968, 1971, 1973); see also *National Suicide: Military Aid to the Soviet Union* (New York: Arlington House, 1973).

War—in which 100,000 Americans and countless allies lost their lives to Soviet armaments built with this same imported U.S. technology. What seemed a farsighted, and undoubtedly profitable, policy for a Wall Street syndicate, became a nightmare for millions outside the elitest power circle and the ruling class.

Appendix 1

DIRECTORS OF MAJOR BANKS, FIRMS, AND INSTITUTIONS MENTIONED IN THIS BOOK (AS IN 1917-1918)

AMERICAN INTERNATIONAL CORPORATION (120 Broadway)

J. Ogden Armour
G. J. Baldwin
C. A. Coffin
W. E. Corey
Robert Dollar
Pierre S. du Pont
Philip A. S. Franklin
J. P. Grace
R. F. Herrick
Otto H. Kahn
H. W. Pritchett

Percy A. Rockefeller
John D. Ryan
W. L. Saunders
J. A. Stillman
C. A. Stone
T. N. Vail
F. A. Vanderlip
E. S. Webster
A. H. Wiggin
Beckman Winthrop
William Woodward

CHASE NATIONAL BANK

J. N. Hill
A. B. Hepburn
S. H. Miller
C. M. Schwab
H. Bendicott

Newcomb Carlton
D. C. Jackling
E. R. Tinker
A. H. Wiggin
John J. Mitchell

Guy E. Tripp

EQUITABLE TRUST COMPANY (37-43 Wall Street)

Charles B. Alexander
Albert B. Boardman
Robert C. Clowry
Howard E. Cole
Henry E. Cooper
Paul D. Cravath
Franklin Wm. Cutcheon
Bertram Cutler
Thomas de Witt Cuyler
Frederick W. Fuller
Robert Goelet
Carl R. Gray
Charles Hayden

Henry E. Huntington
Edward T. Jeffrey
Otto H. Kahn
Alvin W. Krech
James W. Lane
Hunter S. Marston
Charles G. Meyer
George Welwood Murray
Henry H. Pierce
Winslow S. Pierce
Lyman Rhoades
Walter C. Teagle
Henry Rogers Winthrop

Bertram G. Work

FEDERAL ADVISORY COUNCIL (1916)

Daniel G. Wing, Boston, District No. 1
J. P. Morgan, New York, District No. 2
Levi L. Rue, Philadelphia, District No. 3
W. S. Rowe, Cincinnati, District No. 4
J. W. Norwood, Greenville, S.C., District No. 5
C. A. Lyerly, Chattanooga, District No. 6
J. B. Forgan, Chicago, Pres., District No. 7
Frank O. Watts, St. Louis, District No. 8
C. T. Jaffray, Minneapolis, District No. 9
E. F. Swinney, Kansas City, District No. 10
T. J. Record, Paris, District No. 11
Herbert Fleishhacker, San Francisco, District No. 12

FEDERAL RESERVE BANK OF NEW YORK (120 Broadway)

William Woodward (1917)
Robert H. Treman (1918)   } Class A
Franklin D. Locke (1919)

Charles A. Stone (1920)
Wm. B. Thompson (1918)   } Class B
L. R. Palmer (1919)

Pierre Jay (1917)
George F. Peabody (1919)   } Class C
William Lawrence Saunders (1920)

182

FEDERAL RESERVE BOARD

William G. M'Adoo

Charles S. Hamlin (1916)

Paul M. Warburg (1918)

Adolph C. Miller (1924)

Frederic A. Delano (1920)

W. P. G. Harding (1922)

John Skelton Williams

GUARANTY TRUST COMPANY (140 Broadway)

Alexander J. Hemphill (Chairman)

Charles H. Allen

A. C. Bedford

Edward J. Berwind

W. Murray Crane

T. de Witt Cuyler

James B. Duke

Caleb C. Dula

Robert W. Goelet

Daniel Guggenheim

W. Averell Harriman

Albert H. Harris

Walter D. Hines

Augustus D. Julliard

Thomas W. Lamont

William C. Lane

Edgar L. Marston

Grayson M-P Murphy

Charles A. Peabody

William C. Potter

John S. Runnells

Thomas F. Ryan

Charles H. Sabin

John W. Spoor

Albert Straus

Harry P. Whitney

Thomas E. Wilson

London Committee:

Arthur J. Fraser (Chairman)

Cecil F. Parr

Robert Callander

NATIONAL CITY BANK

P. A. S. Franklin

J. P. Grace

G. H. Dodge

H. A. C. Taylor

R. S. Lovett

F. A. Vanderlip

G. H. Miniken

E. P. Swenson

Frank Trumbull

Edgar Palmer

P. A. Rockefeller

James Stillman

W. Rockefeller

J. O. Armour

J. W. Sterling

J. A. Stillman

M. T. Pyne

E. D. Bapst

J. H. Post

W. C. Procter

NATIONALBANK FÜR DEUTSCHLAND
(As in 1914, Hjalmar Schacht joined board in 1918)

Emil Wittenberg

Hjalmar Schacht

Martin Schiff

Hans Winterfeldt

Th Marba

Paul Koch

Franz Rintelen

SINCLAIR CONSOLIDATED OIL CORPORATION (120 Broadway)

Harry F. Sinclair
H. P. Whitney
Wm. E. Corey
Wm. B. Thompson

James N. Wallace
Edward H. Clark
Daniel C. Jackling
Albert H. Wiggin

J. G. WHITE ENGINEERING CORPORATION

James Brown
Douglas Campbell
G. C. Clark, Jr.
Bayard Dominick, Jr.
A. G. Hodenpyl
T. W. Lamont
Marion McMillan
J. H. Pardee
G. H. Walbridge
E. N. Chilson

C. E. Bailey
J. G. White
Gano Dunn
E. G. Williams
A. S. Crane
H. A. Lardner
G. H. Kinniat
A. F. Kountz
R. B. Marchant
Henry Parsons

A. N. Connett

Appendix 2

THE JEWISH-CONSPIRACY THEORY OF THE BOLSHEVIK REVOLUTION

There is an extensive literature in English, French, and German reflecting the argument that the Bolshevik Revolution was the result of a "Jewish conspiracy"; more specifically, a conspiracy by Jewish world bankers. Generally, world control is seen as the ultimate objective; the Bolshevik Revolution was but one phase of a wider program that supposedly reflects an age-old religious struggle between Christianity and the "forces of darkness."

The argument and its variants can be found in the most surprising places and from quite surprising persons. In February 1920 Winston Churchill wrote an article—rarely cited today—for the *London Illustrated Sunday Herald* entitled "Zionism Versus Bolshevism." In this article Churchill concluded that it was "particularly important . . . that the National Jews in every country who are loyal to the land of their adoption should come forward on every occasion . . . and take a prominent part in every measure for combatting the Bolshevik conspiracy." Churchill draws a line between "national Jews" and what he calls "international Jews." He argues that the "international and for the most atheistical Jews" certainly had a "very great" role in the creation of Bolshevism and bringing about the Russian Revolution. He asserts (contrary to fact) that with the exception of Lenin, "the majority" of the leading figures in the revolution were Jewish, and adds (also contrary to fact) that in many cases Jewish interests and Jewish places of worship were excepted by the Bolsheviks from their policies of seizure. Churchill calls the international Jews a "sinister confederacy" emergent from the persecuted populations of countries where Jews have been persecuted on account of their race. Winston Churchill traces this movement back to Spartacus-Weishaupt, throws his literary net around Trotsky, Bela Kun, Rosa Luxemburg, and Emma Goldman, and charges: "This world-wide conspiracy for the overthrow of civilisation and for the reconstitution of society on the basis of arrested development, of envious malevolence, and impossible equality, has been steadily growing."

Churchill then argues that this conspiratorial Spartacus-Weishaupt group has been the mainspring of every subversive movement in the nineteenth century. While pointing out that Zionism and Bolshevism are competing for the soul of the Jewish people, Churchill (in 1920) was preoccupied with the role of the Jew in the Bolshevik Revolution and the existence of a worldwide Jewish conspiracy.

Another well-known author in the 1920s, Henry Wickham Steed describes in the second volume of his *Through 30 Years 1892-1922* (p. 302) how he attempted to bring the Jewish-conspiracy concept to the attention of Colonel Edward M. House and President Woodrow Wilson. One day in March 1919 Wickham Steed called Colonel House and found him disturbed over Steed's recent criticism of U.S. recognition of the Bolsheviks. Steed pointed out to House that Wilson would be discredited among the many peoples and nations of Europe and "insisted that, unknown to him, the prime movers were Jacob Schiff, Warburg and other international financiers, who wished above all to bolster up the Jewish Bolshevists in order to secure a field for German and Jewish exploitation of Russia."[1] According to Steed, Colonel House argued for the establishment of economic relations with the Soviet Union.

Probably the most superficially damning collection of documents on the Jewish conspiracy is in the State Department Decimal File (861.00/5339). The central document is one entitled "Bolshevism and Judaism," dated November 13, 1918. The text is in the form of a report, which states that the revolution in Russia was engineered "in February 1916" and "it was found that the following persons and firms were engaged in this destructive work":

(1) Jacob Schiff .... Jew
(2) Kuhn, Loeb & Company .... Jewish Firm

1. See Appendix 3 for Schiff's actual role.

186

Management: Jacob Schiff .... Jew
              Felix Warburg .... Jew
              Otto H. Kahn .... Jew
              Mortimer L. Schiff .... Jew
              Jerome J. Hanauer .... Jew
(3) Guggenheim .... Jew
(4) Max Breitung .... Jew
(5) Isaac Seligman .... Jew

The report goes on to assert that there can be no doubt that the Russian Revolution was started and engineered by this group and that in April 1917

> Jacob Schiff in fact made a public announcement and it was due to his financial influence that the Russian revolution was successfully accomplished and in the Spring 1917 Jacob Schiff started to finance Trotsky, a Jew, for the purpose of accomplishing a social revolution in Russia.

The report contains other miscellaneous information about Max Warburg's financing of Trotsky, the role of the Rheinish-Westphalian syndicate and Olof Aschberg of the Nya Banken (Stockholm) together with Jivotovsky. The anonymous author (actually employed by the U.S. War Trade Board)[2] states that the links between these organizations and their financing of the Bolshevik Revolution show how "the link between Jewish multi-millionaires and Jewish proletarians was forged." The report goes on to list a large number of Bolsheviks who were also Jews and then describes the actions of Paul Warburg, Judus Magnes, Kuhn, Loeb & Company, and Speyer & Company.

The report ends with a barb at "International Jewry" and places the argument into the context of a Christian-Jewish conflict backed up by quotations from the Protocols of Zion. Accompanying this report is a series of cables between the State Department in Washington and the American embassy in London concerning the steps to be taken with these documents:[3]

5399 Great Britain, TEL. 3253 i pm

   October 16, 1919 In Confidential File

Secret for Winslow from Wright. Financial aid to Bolshevism & Bolshevik Revolution in Russia from prominent Am. Jews: Jacob Schiff, Felix Warburg, Otto Kahn, Mendell Schiff, Jerome Hanauer, Max

---

2. The anonymous author was a Russian employed by the U.S. War Trade Board. One of the three directors of the U.S. War Trade Board at this time was John Foster Dulles.

3. U.S. State Dept. Decimal File, 861.00/5399.

Breitung & one of the Guggenheims. Document re- in possession of Brit. police authorities from French sources. Asks for any facts re-.

*   *   *   *   *

Oct. 17 Great Britain TEL. 6084, noon r c-h 5399 Very secret. Wright from Winslow. Financial aid to Bolshevik revolution in Russia from prominent Am. Jews. No proof re- but investigating. Asks to urge Brit. authorities to suspend publication at least until receipt of document by Dept.

*   *   *   *   *

Nov. 28 Great Britain TEL. 6223 R 5 pm. 5399
FOR WRIGHT. Document re financial aid to Bolsheviki by prominent American jews. Reports—identified as French translation of a statement originally prepared in English by Russian citizen in Am. etc. Seem most unwise to give—the distinction of publicity.

It was agreed to suppress this material and the files conclude, "I think we have the whole thing in cold storage."

Another document marked "Most Secret" is included with this batch of material. The provenance of the document is unknown; it is perhaps FBI or military intelligence. It reviews a translation of the Protocols of the Meetings of the Wise Men of Zion, and concludes:

> In this connection a letter was sent to Mr. W. enclosing a memorandum from us with regard to certain information from the American Military Attache to the effect that the British authorities had letters intercepted from various groups of international Jews setting out a scheme for world dominion. Copies of this material will be very useful to us.

This information was apparently developed and a later British intelligence report makes the flat accusation:

> SUMMARY: There is now definite evidence that Bolshevism is an international movement controlled by Jews; communications are passing between the leaders in America, France, Russia and England with a view to concerted action. . . . [4]

However, none of the above statements can be supported with hard empirical evidence. The most significant information is contained in the paragraph to the effect that the British authorities possessed "letters intercepted from various groups of international Jews setting out a scheme for world dominion." If indeed such let-

---

4. Great Britain, Directorate of Intelligence, *A Monthly Review of the Progress of Revolutionary Movements Abroad,* no. 9, July 16, 1913 (861.99/5067).

ters exist, then they would provide support (or nonsupport) for a presently unsubstantiated hypothesis: to wit, that the Bolshevik Revolution and other revolutions are the work of a worldwide Jewish conspiracy.

Moreover, when statements and assertions are not supported by hard evidence and where attempts to unearth hard evidence lead in a circle back to the starting point—particularly when everyone is quoting everyone else—then we must reject the story as spurious. *There is no concrete evidence that Jews were involved in the Bolshevik Revolution because they were Jewish.* There may indeed have been a higher proportion of Jews involved, but given tsarist treatment of Jews, what else would we expect? There were probably many Englishmen or persons of English origin in the American Revolution fighting the redcoats. So what? Does that make the American Revolution an English conspiracy? Winston Churchill's statement that Jews had a "very great role" in the Bolshevik Revolution is supported only by distorted evidence. The list of Jews involved in the Bolshevik Revolution must be weighed against lists of non-Jews involved in the revolution. When this scientific procedure is adopted, the proportion of foreign Jewish Bolsheviks involved falls to less than twenty percent of the total number of revolutionaries—and these Jews were mostly deported, murdered, or sent to Siberia in the following years. Modern Russia has in fact maintained tsarist anti-Semitism.

It is significant that documents in the State Department files confirm that the investment banker Jacob Schiff, often cited as a source of funds for the Bolshevik Revolution, was in fact *against* support of the Bolshevik regime.[5] This position, as we shall see, was in direct contrast to the Morgan-Rockefeller promotion of the Bolsheviks.

The persistence with which the Jewish-conspiracy myth has been pushed suggests that it may well be a deliberate device to divert attention from the real issues and the real causes. The evidence provided in this book suggests that the New York bankers who were also Jewish had relatively minor roles in supporting the Bolsheviks, while the New York bankers who were also Gentiles (Morgan, Rockefeller, Thompson) had major roles.

What better way to divert attention from the *real* operators than by the medieval bogeyman of anti-Semitism?

5. See Appendix 3.

189

Appendix 3

SELECTED DOCUMENTS FROM GOVERNMENT FILES OF THE UNITED STATES AND GREAT BRITAIN

Note: Some documents comprise several papers that form a related group.

DOCUMENT NO. 1 Cable from Ambassador Francis in Petrograd to U.S. State Department and related letter from Secretary of State Robert Lansing to President Woodrow Wilson (March 17, 1917)

DOCUMENT NO. 2 British Foreign Office document (October 1917) claiming Kerensky was in the pay of the German government and aiding the Bolsheviks

DOCUMENT NO. 3 Jacob Schiff of Kuhn, Loeb & Company and his position on the Kerensky and Bolshevik regimes (November 1918)

DOCUMENT NO. 4 Memorandum from William Boyce Thompson, director of the Federal Reserve Bank of New York, to the British prime minister David Lloyd George (December 1917)

DOCUMENT NO. 5 Letter from Felix Frankfurter to Soviet agent Santeri Nuorteva (May 9, 1918)

DOCUMENT NO. 6 Personnel of the Soviet Bureau, New York, 1920; list from the New York State Lusk Committee files

DOCUMENT NO. 1

Cable from Ambassador Francis in Petrograd to the Department of State in Washington, D.C., dated March 14, 1917, and reporting the first stage of the Russian Revolution (861.00/273).

Petrograd
Dated March 14, 1917,
Recd. 15th, 2:30 a.m.

Secretary of State,
Washington

1287. Unable to send a cablegram since the eleventh. Revolutionists have absolute control in Petrograd and are making strenuous efforts to preserve order, which successful except in rare instances. No cablegrams since your 1251 of the ninth, received March eleventh. Provisional government organized under the authority of the Douma which refused to obey the Emperor's order of the adjournment. Rodzianko, president of the Douma, issuing orders over his own signature. Ministry reported to have resigned. Ministers found are taken before the Douma, also many Russian officers and other high officials. Most if not all regiments ordered to Petrograd have joined the revolutionists after arrival. American colony safe. No knowledge of any injuries to American citizens.

FRANCIS,
American Ambassador

On receipt of the preceding cable, Robert Lansing, Secretary of State, made its contents available to President Wilson (861.00/273):

PERSONAL AND CONFIDENTIAL

My Dear Mr. President:

I enclose to you a very important cablegram which has just come from Petrograd, and also a clipping from the New York WORLD of this morning, in which a statement is made by Signor Scialoia, Minister without portfolio in the Italian Cabinet, which is significant in view of Mr. Francis' report. My own impression is that the Allies know of this matter and I presume are favorable to the revolutionists since the Court party has been, throughout the war, secretely pro-German.

Faithfully yours,
ROBERT LANSING

Enclosure:
The President,
The White House

COMMENT

The significant phrase in the Lansing-Wilson letter is "My own impression is that the Allies know of this matter and I presume are favorable to the revolutionists since the Court party has been, throughout the war, secretely pro-German." It will be recalled (chapter two) that Ambassador Dodd claimed that Charles R. Crane, of Westinghouse and of Crane Co. in New York and an adviser to President Wilson, was involved in this first revolution.

DOCUMENT NO. 2

Memorandum from Great Britain Foreign Office file FO 371/2999 (The War—Russia), October 23, 1917, file no. 3743.

DOCUMENT

Personal (and) Secret.

Disquieting rumors have reached us from more than one source that Kerensky is in German pay and that he and his government are doing their utmost to weaken (and) disorganize Russia, so as to arrive at a situation when no other course but a separate peace would be possible. Do you consider that there is any ground for such insinuations, and that the government by refraining from any effective action are purposely allowing the Bolshevist elements to grow stronger?

If it should be a question of bribery we might be able to compete successfully if it were known how and through what agents it could be done, although it is not a pleasant thought.

COMMENT

Refers to information that Kerensky was in German pay.

DOCUMENT NO. 3

Consists of four parts:

(a) Cable from Ambassador Francis, April 27, 1917, in Petrograd to Washington, D.C., requesting transmission of a message from prominent Russian Jewish bankers to prominent Jewish bankers in New York and requesting their subscription to the Kerensky Liberty Loan (861.51/139).

(b) Reply from Louis Marshall (May 10, 1917) representing American Jews; he declined the invitation while expressing support for the American Liberty Loan (861.51/143).

(c) Letter from Jacob Schiff of Kuhn, Loeb (November 25, 1918) to State Department (Mr. Polk) relaying a message from Russian Jewish banker Kamenka calling for Allied help *against* the Bolsheviks ("because Bolshevist government does not represent Russian People").

(d) Cable from Kamenka relayed by Jacob Schiff.

DOCUMENTS

(a) Secretary of State
    Washington.
    1229, twenty-seventh.

Please deliver following to Jacob Schiff, Judge Brandies [sic], Professor Gottheil, Oscar Strauss [sic], Rabbi Wise, Louis Marshall and Morgenthau:

"We Russian Jews always believed that liberation of Russia meant also our liberation. Being deeply devoted to country we placed implicit trust temporary Government. We know the unlimited economic power of Russia and her immense natural resources and the emancipation we obtained will enable us to participate development country. We firmly believe that victorious finish of the war owing help our allies and United States is near.

194

Temporary Government issuing now new public loan of freedom and we feel our national duty support loan high vital for war and freedom. We are sure that Russia has an unshakeable power of public credit and will easily bear all necessary financial burden. We formed special committee of Russian Jews for supporting loan consisting representatives financial, industrial trading circles and leading public men.

We inform you here of and request our brethern beyong [*sic*] the seas to support freedom of Russian which became now case humanity and world's civilization. We suggest you form there special committee and let us know of steps you may take Jewish committee support success loan of freedom. Boris Kamenka, Chairman, Baron Alexander Gunzburg, Henry Sliosberg."   FRANCIS

*   *   *   *   *

(b) Dear Mr. Secretary:

After reporting to our associates the result of the interview which you kindly granted to Mr. Morgenthau, Mr. Straus and myself, in regard to the advisability of calling for subscriptions to the Russian Freedom Loan as requested in the cablegram of Baron Gunzburg and Messrs. Kamenka and Sliosberg of Petrograd, which you recently communicated to us, we have concluded to act strictly upon your advice. Several days ago we promised our friends at Petrograd an early reply to their call for aid. We would therefore greatly appreciate the forwarding of the following cablegram, provided its terms have your approval:

"Boris Kamenka,
Don Azov Bank, Petrograd.

Our State Department which we have consulted regards any present attempt toward securing public subscriptions here for any foreign loans inadvisable; the concentration of all efforts for the success of American war loans being essential, thereby enabling our Government to supply funds to its allies at lower interest rates than otherwise possible. Our energies to help the Russian cause most effectively must therefore necessarily be directed to encouraging subscriptions to American Liberty Loan. Schiff, Marshall, Straus, Morgenthau, Wise, Gottheil."

You are of course at liberty to make any changes in the phraseology of this suggested cablegram which you may deem desirable and which will indicate that our failure to respond directly to the request that has come to us is due to our anxiety to make our activities most efficient.

195

May I ask you to send me a copy of the cablegram as forwarded, with a memorandum of the cost so that the Department may be promptly reimbursed.

I am, with great respect,
Faithfully yours,
[sgd.] Louis Marshall

The Secretary of State
Washington, D.C.

*   *   *   *   *

(c) Dear Mr. Polk:

Will you permit me to send you copy of a cablegram received this morning and which I think, for regularity's sake, should be brought to the notice of the Secretary of State or your good self, for such consideration as it might be thought well to give this.

Mr. Kamenka, the sender of this cablegram, is one of the leading men in Russia and has, I am informed, been financial advisor both of the Prince Lvoff government and of the Kerensky government. He is President of the Banque de Commerce de l'Azov Don of Petrograd, one of the most important financial institutions of Russia, but had, likely, to leave Russia with the advent of Lenin and his "comrades."

Let me take this opportunity to send sincere greetings to you and Mrs. Polk and to express the hope that you are now in perfect shape again, and that Mrs. Polk and the children are in good health.

Faithfully yours,
[sgd.] Jacob H. Schiff

Hon. Frank L. Polk
Counsellor of the State Dept.
Washington, D.C.

MM-Encl.

[Dated November 25, 1918]

*   *   *   *   *

(d) Translation:

The complete triumph of liberty and right furnishes me a new opportunity to repeat to you my profound admiration for the noble American nation. Hope to see now quick progress on the part of the Allies to help Russia in reestablishing order. Call your attention also to pressing necessity of replacing in Ukraine enemy troops at the very moment of their retirement in order to avoid Bolshevist devastation. Friendly intervention of Allies would be greeted everywhere with enthusiasm and looked upon as democratic action, because Bolshevist government does not represent Russian people. Wrote you September 19th. Cordial greetings.

[sgd.] Kamenka

COMMENT

This is an important series because it refutes the story of a Jewish bank conspiracy behind the Bolshevik Revolution. Clearly Jacob Schiff of Kuhn, Loeb was not interested in supporting the Kerensky Liberty Loan and Schiff went to the trouble of drawing State Department attention to Kamenka's pleas for Allied intervention against the Bolsheviks. Obviously Schiff and fellow banker Kamenka, unlike J. P. Morgan and John D. Rockefeller, were as unhappy about the Bolsheviks as they had been about the tsars.

DOCUMENT NO. 4

Description
Memorandum from William Boyce Thompson (director of the Federal Reserve Bank of New York) to Lloyd George (prime minister of Great Britain), December 1917.

DOCUMENT
FIRST

The Russian situation is lost and Russia lies entirely open to unopposed German exploitation unless a radical reversal of policy is at once undertaken by the Allies.

SECOND
Because of their shortsighted diplomacy, the Allies since the Revolution have accomplished nothing beneficial, and have done considerable harm to their own interests.

THIRD
The Allied representatives in Petrograd have been lacking in sym-

pathetic understanding of the desire of the Russian people to attain democracy. Our representatives were first connected officially with the Czar's regime. Naturally they have been influenced by that environment.

FOURTH

Meanwhile, on the other hand, the Germans have conducted propaganda that has undoubtedly aided them materially in destroying the Government, in wrecking the army and in destroying trade and industry. If this continues unopposed it may result in the complete exploitation of the great country by Germany against the Allies.

FIFTH

I base my opinion upon a careful and intimate study of the situation both outside and inside official circles, during my stay in Petrograd between August 7 and November 29, 1917.

SIXTH

"What can be done to improve the situation of the Allies in Russia"?

The diplomatic personnel, both British and American, should be changed to one democratic in spirit and capable of sustaining democratic sympathy.

There should be erected a powerful, unofficial committee, with headquarters in Petrograd, to operate in the background, so to speak, the influence of which in matters of policy should be recognized and accepted by the DIPLOMATIC, CONSULAR and MILITARY officials of the Allies. Such committee should be so composed in personnel as to make it possible to entrust to it wide discretionary powers. It would presumably undertake work in various channels. The nature of which will become obvious as the task progresses; it would aim to meet all new conditions as they might arise.

SEVENTH

It is impossible now to define at all completely the scope of this new Allied committee. I can perhaps assist to a better understanding of its possible usefulness and service by making a brief reference to the work which I started and which is now in the hands of Raymond Robins, who is well and favorably known to Col. Buchan—a work which in the future will undoubtedly have to be somewhat altered and added to in order to meet new conditions. My work has been performed chiefly through a Russian "Committee on Civic Education" aided by Madame Breshkovsky, the Grandmother of the Revolution. She was assisted by Dr. David Soskice, the private secretary of the then Prime Minister Kerensky (now of London); Nicholas Basil Tchaikovsky, at one time Chairman of the Peasants Co-operative Society, and by other substantial social revolutionaries constituting the saving element of democracy as between the extreme "Right" of the official and property-owning class, and the extreme "Left" embodying the most radical elements of the socialistic parties. The aim of this committee, as stated in a cable message from Madame Breshkovsky to President Wilson, can be gathered from this quotation: "A widespread education is necessary to make Russia an orderly democracy. We plan to bring this education to the soldier in the camp, to the workman in the factory, to the peasant in the village." Those aiding in this work realized that for centuries the masses had been under the heel of Autocracy which had given them not protection but oppression; that a democratic form of government in Russian could be maintained only BY THE DEFEAT OF THE GERMAN ARMY; BY THE OVERTHROW OF GERMAN AUTOCRACY. Could free Russia, unprepared for great governmental responsibilities, uneducated, untrained, be expected long to survive with imperial Germany her next door neighbor? Certainly not. Democratic Russia would become speedily the greatest war prize the world has even known.

The Committee designed to have an educational center in each regiment of the Russian army, in the form of Soldiers' Clubs. These clubs were organized as rapidly as possible, and lecturers were employed to address the soldiers. The lecturers were in reality teachers, and it should be remembered that there is a percentage of 90 among the soldiers of Russia who can neither read nor write. At the time of the Bolshevik outbreak many of these speakers were in the field making a fine impression and obtaining excellent results. There were 250 in the city of Moscow alone. It was contemplated by the Committee to have at least 5000 of these lecturers. We had under publication many newspapers of the "A B C" class, printing matter in the simplest style, and were assisting about 100 more. These papers carried the appeal for patriotism, unity and co-ordination into the homes of the workmen and the peasants.

After the overthrow of the last Kerensky government we materially aided the dissemination of the Bolshevik literature, distributing it through agents and by aeroplanes to the German army. If the suggestion is permissible, it might be well to consider whether it would not be desirable to have this same Bolshevik literature sent into Germany and Austria across the West and Italian fronts.

EIGHTH

The presence of a small number of Allied troops in Petrograd would certainly have done much to prevent the overthrow of the Kerensky government in November. I should like to suggest for your consideration, if present conditions continue, the concentration of all the British and French Government employes in Petrograd, and if the necessity should arise it might be formed into a fairly effective force. It might be advisable even to pay a small sum to a Russian force. There is also a large body of volunteers recruited in Russia, many of them included in the Inteligentzia of "Center" class, and these have done splendid work in the trenches. They might properly be aided.

NINTH

If you ask for a further programme I should say that it is impossible to give it now. I believe that intelligent and courageous work will still prevent Germany from occupying the field to itself and thus exploiting Russia at the expense of the Allies. There will be many ways in which this service can be rendered which will become obvious as the work progresses.

COMMENT

Following this memorandum the British war cabinet changed its policy to one of tepid pro-Bolshevism. Note that Thompson admits to distribution of Bolshevik literature by his agents. The confusion over the date on which Thompson left Russia (he states November 29th in this document) is cleared up by the Pirnie papers at the Hoover Institution. There were several changes of travel plans and Thompson was still in Russia in early December. The memorandum was probably written in Petrograd in late November.

DOCUMENT NO. 5
DESCRIPTION

Letter dated May 9, 1918, from Felix Frankfurter (then special assistant to the secretary of war) to Santeri Nuorteva (alias for Alexander Nyberg), a Bolshevik agent in the United States. Listed as Document No. 1544 in the Lusk Committee files, New York:

DOCUMENT

WAR DEPARTMENT
WASHINGTON
May 9, 1918

My dear Mr. Nhorteva [sic]:

Thank you very much for your letter of the 4th. I knew you would understand the purely friendly and wholly unofficial character of our talk, and I appreciate the prompt steps you have taken to correct your Sirola* letter. Be wholly assured that nothing has transpired which diminishes my interest in the questions which you present. Quite the contrary. I am much interested in** the considerations you are advancing and for the point of view you are urging. The issues*** at stake are the interests that mean much for the whole world. To meet them adequately we need all the knowledge and wisdom we can possibly get****.

Cordially yours,
Felix Frankfurter

Santeri Nuorteva, Esq.

*   Yrjo Sirola was a Bolshevik and commissar in Finland.
**   Original text, "continually grateful to you for."
***   Original text, "interests."
****   Original text added "these days."

COMMENT

This letter by Frankfurter was written to Nuorteva/Nyberg, a Bolshevik agent in the United States, at a time when Frankfurter held an official position as special assistant to Secretary of War Baker in the War Department. Apparently Nyberg was willing to change a letter to commissar "Sirola" according to Frankfurter's instructions. The Lusk Committee acquired the original Frankfurter draft including Frankfurter's changes and not the letter received by Nyberg.

DOCUMENT NO. 6

THE SOVIET BUREAU IN 1920

Position	Name	Citizenship	Born	Former Employment
Representative of USSR	Ludwig c.a.k. MARTENS	German	Russia	V-P of Weinberg & Posner Engineering (120 Broadway)
Office manager	Gregory WEINSTEIN	Russian	Russia	Journalist
Secretary	Santeri NUORTEVA	Finnish	Russia	Journalist
Assistant secretary	Kenneth DURANT	U.S.	U.S.	(1) U.S. Committee on Public Information (2) Former aide to Colonel House
Private secretary to NUORTEVA	Dorothy KEEN	U.S.	U.S.	High school
Translator	Mary MODELL	Russian	Russia	School in Russia
File clerk	Alexander COLEMAN	U.S.	U.S.	High school
Telephone clerk	Blanche ABUSHEVITZ	Russian	Russia	High school
Office attendant	Nestor KUNTZEVICH	Russian	Russia	—
Military expert	Lt. Col. Boris Tagueeff Roustam BEK	Russian	Russia	Military critic on *Daily Express* (London)
Commercial Department				
Director	A. HELLER	Russian	U.S.	International Oxygen Company
Secretary	Ella TUCH	Russian	U.S.	U.S. firms
Clerk	Rose HOLLAND	U.S.	U.S.	Gary School League
Clerk	Henrietta MEEROWICH	Russian	Russia	Social worker
Clerk	Rose BYERS	Russian	Russia	School
Statistician	Vladimir OLCHOVSKY	Russian	Russia	Russian Army
Information Department				
Director	Evans CLARK	U.S.	U.S.	Princeton University
Clerk	Nora G. SMITHEMAN	U.S.	U.S.	Ford Peace Expedition
Steno	Etta FOX	U.S.	U.S.	War Trade Board
—	Wilfred R. HUMPHRIES	U.K.	—	American Red Cross
Technical Dept.				
Director	Arthur ADAMS	Russian	U.S.	—
Educational Dept.				
Director	William MALISSOFF	Russian	U.S.	Columbia University
Medical Dept.				
Director	Leo A. HUEBSCH	Russian	U.S.	Medical doctor
	D. H. DUBROWSKY	Russian	U.S.	Medical doctor

Legal Dept.

Director	Morris HILLQUIT	Lithuanian	—	—
	Counsel retained:			
	Charles RECHT			
	Dudley Field MALONE			
	George Gordon BATTLE			
Dept. of Economics & Statistics				
Director	Isaac A. HOURWICH	Russian	U.S.	U.S. Bureau of Census
	Eva JOFFE	Russian	U.S.	National Child Labor Commission
Steno	Elizabeth GOLDSTEIN	Russian	U.S.	Student
Editorial Staff of Soviet Russia				
Managing editor	Jacob W. HARTMANN	U.S.	U.S.	College of City of New York
Steno	Ray TROTSKY	Russian	Russia	Student
Translator	Theodore BRESLAUER	Russian	Russia	—
Clerk	Vasily IVANOFF	Russian	Russia	—
Clerk	David OLDFIELD	Russian	Russia	—
Translator	I. BLANKSTEIN	Russian	Russia	—

SOURCE: U.S., House, *Conditions in Russia* (Committee on Foreign Affairs), 66th Cong., 3rd sess. (Washington, D.C., 1921).
See also British list in U.S. State Department Decimal File, 316-22-656, which also has the name of Julius Hammer.

DOCUMENT NO. 7

DESCRIPTION

Letter from National City Bank of New York to the U.S. Treasury, April 15, 1919, with regard to Ludwig Martens and his associate Dr. Julius Hammer (316-118).

DOCUMENT

The National City Bank of New York
New York, April 15, 1919

Honorable Joel Rathbone,
Assistant Secretary of the Treasury
Washington, D.C.

Dear Mr. Rathbone:

I beg to hand you herewith photographs of two documents which we have received this morning by registered mail from a Mr. L. Martens who claims to be the representative in the United States of the Russian Socialist Federal Soviet Republic, and witnessed by a

Dr. Julius Hammer for the Acting Director of the Financial Department.

You will see from these documents that there is a demand being made upon us for any and all funds on deposit with us in the name of Mr. Boris Bakhmeteff, alleged Russian Ambassador in the United States, or in the name of any individual, committee, or mission purporting to act in behalf of the Russian Government in subordination to Mr. Bakhmeteff or directly.

We should be very glad to receive from you whatever advice or instructions you may care to give us in this matter.

Yours respectfully,
[sgd.] J. H. Carter,
Vice President.

JHC:M
Enclosure

COMMENTS

The significance of this letter is related to the long-time association (1917-1974) of the Hammer family with the Soviets.

DOCUMENT NO. 8
DESCRIPTION

Letter dated August 3, 1920, from Soviet courier "Bill" Bobroff to Kenneth Durant, former aide to Colonel House. Taken from Bobroff by U.S. Department of Justice.

DOCUMENT

Department of Justice
Bureau of Investigation,
15 Park Row, New York City, N. Y.,
August 10, 1920

Director Bureau of Investigation
United States Department of Justice, Washington, D.C.

Dear Sir: Confirming telephone conversation with Mr. Ruch today, I am transmitting herewith original documents taken from the effects of B. L. Bobroff, steamship *Frederick VIII*.

The letter addressed Mr. Kenneth Durant, signed by Bill, dated August 3, 1920, together with the translation from "Pravda," July 1, 1920, signed by Trotzki, and copies of cablegrams were found inside the blue envelope addressed Mr. Kenneth Durant, 228 South Nineteenth Street, Philadelphia, Pa. This blue envelope was in turn sealed inside the white envelope attached.

Most of the effects of Mr. Bobroff consisted of machinery catalogues, specifications, correspondence regarding the shipment of various equipment, etc., to Russian ports. Mr. Bobroff was closely questioned by Agent Davis and the customs authorities, and a detailed report of same will be sent to Washington.

Very truly yours,
G. F. Lamb,
Division Superintendent

LETTER TO KENNETH DURANT

Dear Kenneth: Thanks for your most welcome letter. I have felt very much cut off and hemmed in, a feeling which has been sharply emphasized by recent experiences. I have felt distressed at inability to force a different attitude toward the bureau and to somehow get funds to you. To cable $5,000 to you, as was done last week, is but a sorry joke. I hope the proposal to sell gold in America, about which we have been cabling recently, will soon be found practicable. Yesterday we cabled asking if you could sell 5,000,000 rubles at a minimum of 45 cents, present market rate being 51.44 cents. That would net at least $2,225,000. L's present need is $2,000,000 to pay Niels Juul & Co., in Christiania, for the first part of the coal shipment from America to Vardoe, Murmansk, and Archangel. The first ship is nearing Vardoe and the second left New York about July 28. Altogether, Niels Juul & Co., or rather the Norges' Bank, of Christiania, on their and our account, hold $11,000,000 gold rubles of ours, which they themselves brought from Reval to Christiania, as security for our coal order and the necessary tonnage, but the offers for purchase of this gold that they have so far been able to get are very poor, the best being $575 per kilo, whereas the rate offered by the American Mint or Treasury Department is now $644.42, and considering the large sum involved it would be a shame to let it go at too heavy a loss. I hope that ere you get this you will have been able to effect the sale, at the same time thus getting a quarter of a million dollars or more for the bureau. If we can't in some way pay the $2,000,000 in Christiania, that was due four days ago, within a very short time, Niels Juul & Co. will have the right to sell our gold that they now hold at the best price then obtainable, which, as stated above, is quite low.

We don't know yet how the Canadian negotiations are going on. We understand Nuorteva turned over the strings to Shoen when N.'s arrest seemed imminent. We don't at this writing know where Nuorteva is. Our guess is that after his enforced return to England from Esbjerg, Denmark, Sir Basil Thomson had him shipped aboard a steamer for Reval, but we have not yet heard from Reval that he has arrived there, and we certainly would hear from Goukovski or from N. himself. Humphries saw Nuorteva at Esbjerg, and is himself in difficulties with the Danish police because of it. All his connections are being probed for; his passport has been taken away: he has been up twice for examination, and it looks as if he will be lucky if he escapes deportation. It was two weeks ago that Nuorteva arrived at Esbjerg, 300 miles from here, but having no Danish visé, the Danish authorities refused to permit him to land, and he was transferred to a steamer due to sail at 8 o'clock the following morning. By depositing 200 kroner he was allowed shore leave for a couple of hours. Wanting to get Copenhagen on long-distance wire and having practically no more money, he once more pawned that gold watch of his for 25 kroner, therewith getting in touch with Humphries, who within half an hour jumped aboard the night train, slept on the floor, and arrived at Esbjerg at 7:30. Humphries found Nuorteva, got permission from the captain to go aboard, had 20 minutes with N., then had to go ashore and the boat sailed. Humphries was then invited to the police office by two plain-clothes men, who had been observing the proceedings. He was closely questioned, address taken, then released, and that night took train back to Copenhagen. He sent telegrams to Ewer, of Daily Herald, Shoen, and to Kliskho, at 128 New Bond Street, urging them to be sure and meet Nuorteva's boat, so that N. couldn't again be spirited away, but we don't know yet just what happened. The British Government vigorously denied that they had any intention of sending him to Finland. Moscow has threatened reprisals if anything happens to him. Meantime, the investigation of H. has begun. He was called upon at his hotel by the police, requested to go to headquarters (but not arrested), and we understand that his case is now before the minister of justice. Whatever may be the final outcome, Humphries comments upon the reasonable courtesy shown him, contrasting it with the ferocity of the Red raids in America.

He found that at detective headquarters they knew of some of his outgoing letters and telegrams.

I was interested in your favorable comment upon the Krassin interview of Tobenken's (you do not mention the Litvinoff one), because I had to fight like a demon with L. to get the opportunities for Tobenken. Through T. arrived with a letter from Nuorteva, as also did Arthur Ruhl, L. brusquely turned down in less than one minute the application T. was making to go into Russia, would hardly take time to hear him, saying it was impossible to allow two correspondents from the same paper to enter Russia. He gave a visé to Ruhl, largely because of a promise made last summer to Ruhl by L. Ruhl then went off to Reval, there to await the permission that L. had cabled asking Moscow to give. Tobenken, a nervous, almost a broken man because of his turn down, stayed here. I realized the mistake that had been made by the snap judgment, and started in on the job of getting it changed. Cutting a long story short, I got him to Reval with a letter to Goukovsky from L. In the meantime Moscow refused Ruhl, notwithstanding L's visé. L. was maddened at affront to his visé, and insisted that it be honored. It was, and Ruhl prepared to leave. Suddenly word came from Moscow to Ruhl revoking the permission and to Litvinoff, saying that information had reached Moscow that Ruhl was in service of State Department. At time of writing, both Tobenken and Ruhl are in Reval, stuck.

I told L. this morning of the boat leaving to-morrow and of the courier B. available, asked him if he had anything to write to Martens, offered to take it in shorthand for him, but no, he said he had nothing to write about that I might perhaps send duplicates of our recent cables to Martens.

Kameneff passed by here on a British destroyer en route to London, and didn't stop off here at all, and Krassin went direct from Stockholm. Of the negotiations, allied and Polish, and of the general situation you know about as much as we do here. L's negotiations with the Italians have finally resulted in establishing of mutual representation. Our representative, Vorovsky, has already gone to Italy and their representative, M. Gravina, is en route to Russia. We have just sent two ship loads of Russian wheat to Italy from Odessa.

Give my regards to the people of your circle that I know. With all good wishes to you.

Sincerely yours,
Bill

The batch of letters you sent —— —— 5 Cranbourne Road, Charlton cum Hardy, Manchester, has not yet arrived.

L's recommendation to Moscow, since M. asked to move to Canada, is that M. should be appointed there, and that N., after having some weeks in Moscow acquainting himself first hand, should be appointed representative to America.

L. is sharply critical of the bureau for giving too easily visés and recommendations. He was obviously surprised and incensed when B. reached here with contracts secured in Moscow upon strength of letters given to him by M. The later message from M. evidently didn't reach Moscow. What L. plans to do about it I don't know. I would suggest that M. cable in cipher his recommendation to L. in this matter. L. would have nothing to do with B. here. Awkward situation may be created.

L. instanced also the Rabinoff recommendation.

Two envelopes, Mr. Kenneth Durant, 228 South Nineteenth Street, Philadelphia, Pa., U.S.A.

Source: U.S. State Department Decimal File, 316-119-458/64.

NOTE: IDENTIFICATION OF INDIVIDUALS

William (Bill) L. BOBROFF	Soviet courier and agent. Operated Bobroff Foreign Trading and Engineering Company of Milwaukee. Invented the voting system used in the Wisconsin Legislature.
Kenneth DURANT	Aide to Colonel House; see text.
SHOEN	Employed by International Oxygen Co., owned by Heller, a prominent financier and Communist.
EWER	Soviet agent, reporter for *London Daily Herald.*
KLISHKO	Soviet agent in Scandinavia
NUORTEVA	Also known as Alexander Nyberg, first Soviet representative in United States; see text.
Sir Basil THOMPSON	Chief of British Intelligence

"L"	Litvinoff.
"H"	Wilfred Humphries, associated with Martens and Litvinoff, member of Red Cross in Russia.
KRASSIN	Bolshevik commissar of trade and labor, former head of Siemens-Schukert in Russia.

COMMENTS

This letter suggests close ties between Bobroff and Durant.

DOCUMENT NO. 9

DESCRIPTION

Memorandum referring to a request from Davison (Morgan partner) to Thomas Thacher (Wall Street attorney associated with the Morgans) and passed to Dwight Morrow (Morgan partner), April 13, 1918.

DOCUMENT

The Berkeley Hotel, London
April 13th, 1918.

Hon. Walter H. Page,
American Ambassador to England,
London.

Dear Sir:

Several days ago I received a request from Mr. H. P. Davison, Chairman of the War Council of the American Red Cross, to confer with Lord Northcliffe regarding the situation in Russia, and then to proceed to Paris for other conferences. Owing to Lord Northcliffe's illness I have not been able to confer with him, but am leaving with Mr. Dwight W. Morrow, who is now staying at the Berkeley Hotel, a memorandum of the situation which Mr. Morrow will submit to Lord Northcliffe on the latter's return to London.

For your information and the information of the Department I enclose to you, herewith, a copy of the memorandum.

Respectfully yours,
[sgd.] Thomas D. Thacher.

COMMENT

Lord Northcliffe had just been appointed director of propaganda. This is interesting in the light of William B. Thompson's subsidizing of Bolshevik propaganda and his connection with the Morgan-Rockefeller interests.

DOCUMENT NO. 10
DESCRIPTION

This document is a memorandum from D. C. Poole, Division of Russian Affairs in the Department of State, to the secretary of state concerning a conversation with Mr. M. Oudin of General Electric.

DOCUMENT

May 29, 1922

Mr. Secretary:

Mr. Oudin, of the General Electric Company, informed me this morning that his company feels that the time is possibly approaching to begin conversations with Krassin relative to a resumption of business in Russia. I told him that it is the view of the Department that the course to be pursued in this matter by American firms is a question of business judgment and that the Department would certainly interpose no obstacles to an American firm resuming operations in Russia on any basis which the firm considered practicable.

He said that negotiations are now in progress between the General Electric Company and the Allgemeine Elektrizitäts Gesellschaft for a resumption of the working agreement which they had before the war. He expects that the agreement to be made will include a provision for cooperation of Russia.

Respectfully,
DCP
D. C. Poole

COMMENT

This is an important document as it relates to the forthcoming resumption of relations with Russia by an important American company. It illustrates that the initiative came from the company, not from the State Department, and that no consideration was given to the effect of transfer of General Electric technology to a self-declared enemy. This GE agreement was the first step down a road of major technical transfers that led directly to the deaths of 100,000 Americans and countless allies.

SELECTED BIBLIOGRAPHY

Adam, George. *Treason and Tragedy: An Account of French War Trials.* London: Jonathan Cape, 1929.

American Red Cross Archives. Minutes of the War Council of the American National Red Cross, Washington, D.C., May 1917; and Billings report to Henry P. Davison, October 22, 1917, Washington, D.C.

Aschberg, Olof. *En Vandrande Jude Frän Glasbruksgatan.* Stockholm: Albert Bonniers Förlag, n.d.

Binion, Rudolph. *Defeated Leaders.* New York: Columbia University Press, 1960.

Bradley, John. *Allied Intervention in Russia* London: Weidenfeld and Nicolson, 1968.

British War Cabinet Papers. Public Records Office, London.

Browder, Robert Paul, and Kerensky, Alexander F. *The Russian Provisional Government, 1917.* Stanford, Calif.: Stanford University Press, 1961.

Bruntz, George G. *Allied Propaganda and the Collapse of the German Empire in 1918.* Stanford, Calif.: Stanford University Press, 1936.

Buley, R. Carlyle. *The Equitable Life Assurance Society of the United States.* New York: Appleton-Century-Crofts, n.d.

Collman, Charles U. *Die Kriegstreiber in Wall Street.* (Leipzig: Berlag von Rudolf Schick, 1917.

Corey, Lewis. *House of Morgan: A Social Biography of the Masters of Money.* New York: G. H. Watt, 1930.

Crankshaw, Edward. *The Forsaken Idea: A Study of Viscount Milner.* London: Longmans Green, 1952.

Cumming, C. K., and Pettit, Walter W. *Russian-American Relations, Documents and Papers.* New York: Harcourt, Brace & Howe, 1920.

Diggins, John P. *Mussolini and Fascism: The View from America*. Princeton, N.J.: Princeton University Press, 1972.

Dodd, William E. *Ambassador Dodd's Diary, 1933-1938*. New York: Harcourt, Brace, 1941.

Domhoff, G. William. *Who Rules America?* Englewood Cliffs, N.J.: Prentice-Hall, 1967.

Dulles, John Foster. *American Red Cross*. New York: Harper, 1950.

Futrell, Michael. *Northern Underground*. London: Faber and Faber, 1963.

Hagedorn, Hermann. *The Magnate: William Boyce Thompson and His Time (1869-1930)*. New York: Reynal & Hitchcock, 1935.

Hicks, Granville. *John Reed, 1887-1920*. New York: Macmillan, 1936.

Hillquit, Morris. *Loose Leaves from a Busy Life*. New York: Macmillan, 1934.

Howe, Frederick C. *The Confessions of a Monopolist*. Chicago: Public Publishing, 1906.

Johnson. Severance. *The Enemy Within*. London: George Allen & Unwin, 1920.

Katkov, George. "German Foreign Office Documents on Financial Support to the Bolsheviks in 1917." *International Affairs* 32 (1956).

Kennan, George F. *Decision to Intervene: Soviet-American Relations, 1917-1920*. Princeton, N.J.: Princeton University Press, 1958.

———. *Russia Leaves the War*. New York: Atheneum, 1967.

———. "The Sisson Documents." *Journal of Modern History* 27-28 (1955-56).

Kolko, Gabriel. *Railroads and Regulation 1877-1916*. New York: W. W. Norton, 1965.

Lamont, Thomas W. *Across World Frontiers*. New York: Harcourt, Brace, 1950.

Lenin, V. I. *Polnoe Sobranie Sochinenii*. 5th ed., vol. 53. Moscow, 1958.
———. Report to the Tenth Congress of the Russian Communist Party (Bolshevik), March 15, 1921.

Lockhart, Robert Hamilton Bruce. *British Agent*. New York: Putnam's, 1933.

McCormick, Donald. *The Mask of Merlin*. London: MacDonald, 1963; New York: Holt, Rinehart and Winston, 1964.

Moody, John. *The Truth about the Trusts*. New York: Moody Publishing, 1904.

Nedava, Joseph. *Trotsky and the Jews*. Philadelphia: Jewish Publication Society of America, 1972.

214

North, Joseph. *Robert Minor: Artist and Crusader.* New York: International Publishers, 1956.

Possony, Stefan. *Lenin: The Compulsive Revolutionary.* London: George Allen & Unwin, 1966.

Quigley, Carroll. *Tragedy and Hope.* New York: Macmillan, 1966.

Reed, John. *The Sisson Documents.* New York: Liberator Publishing, n.d.

Report of Court Proceedings in the Case of the Anti-Soviet "Bloc of Rights and Trotskyites" Heard Before the Military Collegium of the Supreme Court of the USSR. Moscow: People's Commissariat of Justice of the USSR, 1938.

Reswick, William. *I Dreamt Revolution.* Chicago: Henry Regnery. 1952.

Rockefeller, John D. *The Second American Revolution.* Chicago: Public Publishing, 1973.

Rubin, Jacob H. *I Live to Tell: The Russian Adventures of an American Socialist.* Indianapolis: Bobbs-Merrill, 1934.

Sadoul, Jacques. *Notes sur la revolution bolchevique.* Paris: Editions de la sirene, 1919.

Sands, William Franklin. *Our Jungle Diplomacy.* Chapel Hill: University of North Carolina Press, 1944.

———. *Undiplomatic Memories.* New York: McGraw-Hill, 1930.

Schulz, Ernst. *Weltdiktator Morgan.* Hamburg: Hoffmann und Campe Verlag, 1924.

Steffens, Lincoln. *The Letters of Lincoln Steffens.* New York: Harcourt, Brace, 1941.

Strothers, French. *Fighting Germany's Spies.* New York: Doubleday, Page, 1918.

Sutton, Antony C. *National Suicide: Military Aid to the Soviet Union.* New York: Arlington House, 1973.

———, **Western Technology and Soviet Economic Development,** 3 vols. Stanford, Calif.: Hoover Institution, 1968, 1971, 1973.

Thompson, Polkovnik' Villiam' Boic'. "Pravda o Rossiia i Bol'shevikakh." New York: Russian-American Publication Society, 1918.

Trotsky, Leon. *The Bolsheviki and World Peace.* New York: Boni & Liveright, 1918.

———. *My Life.* New York: Scribner's, 1930.

Ullman, Richard H. *Intervention and the War.* Princeton, N.J.: Princeton University Press, 1961.

United States, Committee on Public Information. *The German-Bolshevik Conspiracy.* War Information Series, no. 20, October 1918.

United States, House. *The Story of Panama*. Hearings of the Committee on Foreign Affairs on the Rainey Resolution, 1913.

United States, Senate. *Bolshevik Propaganda*. Hearings before a subcommittee of the Committee on the Judiciary, 65th Cong., 1919.

United States, Senate. *Brewing and Liquor Interests and German and Bolshevik Propaganda*. Hearings before a subcommittee of the Committee on the Judiciary, 65th Cong., 1919.

United States, Senate, Committee on Foreign Relations. *Investigation of Mexican Affairs*, 1920.

United States, Senate. *Russian Propaganda*. Hearings before a subcommittee of the Committee on Foreign Relations pursuant to S. Res. 263, directing the Committee on Foreign Relations to investigate the status and activities of Ludwig C. A. K. Martens, who claimed to be a representative of the Russian Socialist Soviet Republic, 1920.

United States, Senate. *Russian Propaganda*. Hearings before a subcommittee of the Committee on Foreign Relations. Report pursuant to S. Res. 263, etc., submitted to Mr. Moses, April 14, 1920. S. report 526, 66th Cong., 1920.

United States, Senate. *Russian Propaganda*. Hearings before a subcommittee of the Committee on Foreign Relations, 66th Cong., 1920.

United States, State Department Decimal File. Cited in two series: (a) by National Archives microfilm number for documents available for purchase on microfilm—example 316-18-1306 (i.e., microcopy 316, roll 18, frame 1306); and (b) United States, State Department Decimal File, 861.51/649 (i.e., document sub no. 649 in Decimal File 861.51), available at National Archives.

Vanderlip, Frank A. *From Farm Boy to Financier*. New York: A. Appleton-Century, 1935.

Voline (V. M. Eichenbaum). *Nineteen-Seventeen: The Russian Revolution Betrayed*. New York: Libertarian Book Club, n.d.

Von Bernstorff, Count. *My Three Years in America*. New York: Scribner's, 1920.

Ware, Louis. *George Foster Peabody*. Athens: University of Georgia Press, 1951.

Wise, Jennings C. *Woodrow Wilson: Disciple of Revolution*. New York: Paisley Press, 1938.

Zeman, Z. A. B., and Scharlau, W. B. *The Merchant of Revolution: The Life of Alexander Israel Helphand (Parvus), 1867-1924*. New York: Oxford University Press, 1965.

ADDENDA

Bardanne, Jean. *Le Colonel Nicolai: espion de genie.* Paris Editions Siboney, n.d.

Cours de Justice. *L'Affaire Caillaux, Loustalot et Comby: Procedure Generale Interrogatoires.* Paris, 1919.

Guernut, Henri; Kahn, Emile; and Lemercier, Camille M. *Etudes documentaires sur L'Affaire Caillaux.* Paris, n.d.

Vergnet, Paul. *L'Affaire Caillaux.* Paris, 1918. Chap., "Marx de Mannheim."

INDEX